PROMOTING GLOBAL MONETARY AND FINANCIAL STABILITY

As the global organisation of central banks, the Bank for International Settlements (BIS) has played a significant role in the momentous changes the international monetary and financial system has undergone over the past half-century. This book offers a key contribution to understanding these changes. It explores the rise of the emerging-market economies, the resulting shifts in the governance of the international financial system and the role of central-bank cooperation in this process. In this truly multidisciplinary effort, scholars from the fields of economics, history, political science and law unravel the most poignant episodes that marked this period, including European monetary unification, the paradigm shifts in economic and financial analysis, the origins and influence of macro-financial stability frameworks, the rise of soft law in international financial governance, central bank crisis management in the wake of the Great Financial Crisis and, finally, the institutional evolution of the BIS itself.

Claudio Borio is Head of the Monetary and Economic Department at the BIS.

Stijn Claessens is Head of Financial Stability Policy and Deputy Head of the Monetary and Economic Department at the BIS.

Piet Clement is Historian at the BIS. He is a member of the Academic Council of the European Association for Banking and Financial History.

Robert N. McCauley was a senior economist and adviser at the BIS from 1994 until his retirement in 2019.

Hyun Song Shin is Economic Adviser and Head of Research at the BIS.

STUDIES IN MACROECONOMIC HISTORY

SERIES EDITOR: Michael D. Bordo, *Rutgers University*

EDITORS:

Owen F. Humpage, *Federal Reserve Bank of Cleveland*
Christopher M. Meissner, *University of California, Davis*
Kris James Mitchener, *Santa Clara University*
David C. Wheelock, *Federal Reserve Bank of St. Louis*

The titles in this series investigate themes of interest to economists and economic historians in the rapidly developing field of macroeconomic history. The four areas covered include the application of monetary and finance theory, international economics, and quantitative methods to historical problems; the historical application of growth and development theory and theories of business fluctuations; the history of domestic and international monetary, financial, and other macroeconomic institutions; and the history of international monetary and financial systems. The series amalgamates the former Cambridge University Press series Studies in Monetary and Financial History and Studies in Quantitative Economic History.

Other Books in the Series:

Patrick Honohan, *Currency, Credit and Crisis: Central Banking in Ireland and Europe* (2019)

William A. Allen, *The Bank of England and the Government Debt: Operations in the Gilt-Edged Market, 1928–1972* (2019)

Eric Monnet, *Controlling Credit: Central Banking and the Planned Economy in Postwar France, 1948–1973* (2018)

Laurence M. Ball, *The Fed and Lehman Brothers: Setting the Record Straight on a Financial Disaster* (2018)

Rodney Edvinsson, Tor Jacobson, and Daniel Waldenström, Editors, *Sveriges Riksbank and the History of Central Banking* (2018)

(*Continued after Index*)

Promoting Global Monetary and Financial Stability

The Bank for International Settlements after Bretton Woods, 1973–2020

Edited by

CLAUDIO BORIO

Bank for International Settlements

STIJN CLAESSENS

Bank for International Settlements

PIET CLEMENT

Bank for International Settlements

ROBERT N. MCCAULEY

Bank for International Settlements

HYUN SONG SHIN

Bank for International Settlements

CAMBRIDGE
UNIVERSITY PRESS

CAMBRIDGE
UNIVERSITY PRESS

University Printing House, Cambridge CB2 8BS, United Kingdom

One Liberty Plaza, 20th Floor, New York, NY 10006, USA

477 Williamstown Road, Port Melbourne, VIC 3207, Australia

314–321, 3rd Floor, Plot 3, Splendor Forum, Jasola District Centre,
New Delhi – 110025, India

79 Anson Road, #06–04/06, Singapore 079906

Cambridge University Press is part of the University of Cambridge.

It furthers the University's mission by disseminating knowledge in the pursuit of
education, learning, and research at the highest international levels of excellence.

www.cambridge.org
Information on this title: www.cambridge.org/9781108495981
DOI: 10.1017/9781108856522

© Bank for International Settlements, Basel 2020

First published 2020

Printed in the United Kingdom by TJ International Ltd, Padstow Cornwall

A catalogue record for this publication is available from the British Library.

Library of Congress Cataloging-in-Publication Data
Names: Borio, C. E. V., editor. | Claessens, Stijn, editor. | Clement, Piet, editor. | McCauley,
Robert, editor. | Shin, Hyun Song, editor.
Title: Promoting global monetary and financial stability : the Bank for International
Settlements after Bretton Woods, 1973–2020 / edited by Claudio Borio, Bank for
International Settlements, Stijn Claessens, Bank for International Settlements, Piet Clement,
Bank for International Settlements, Robert N. McCauley, Bank for International Settlements,
Hyun Song Shin, Bank for International Settlements.
Description: Cambridge, United Kingdom ; New York, NY : Cambridge University Press,
2020. | Series: Studies in macroeconomic history | Includes bibliographical references and
index.
Identifiers: LCCN 2019059908 (print) | LCCN 2019059909 (ebook) | ISBN 9781108495981
(hardback) | ISBN 9781108856522 (ebook)
Subjects: LCSH: Bank for International Settlements. | Monetary policy.
Classification: LCC HG3881.5.B38 P76 2020 (print) | LCC HG3881.5.B38 (ebook) | DDC
332.1/5509045–dc23
LC record available at https://lccn.loc.gov/2019059908
LC ebook record available at https://lccn.loc.gov/2019059909

ISBN 978-1-108-49598-1 Hardback

Contents

Graphs and Tables

Graphs

Tables

Contributors

Andrew Baker is Professor of Political Economy in the Department of Politics at the University of Sheffield. He researches various aspects of financial and economic governance and has authored over fifty articles and chapters and two books: *The Group of Seven: Finance Ministries, Central Banks and Global Financial Governance* (2006) and *Governing Financial Globalization: International Political Economy and Multi-level Governance* (2005). He has been a visiting scholar at Copenhagen Business School and Griffith University, Australia. He was formerly the editor of the *British Journal of Politics and International Relations* and is currently a co-editor of the journal *New Political Economy.*

Claudio Borio is Head of the Monetary and Economic Department at the BIS. Since 1987, Mr Borio has held various positions at the BIS, including Director of Research and Statistics and Head of Secretariat for the Committee on the Global Financial System and the Gold and Foreign Exchange Committee (now the Markets Committee). From 1985 to 1987, he was an economist at the OECD. Prior to that, he was Lecturer and Research Fellow at Brasenose College, Oxford University. He holds a DPhil and an MPhil in economics and a BA in politics, philosophy and economics from Oxford. Claudio Borio is author of numerous publications in the fields of monetary policy, banking, finance and issues related to financial stability.

Chris Brummer is the Agnes N. Williams Research Professor and Faculty Director of Georgetown's Institute of International Economic Law. He earned his JD with honours from Columbia Law School and holds a PhD in Germanic studies from the University of Chicago. Before becoming a professor, he practised law in the New York and London offices of Cravath, Swaine & Moore LLP. He is the author of *Soft Law and the*

Global Financial System: Rule Making in the 21st Century (2012);
*Minilateralism: How Trade Alliances, Soft Law and Financial
Engineering Are Redefining Economic Statecraft* (2014); and *Fintech
Law in a Nutshell* (2019). He is the editor of *Cryptoassets: Legal,
Regulatory and Monetary Perspectives* (2019).

Agustín Carstens became General Manager of the BIS on
1 December 2017. He was Governor of the Bank of Mexico from 2010
to 2017. A member of the BIS Board from 2011 to 2017, he was chair of
the Global Economy Meeting and the Economic Consultative
Committee from 2013 until 2017. He also chaired the International
Monetary and Financial Committee, the IMF's policy advisory committee, from 2015 to 2017. Mr Carstens began his career in 1980 at the Bank
of Mexico. From 1999 to 2000, he was Executive Director at the IMF. He
later served as Mexico's deputy finance minister (2000–3) and as deputy
managing director at the IMF (2003–6). He was Mexico's finance minister from 2006 to 2009. Mr Carstens has been a member of the Financial
Stability Board since 2010 and is a member of the Group of Thirty. He
holds an MA and a PhD in economics from the University of Chicago.

Stijn Claessens is Head of Financial Stability Policy and Deputy Head of
the Monetary and Economic Department at the BIS. He represents the
BIS externally in the Financial Stability Board, Basel Committee on
Banking Supervision and G20. Within the BIS, he leads policy-based
analyses of financial sector issues and oversees the work of the
Committee on the Global Financial System and Committee on
Payments and Market Infrastructures. Earlier, he worked at the World
Bank (1987–2006), the IMF (2007–14) and the Federal Reserve Board
(2015–17). He holds a PhD from the Wharton School of the University
of Pennsylvania and a master's degree from Erasmus University,
Rotterdam, and has taught at New York University and the University
of Amsterdam.

Piet Clement has been historian at the BIS since 1995. He holds a PhD in
history from the Catholic University of Leuven, Belgium. He assisted
Gianni Toniolo in writing the history of the BIS for the Bank's 75th
anniversary: *Central Bank Cooperation at the Bank for International
Settlements, 1930–1973* (2005). He has published extensively on the
history of international cooperation and of the BIS. He is a member of
the Academic Council of the European Association for Banking and
Financial History.

William C. Dudley is a senior research scholar at Princeton University. From 2009 to 2018, Mr Dudley was the President of the Federal Reserve Bank of New York, Vice Chairman of the Federal Open Market Committee and a director on the BIS Board of Directors. At the BIS, he chaired the Committee on Payments and Settlement Systems (now the Committee on Payments and Market Infrastructures) and the Committee on the Global Financial System. Prior to being President of the New York Fed, Mr Dudley served as Executive Director of the Markets Group there and was the Chief US Economist at Goldman Sachs.

Barry Eichengreen is George C. Pardee and Helen N. Pardee Professor of Economics and Political Science at the University of California, Berkeley; Research Associate of the National Bureau of Economic Research; and Research Fellow of the Centre for Economic Policy Research. He has published extensively on the history and functioning of the international monetary and financial system, including *Golden Fetters: The Gold Standard and the Great Depression 1919–1939* (1992) and *Exorbitant Privilege: The Rise and Fall of the Dollar and the Future of the International Monetary System* (2010). His most recent books include *How Global Currencies Work: Past, Present and Future* (2017, with Arnaud Mehl and Livia Chitu) and *The Populist Temptation: Economic Grievance and Political Reaction in the Modern Era* (2018).

Harold James, the Claude and Lore Kelly Professor in European Studies at Princeton University, is Professor of History and International Affairs at the Woodrow Wilson School and Director of the Program in Contemporary European Politics and Society. His books include a study of the interwar depression in Germany, *The German Slump* (1986); *International Monetary Cooperation since Bretton Woods* (1996); and *The End of Globalization* (2001), which is available in eight languages. He is also co-author of a history of Deutsche Bank, *The Deutsche Bank, 1870–1995* (1995). His most recent books include *The Creation and Destruction of Value: The Globalization Cycle* (2009), *Making the European Monetary Union* (2012) and *The Euro and the Battle of Economic Ideas* (2016, with Markus K. Brunnermeier and Jean-Pierre Landau). He is currently working on a history of the Bank of England and is the official historian at the IMF.

Robert N. McCauley was a senior economist and adviser at the BIS from 1994 until his retirement in 2019. He was Chief Representative of the BIS

Office for Asia and the Pacific from 2003 until 2008. He does policy-relevant and market-savvy research on international financial markets, the international monetary system and corporate finance. He combines deep analysis with broad communication: the *Financial Times, Economist, Wall Street Journal* and *New York Times* cite his work extensively. His research spans the international monetary system, reserve management, foreign exchange markets and renminbi internationalisation. At the time of his retirement in 2019, he represented the BIS Monetary and Economic Department on the Basel-based Markets Committee.

Catherine R. Schenk, FRHS, FRSA, FAcSS, is Professor of Economic and Social History at St Hilda's College, University of Oxford. After completing her undergraduate and master's degrees at the University of Toronto in economics, international relations and Chinese studies, she went to the London School of Economics to complete her PhD in economic history. Since then she has held academic positions at Victoria University of Wellington, New Zealand, Royal Holloway, the University of London and the University of Glasgow. She has also been visiting professor at Nankai University, China, and Hong Kong University. She has published extensively on the history of the international monetary and financial system, including *Hong Kong as an International Financial Centre: Emergence and Development 1945–1965* (2002) and *The Decline of Sterling: Managing the Retreat of an International Currency 1945–1992* (2010). She is the president of the Economic History Society and has been visiting fellow at the IMF and Lamfalussy Senior Research Fellow at the BIS.

Hyun Song Shin was appointed Economic Adviser and Head of Research of the BIS in 2014. He is a member of the Bank's Executive Committee. Before joining the BIS, Mr Shin was the Hughes-Rogers Professor of Economics at Princeton University. In 2010, on leave from Princeton, he served as Senior Adviser to the Korean president, taking a leading role in formulating financial stability policy in Korea and developing the agenda for the G20 during Korea's presidency. From 2000 to 2005, he was Professor of Finance at the London School of Economics.

Foreword

Agustín Carstens

This volume, published on the occasion of the BIS's ninetieth anniversary, brings together contributions by six scholars, experts in their fields, who shed light on key aspects of the BIS's recent past and evolution. The starting point is the breakdown of the Bretton Woods system of fixed exchange rates in 1973. That date marks the end of the period economic historian Gianni Toniolo covers in his book on the BIS, published in 2005 to mark the Bank's seventy-fifth anniversary. As such, this volume perfectly complements that book.

The end of Bretton Woods brought momentous changes to the monetary and financial system and ushered in a new era in central banking and in international central-bank cooperation. A world of strict monetary regulations, financial repression and omnipresent capital controls made way for a market-based monetary system of floating rates, deregulation and rapid financial globalisation. The key characteristics and paradigms of the post–Bretton Woods monetary and financial system generally still hold nearly fifty years later. It therefore seems appropriate to treat the near half-century since 1973 as one period, one reference frame for analysis, as this volume does.

The volume shows that, over the past five decades, the BIS has played a very varied and at times critical role in the international monetary and financial system. Its specific origins, history and institutional traits set the BIS apart from most other international organisations. As the book indicates, this idiosyncrasy perhaps results in certain limitations, but it also creates important opportunities. It is precisely thanks to its specific role and activities over the past decades that the BIS has remained the prime locus for central-bank cooperation, and as such has become firmly embedded in the global financial architecture. As William Dudley notes in his contribution, 'if the BIS didn't exist, it would have to be invented'.

Throughout its history, the BIS has sought – usually with success – to adapt to changing circumstances, reinventing itself when faced with major challenges. Since the 1970s, the BIS has dramatically expanded the scope and breadth of its activities in response to the evolving international monetary and financial system and demands from the central bank community. A strong focus on financial stability issues has complemented the traditional one on monetary policy and exchange rates. Moreover, with the creation of key policy committees such as the Basel Committee on Banking Supervision and the Committee on Payments and Market Infrastructures, the BIS has established itself as a focal point for the development of best-practice principles and standards for the global financial system. The Bank has also considerably expanded its balance sheet and the customer base of its banking services to include almost all central banks worldwide, offering increasingly sophisticated financial products. And since the 1990s – when monetary cooperation among the European Union countries moved away from Basel to Frankfurt – the BIS has transformed itself from a largely European into a truly global organisation. Today, sixty-three central banks from around the world are shareholding members of the BIS. These sixty-three represent countries that together make up nearly 95 per cent of global GDP. All major central banks of the world are part of the BIS Board of Directors and of the BIS's other governance bodies.

Of course, the story does not end here. There is no dearth of challenges ahead. Old challenges remain, sometimes in new guises. Think of the growth of volatile gross capital flows or the conduct of monetary policy, today in an environment of stubbornly low inflation. At the same time, the Great Financial Crisis of 2007–9 has profoundly affected central banking. Views on the goals and tools of monetary policy and on how best to deal with financial stability risks have changed significantly. Central banks have started to think in terms of macro-financial stability frameworks that encompass monetary and financial stability and microprudential policies, with all the difficulties that entails.

New challenges are emerging. Financial innovation through new technologies has gathered pace. Digital currencies (including central bank digital currencies) and 'real-time' payment systems are just two examples of technological advances that have the potential to fundamentally change monetary policy and financial intermediation as we know them. Central banks have a major role to play in making sure that such innovations promote the resilience of the financial system, level the playing field for fair competition and enhance the well-being of society at large (BIS AR 2019: 55–79; Carstens 2019b).

The central bank community and the BIS have the ambition to rise to these challenges, old and new. Policy discussions in the Basel-based Committees and the BIS's own research will continue to feed into the design of monetary policy and financial stability frameworks. How to integrate financial stability objectives in the monetary policy framework is of great interest to the central banks of advanced and emerging-market economies alike. In 2018, the BIS Board of Directors approved the BIS 2025 innovation strategy. A first practical manifestation of our strategic focus on financial innovation has been the opening of a series of Innovation Hubs with and at the central banks of the Hong Kong Special Administrative Region, Singapore and Switzerland. The role of these Innovation Hubs is to identify and develop in-depth insights into critical trends in technology affecting central banking; develop public goods in the technology space geared towards improving the functioning of the global financial system; and serve as a focal point for a network of central bank experts on innovation. They will also enable central banks to keep abreast of the need to adapt regulations with the objective of safeguarding financial stability.

These are indeed challenging and exciting times. I am confident that the next time the BIS looks back at its history, it will be with the satisfaction that it has made the right choices and that it has continued to grow and adapt in fulfilling its role of promoting global monetary and financial stability through international cooperation.

Acknowledgements

The editors would like to express their thanks to all who have contributed to this volume. As always, publishing a book like this is a collective effort, and all the more enjoyable for it.

First of all, thanks are due to the editors at Cambridge University Press, Rachel Blaifeder, Robert Dreesen, Valarie Guagnini, Adam Hooper, Karen Maloney, Erika Walsh and Katie Walsh, as well as to the series editor Michael Bordo. Their support and excellent advice throughout this project have been greatly appreciated.

At the BIS, we are especially grateful to Oriana Harte for her tireless dedication and eye for detail. The following have been very generous with their time, providing crucial input and kindly reviewing drafts: Svein Andresen, Agustín Carstens, Jaime Caruana, Mathias Drehmann, Hermann Greve, Hervé Hannoun, Richard Jones, Malcolm Knight, Pierre Panchaud, Jean-François Rigaudy, Rupert Thorne, Kostas Tsatsaronis and David Williams. We benefited from the expertise and support of James Connor-Hughes, Karl-Heinrich Rangenau, Han-Chih Yang and Christine Zimmerli. In the BIS Editorial Services team, Doris Berger-Lässer, Emma Claggett, Martin Hood, Tomislav Minić and Nathalie Savary provided valuable assistance. Nigel Hulbert proved to be a meticulous and reliable language editor – as always. The ever-resourceful BIS Library and Records and Archives teams came to the rescue more than once. Márcia Cavalinhos and Mihaiela Donisa helped with the photo material. Alan Villegas kindly drew the graphs for this volume, based on data carefully compiled by Pablo Echagüe.

Abbreviations

ACC	Asian Consultative Council (BIS)
APEC	Asia-Pacific Economic Cooperation
BCBS	Basel Committee on Banking Supervision
BIS	Bank for International Settlements
C20	Committee of Twenty (IMF)
CCA	Consultative Council for the Americas (BIS)
CCyB	Countercyclical capital buffer
CEMLA	Center for Latin American Monetary Studies
CGFS	Committee on the Global Financial System
CPMI	Committee on Payments and Market Infrastructures
CPSS	Committee on Payment and Settlement Systems
ECB	European Central Bank
ECC	Economic Consultative Committee (BIS)
ECSC	Euro-currency Standing Committee
EMEAP	Executives' Meeting of East Asia and Pacific Central Banks
EMI	European Monetary Institute
EMS	European Monetary System
EMU	Economic and Monetary Union (EU)
FSAP	Financial Sector Assessment Program (IMF/World Bank)
G10	Group of Ten countries
G20	Group of Twenty systemically important countries (with focus on financial stability)
GAB	General Arrangements to Borrow (IMF/G10)
GEM	Global Economy Meeting (BIS)
GFC	Great Financial Crisis (2007–9)
GHOS	Group of Governors and Heads of Supervision (BIS)
G-SIFI	Global systemically important financial institution

IADI	International Association of Deposit Insurers
IAIS	International Association of Insurance Supervisors
IFI	International financial institution
IGC	Intergovernmental Conference
IMF	International Monetary Fund
IO	International organisation
IOSCO	International Organization of Securities Commissions
LTCM	Long-Term Capital Management
LTI	Loan-to-income
LTV	Loan-to-value
MC	Markets Committee
MED	Monetary and Economic Department (BIS)
OECD	Organisation for Economic Co-operation and Development
PFMI	Principles for Financial Market Infrastructures
SDR	Special Drawing Right (IMF)
SEACEN	South East Asian Central Banks
UN	United Nations
VaR	Value-at-risk

Introduction

Claudio Borio, Stijn Claessens, Piet Clement,
Robert N. McCauley and Hyun Song Shin

It is a commonplace to state that we live in a time of continuous change. But that doesn't make it any less true. The force and impact of change become all the more obvious when considering a horizon that spans two generations. Fifty years ago, a mere handful of advanced industrial economies dominated the global economy. Since then, a wide array of countries have emerged as new economic powerhouses. Economic development and prosperity are now more equally spread across the globe than at any other time over at least the past two centuries. Thanks to the often breathtaking growth of emerging-market economies, the share of the world's population living in extreme poverty has dropped from more than 30 per cent to about 10 per cent (World Bank Group 2018). Future historians may very well see this as *the* change that defined our time.

Money and finance are at the heart of economic development. Financial intermediation is a key lubricant of modern economic growth. The last fifty years have witnessed momentous changes in the monetary and financial areas. Since the early 1970s, a gold-based system of fixed exchange rates ('Bretton Woods') has given way to a world of full fiat money with floating – even if still managed – exchange rates. Financial deregulation and the lifting of capital controls have contributed to a boom in banking and unprecedented financial globalisation (even surpassing the first globalisation wave of the late nineteenth century). These developments not only have supported economic growth worldwide but have also brought old and new challenges to the fore: inflation risks, bank fragility, excessive indebtedness, financial instability, managing financial innovation.

Central banks have a mandate to promote and safeguard monetary and financial stability as the essential foundation of economic growth and prosperity. They have been key to how the world has coped (and is coping) with the post–Bretton Woods challenges. In the process, they have undergone changes too. The roles central banks, or associated organisations, currently perform go far beyond what they were usually tasked to do fifty or one hundred years ago. These expanded roles include regulating and supervising banks, overseeing centralised payment systems, performing broad financial stability mandates, executing orthodox and non-orthodox monetary policies, and acting as lenders of last resort (Carstens 2019a).

Given the global economy's growing interconnectedness and the challenges posed by financial globalisation, it is not surprising that the need for central banks to cooperate internationally has also increased. Since its creation in 1930, the Bank for International Settlements (BIS), in Basel, Switzerland, has been the prime venue for international central-bank cooperation. The BIS was set up as an international organisation owned by central banks for this express purpose. Until the early 1960s, the BIS was a predominantly European organisation, as meticulously documented in Gianni Toniolo's history of the first forty years of the Bank (Toniolo 2005). From the 1960s onwards, in the context of the Bretton Woods system of fixed exchange rates, central-bank cooperation became 'transatlantic' and took place mostly within the framework of the Group of Ten (G10) advanced industrialised countries.[1]

How has the BIS facilitated central-bank cooperation since the end of Bretton Woods in 1973? How has it adapted to the momentous changes in the global economy that have marked the past half-century? This is the topic of this volume, published on the occasion of the BIS's ninetieth anniversary in 2020. It explores in what areas the BIS has changed over the past fifty years and how the scope, depth and reach of central-bank cooperation have expanded. Six independent scholars – experts in their respective fields – review and assess key aspects of the BIS's roles and activities since the early 1970s. Their contributions focus on the institutional changes of the BIS and on its intellectual contributions over this period.

Harold James (Princeton University) kicks off the volume with a European story. Just as the global system of fixed exchange rates gave way to generalised floating at the beginning of the 1970s, the BIS served as the venue for a regional experiment aimed at reducing exchange rate fluctuations among a group of European countries. This experiment had its origin in the 1957 Treaty of Rome creating the European Economic Community (EEC) and, more particularly, in the establishment of the Committee of Governors of the Central Banks of the Member States of the European Economic Community (Committee of Governors) in 1964. The Committee of Governors, initially tasked by the EEC to consult on monetary policy issues relevant to the Community, was soon also expected to coordinate monetary and foreign exchange policies across the EEC in preparation for an eventual monetary union. This cast the central banks of what became the European Union (EU) in a dual, and potentially conflicting, role of guardians of orthodoxy and innovators, as it drew them into an essentially political project.

As pointed out by James, the central banks' immediate and perhaps natural reaction was to keep Brussels – the political heart of the European project – at arm's length by organising their cooperation within the much more familiar and secluded confines of the BIS. For thirty years, from the first meeting of the Committee of Governors in 1964 until the creation of the European Monetary Institute (EMI) in Frankfurt in 1994, the BIS played host to the intensifying cooperation among EU central banks and provided the Committee with secretariat services as well as important technical assistance.

As Harold James argues, the BIS's direct involvement in the European monetary cooperation and unification project provides an excellent illustration of the strengths and limitations of the institution as a non-political, cooperative international organisation. For as long as the European project was mostly about aligning the positions of the individual EU central banks, or about finding technical solutions to reduce tensions in the foreign exchange markets, the BIS proved to be the ideal venue for cooperation. As soon as the European monetary cooperation project became a political one, with the decision to move in stages towards full economic and monetary union (EMU) as enshrined in the 1992 Maastricht Treaty, the BIS could not fulfil such a role any longer.

In 1993, the Committee of Governors transformed itself into the aforementioned EMI. The EMI elected BIS General Manager Alexandre Lamfalussy as its President and promptly moved from Basel to Frankfurt, bringing an end to the involvement of the BIS in European monetary unification. Harold James tells us how the story continued from there. In 1998, the European Central Bank took over from the EMI, and on 1 January 1999 the exchange rates of the participating countries were irrevocably fixed through the introduction of the euro. James goes on to describe the eurozone crisis that followed hot on the heels of the Great Financial Crisis (GFC) of 2007–9 and looks for possible explanations in the origins and lopsided design of the monetary union.

The creation of EMU marked an important turning point in the Bank's history. The BIS was forced to rethink its own future, and more particularly its traditionally strong focus on Europe. It was the starting point of a process of far-reaching institutional reforms.

This is the topic of the second chapter, written by Catherine R. Schenk (Oxford University). Schenk offers an account of how the BIS has responded – particularly since the 1990s – to the momentous shifts in the balance of global economic and financial power over this period by expanding its membership and adapting its governance. For historical reasons, BIS membership up to the 1990s was heavily concentrated in Europe. To be sure, the BIS has traditionally provided cooperative and banking services to *all* central banks – members and non-members – on a global scale and has continuously developed formal and informal ways of interacting with them. For instance, the BIS's Banking Department has maintained active banking relationships with most emerging-market central banks since at least the 1970s. That said, from the 1990s onwards, the conviction grew that the Bank's formal governance too needed to adapt to the realities of globalisation. Significant reforms, set in motion from the mid-1990s, succeeded in turning the BIS from a predominantly European organisation into a truly global one.

Catherine Schenk's thorough analysis shows that this was not a straightforward – let alone easy – process. In addition to the obstacles reflecting binding statutory constraints and tradition, there was an inherent tension between the need to ensure inclusiveness and relevance, on the one hand, and the desire to retain flexibility, informality and confidentiality, on the other. As a result, the reforms of the Bank's formal governance were very gradual. The expansion of the BIS's shareholding membership from thirty-two mostly European central banks at the beginning of the 1990s to currently sixty-three central banks representing all main economic and financial centres globally was in itself uncontroversial but proceeded in steps in order to manage expectations.

The next challenge after the expansion of membership was to broaden the oversight of the BIS-based Committees – under their current names: the Basel Committee on Banking Supervision (BCBS), the Committee on Payments and Market Infrastructures (CPMI), the Committee on the Global Financial System (CGFS) and the Markets Committee. The key was to shift oversight from the G10 Governors-dominated Board to more encompassing bodies. The process, which had already started before the GFC, accelerated in 2008–9 as the G20 took the lead in propagating global post-crisis reforms. As the BIS expanded the membership of the Committees, their oversight was transferred to the Global Economy Meeting (GEM, comprising thirty central banks as members and nineteen more as observers) or to the Group of Governors and Heads of Supervision (GHOS, comprising representatives from twenty-eight jurisdictions).

Changing the composition of the BIS Board of Directors itself required a more formal and lengthier process. As Catherine Schenk points out, it is only since the most recent reform (January 2019) that the Board can be said to be truly representative of the BIS's membership – and thereby of global economic and financial interests. Schenk sees the slow pace of transformation as a clear indication of how highly the G10 Governors prized their informal cooperation through the Board. In the final analysis, she argues, the evolution of the BIS's governance since the 1990s has been determined by external developments – the rise to prominence of the emerging-market economies – as well as by the overriding concern for the BIS to retain not only its legitimacy and authority but also its agility and usefulness to members and non-members alike.

A key innovation in the BIS's functions over the past fifty years is that it has become strongly associated with the development of best-practice principles and standards for the global financial system. As a global organisation, owned by and working for central banks, the BIS is well placed to help develop such standards and rules. But as a non-political (i.e. non-governmental) organisation, it lacks the mandate to impose and implement them.

The solution to this seeming paradox by means of what is commonly termed 'soft law' is the topic of the third chapter by Christopher Brummer (Georgetown University Law Center). He provides a historical account of why the institutional setting of the BIS has been conducive to the emergence of soft law as a critical tool for managing the global financial system. The purpose of creating the BIS was to solve a 'hard law' compliance problem, namely forcing Germany to fulfil the reparation obligations imposed on it after the First World War. But to achieve this, Brummer recounts, the BIS resorted to consensus-building in Committees of neutral experts that would then advise national governments. Something comparable occurred during the post-war Bretton Woods era, when much of the international cooperation in the monetary field took place in more or less informal settings centred on the G10, including the G10 expert Committees meeting at the BIS. Post-Bretton Woods, the same approach was then transposed to standard setting in order to address the growing financial stability concerns. The stage was set for the emergence of modern financial soft law in which the BIS was to play an important part.

Initially, the role of BIS-based Committees of experts, such as the BCBS and the CPMI (or Committee on Payment and Settlement Systems (CPSS) as it was known then), was limited to exchanging information and building common understanding. The sovereign debt crisis of the 1980s prompted key constituencies – foremost the United Kingdom and the United States – to push for more stringent banking regulation not only at home but also globally, to avoid distorting competition. It was natural that they would leverage their participation in the informal setting of the BIS, and in particular in the BCBS. The 1988 Basel Capital Accord (Basel I) was, in Brummer's assessment, a political and regulatory watershed. It was a quintessential piece of soft law – a non-binding code of conduct agreed by an informal, technocratic Committee of experts – subsequently implemented by national legislation in all the main constituencies. It set the tone for other important instances of soft law developed within the BIS framework, such as the Core Principles for Effective Banking Supervision (1997), the Core Principles for Systemically Important Payment Systems (2000) and the Basel II (2004) and Basel III (2011/17) Accords.

Christopher Brummer argues that the relative success of soft law in financial regulation owes a lot to the particular set-up and traditions of the BIS, and has in turn helped to reinforce the BIS's relevance and status in this area. However, recent developments, particularly following the GFC, have changed the nature of soft law. In spite of its informality, Brummer points out, it has become more 'coercive', as international bodies increasingly focus on implementation and surveillance, and as soft-law standards have become true benchmarks, with market participants themselves increasingly serving as discipliners. For Brummer, these developments make clear that, in order to be successful, soft law will have to become ever more inclusive and transparent. By extension, the same applies to the BIS.

The BIS Committees are the natural locus for central-bank cooperation designed to set standards. Here, the BIS's role is to provide the secretariats, which operate at arm's length from the rest of the institution, working for the respective Committees and their Chairs. Adopting the perspective of political science, Andrew Baker (University of Sheffield) discusses a different contribution to central-bank cooperation in Chapter 4. He recounts the story of how the analytical work of the BIS's own staff under the aegis of the General Manager helped reframe the understanding of financial stability issues, laying the ground for important aspects of the post-GFC financial reforms. In this context, he coins the apt term 'measured contrarianism'.

Baker explains how a long intellectual tradition of questioning the inherent efficiency and self-correcting ability of financial markets, reinforced by the sobering experience of the 1997–8 Asian crisis, led the BIS to increasingly emphasise endogenous causes of financial instability. In other words, the BIS consistently articulated the view that financial crises were not the result of exogenous shocks but rather caused or at least reinforced by factors inherent in the financial system itself. This led to a stronger focus on the resilience and risks of the financial system as a whole, rather than on the risks facing individual financial institutions – the macroprudential rather than the microprudential perspective. Indeed, as also highlighted by Barry Eichengreen in Chapter 5, such a macroprudential approach had a long pedigree at the BIS, going back to at least the late 1970s.

BIS research brought the 'procyclicality' of the financial system to the fore. It pointed out the propensity of market participants to underestimate risks during the upswing phase of the cycle, leading to excessive risk-taking and leverage and thereby setting the stage for – and amplifying – a problematic unwinding of risks during the inevitable downswing phase. This was, according to Andrew Baker, an important 'ideational shift' in the way one looks at financial stability issues. In the late 1990s and early 2000s, this analysis and its call for countercyclical macroprudential policies were controversial and lacked broad-based support in policy circles, including in the standard-setting bodies such as the BCBS. The Basel II Capital Accord (2004), for instance, largely ignored macroprudential concerns and relied heavily on financial institutions' own risk management models.

In Andrew Baker's view, the BIS's key contribution was to pursue the macroprudential agenda in the face of relative indifference and even opposition – hence the term 'measured contrarianism'. In this, it was greatly helped by the fact that similar work and ideas were gradually gaining a foothold in some academic circles and central banks. After the GFC broke out in 2007–8, this work was leveraged in the post-crisis financial reform policies overseen by the G20 and implemented by the Financial Stability Board (FSB), the BCBS, the CGFS and the International Monetary Fund (IMF). In this way, Andrew Baker argues, the BIS's measured contrarianism displayed in the previous decades had real impact on the post-crisis policy response. This, according to the author, is where an international organisation like the BIS adds most value. At the same time, it also points to its limitations, as its potential impact is strongly conditioned by the macroeconomic and global political environment. Such measured contrarianism in the pursuit of financial stability is an ongoing process that is far from complete. It can extend also to the conduct of monetary policy.

As mentioned, the BIS view on the financial system – which Baker argues was influential post-GFC – had deep roots. Barry Eichengreen (University of California, Berkeley) has painstakingly gone through all of the BIS's *Annual Reports* from the early 1970s up to the present day to trace the evolution in the Bank's thinking on the international monetary and financial system, which he finds to be fully consistent with its perspective on financial stability.

In Chapter 5, Eichengreen shows how the BIS's analysis over the past half-century has progressively helped shape what he calls a distinctive 'BIS view'. In the 1970s, in the immediate aftermath of Bretton Woods, the focus of the BIS was still very much on exchange rates and their potential impact on monetary stability. Faced with the reality of floating rates, the BIS, from early on, demonstrated a certain scepticism with regard to the supposed shock-absorbing, self-equilibrating properties of floating exchange rates. The rapid growth of the eurocurrency markets and increasing concerns about the operation of the interbank market, especially in the wake of the sovereign-debt crisis of the early 1980s, shifted the attention to international capital flows and to the risks of an increasingly complex and interconnected global banking system. With this, the seeds of the BIS macro-financial approach were sown, contributing to an improved understanding of the workings of the global economy and to the formulation of possible policy solutions. In particular, attention focused on how monetary and (macro)prudential policies could work together to promote lasting macroeconomic and financial stability. Eichengreen highlights how the Mexico crisis of 1995 and the Asian crisis of 1997–8 gave further impetus to this shift in the BIS's analysis.

The belief that lax credit conditions create incentives for risk-taking which in turn might threaten systemic stability naturally led to an overriding concern with the procyclicality of the financial system and its broader implications. Eichengreen concludes that, according to the BIS view, the key weakness of the international monetary and financial system was not so much countries' asymmetric response to current-account imbalances but rather the system's 'excessive elasticity' – that is, its tendency to provide too much liquidity in the upswing phase of the financial cycle.

While the analysis of the threats to financial stability and the BIS view that derives from it are quite clear, Eichengreen points out that the possible solutions may be less so. On the one hand, it is true that the focus on a macro-financial stability framework has contributed significantly to advancing the work of many of the BIS Committees and standard-setting bodies, particularly in the wake of the GFC, through the development of macroprudential frameworks. On the other hand, Eichengreen concludes, there has not been much progress in the international coordination of monetary policies or in addressing the excessive elasticity problem through a fundamental reform of the international monetary system.

Using the term 'BIS view' does not of course imply that the BIS would favour a monolithic or purely institutional way of thinking – far from it. But it is a useful abstraction as an analytical tool, particularly when this view finds itself at loggerheads with the conventional wisdom. As Barry Eichengreen points out, a credible voice of dissent can make a difference, not least in times of crisis – the point Andrew Baker develops earlier in the volume.

The book ends with a personal reflection from William Dudley (Center for Economic Policy Studies, Princeton University). A former senior official and President of the Federal Reserve Bank of New York (2007–18) and Vice-Chairman of the Federal Open Market Committee, Dudley has witnessed and shaped central-bank policies and central-bank cooperation from the front row during the crucial decade following the GFC.

An avowed 'big fan of the BIS', Dudley sees the value of the organisation in three main areas: first, as a forum for information exchange and discussions among central bankers on topics of common interest – certainly valuable in helping them formulate their own domestic policy choices; second, as the ideal environment for building personal relationships that foster mutual trust and common understanding – an invaluable asset to central bankers, particularly in times of crisis; and, third, as a place where policies are studied, developed and internationally agreed with a view to promoting global financial stability – be it through the Basel-based Committees, such as the BCBS, CGFS or CPMI, or through the BIS's own pioneering research and statistical activities.

William Dudley also sees room for improvement in three areas. He fears that the BIS's global, public mission may be somewhat undermined by the stubborn perception that it is 'a secretive organisation outside the control of elected governments'. To counter this perception, he notes, the BIS has already taken important steps to improve its transparency, which should also help to increase its legitimacy. But, in Dudley's view, more should and can be done, without jeopardising the 'candour and willingness to exchange sensitive information on a confidential basis' typical of BIS meetings. In addition, Dudley calls on the BIS to continue its efforts to further broaden its membership and outreach, as well as the diversity in its staff and management. He acknowledges that, as documented in Catherine Schenk's contribution, a lot has been achieved on this account over the past decades – with the most recent changes in the composition of the BIS's Board of Directors (2019) being a landmark. However, Dudley would like the BIS to lead in this area, not just to follow. Finally, he praises the cooperation between the BIS, on the one hand, and the Bretton Woods institutions, the IMF and the World Bank, on the other. A hyperconnected global economic and financial system needs these multilateral organisations working together. But he reminds us that, in order to operate effectively, these organisations should continuously seek to eliminate possible redundancies between them and to improve the ways in which they complement one another.

William Dudley's reflection reminds us that, in spite of all the changes over the past half-century, some things have remained remarkably constant. The BIS's statutory objectives of 'promoting the cooperation of central banks' and, in order to achieve this, of 'associating with the BIS the largest possible number of central banks that make a substantial contribution to international monetary cooperation' remain as valid in 2020 as they were back in 1930. And there is something else that has not really changed since 1930: central-bank Governors and high-level officials still regularly flock to Basel to participate in BIS-hosted meetings and activities. In the 1930s, Governor of the Bank of England Montagu Norman would typically have left his office in Threadneedle Street, London, on a Thursday to catch the boat train at Waterloo Station that would take him to Dover, rolling straight onto the Calais ferry. From Calais, he would have continued his journey, perhaps making a stopover in Paris to meet his colleague, the Governor of the Bank of France. Then both men might have travelled together by train from Paris to Basel, arriving on the Friday evening. A full weekend of bilateral and multilateral meetings and discussions between central bankers followed, after which a doubtless exhausted Norman would have embarked on the return journey, arriving back at his desk at the Bank of England on the Tuesday. For nearly a decade, Governor Norman made this taxing journey ten times a year almost without fail. Since those early days, air travel has reduced journey times dramatically. Even so, the fact that high-level officials from central banks and supervisory authorities from across the world, in spite of their busy agendas, continue coming to Basel regularly to meet with their peers – just as their predecessors did in the 1930s, 1960s or 1990s – surely testifies to the continued value of these meetings. It is only when the BIS provides real value, and remains relevant to its member and non-member central banks alike, that it can successfully fulfil its mission of promoting monetary and financial stability through international cooperation.

Note

1. The G10 had its origin in the IMF General Arrangements to Borrow (GAB (1961)). It comprised Belgium, Canada, France, Italy, Japan, Germany, the Netherlands, Sweden, the United Kingdom and the United States, with Switzerland being an associated member.

1

The BIS and the European Monetary Experiment

Harold James

When the Bank for International Settlements (BIS) was established in 1930 it had two purposes. The most obvious practical concern was to handle a narrow technical issue: to create a painless or crisis-minimising method for making the transfer of German post-war reparation payments. But the new institution also had a more encompassing goal, defined in its statutes, of promoting 'cooperation of central banks' in order to foster monetary stability. The latter was a task for the future, while the reparations question was mired in present politics. One of the members of the Organisation Committee that drew up the plan for the new institution stated his hopes for the 'gradual development' of a 'cooperative society of Central Banks, the governors of which would regularly meet together in concert in order to exchange information, and to devise means for promoting economy in the use of gold and for preventing by a common policy undue fluctuations in its value'.[1] Providing a club-like arrangement for central banks thus became the raison d'être of the BIS, but one of the characteristics of clubs is that, through their success, they may encourage the formation of smaller or tighter clubs within their space.

The institutional setting was thus delicately balanced between political priorities and the logic of cooperation for a common good, both globally and in a European context. That tension remained a constant feature of the BIS's history, especially at moments when major financial tensions called existing arrangements into question. A key moment came in the early 1990s, when two issues came together. First, the European currency and exchange rate crises of 1992–3 discredited the notion of a fixed but adjustable exchange rate regime and made corner solutions seem preferable: either free-floating rates or a completely fixed arrangement through monetary union. Second, the big geopolitical upheaval with the end of communism and the disintegration of the Soviet Union gave a new dynamic to European discussions about cooperation.

It was in large part the interwar origins of the BIS as a reparations bank that explained the heavy (frequently preponderant) European influence and the Eurocentric character of the institution, which remained until it launched a sustained and deliberate push for internationalisation at the end of the twentieth century, at the onset of a new wave of globalisation.[2] It was also inevitable that the institution would be the locus for the creation of narrower European clubs.

1.1 European Coordination

Europe developed its own more intense coordination mechanisms within a framework of a broader and global international framework, in other words a broad multilateralism. In the 1950s, as the original Six moved to establish the European Economic Community (EEC), some voices argued that a customs union conflicted with the most-favoured-nation provisions of the General Agreement on Tariffs and Trade (GATT). The GATT's Article XXIV permitted customs unions and free-trade agreements only if the external tariff were not to be increased, and the European leaders of the 1950s successfully (but not uncontroversially) argued that an arithmetic mean of the different national rates would satisfy that requirement. The same pattern of looking for closer cooperation within a global or universal framework was repeated in the monetary sphere. Already in the 1950s, the Europeans worked closely together to restore currency convertibility in a coordinated manner through the European Payments Union (EPU, 1950–8), with the BIS, as EPU agent, being responsible for the technical aspects of the successful scheme. The International Monetary Fund (IMF) might have been a logical choice for this role, but by this stage it was mistrusted in Washington as being too political and potentially tainted by the involvement of some of its key early leaders, Harry Dexter White and Frank Coe, in Soviet espionage, and the BIS looked a more neutral option. In the late 1960s, with a working international exchange rate regime (the par value system or Bretton Woods) in place, the Europeans looked for a narrower arrangement, as they argued that Bretton Woods allowed movements of European currency pairs to be twice the magnitude of the 1 per cent fluctuation around the US dollar par value.

Much of the concrete planning for European monetary cooperation took place in the setting of the BIS, in its rooms in Basel, but not formally or institutionally in the BIS itself. The critical coordinating mechanism was the cumbersomely named 'Committee of Governors of the Central Banks of the Member States of the European Economic Community', established in 1964 by the EEC (later the European Community, and eventually, after the Treaty of Maastricht, the European Union): for short, it was generally just called the Committee of Governors (CoG).

The origins of the new phase of European central-bank cooperation lie at the same moment as the creation of the EEC through the Treaty of Rome (1957). In a 1957 speech at the Alpbach Economic Forum in Austria, the governor of the Netherlands Bank, Marius Holtrop, had gone further and asked whether a common central-bank policy was necessary in a unified Europe and then went on to answer the question in the affirmative (Holtrop 1957; Vanthoor 1991). On 10 November 1957, Holtrop circulated a note in which he suggested that the five central banks of the EEC countries (Luxembourg had none, as it was in a monetary union with Belgium) should send identical letters to the finance ministers proposing enhanced cooperation between central banks. The Belgian, French and German governors responded sceptically, arguing that such a move would look like a concerted effort and only raise mutual national suspicions.

One country in particular was persistently sceptical of all the cooperation talk and always found the compromise of monetary sovereignty difficult. Here is an example of the common pattern: that cooperation is more attractive as it seems to provide more benefits for smaller countries, and it is the heavyweights who are likely to think that they can go it on their own. In the late 1950s, German current-account surpluses started to increase, setting off a pattern of discussion that was echoed not only in the 1960s, the late 1970s, and the late 1980s but also in the late 2000s after the establishment of a monetary union. From the perspective of Germany's central bank, the Deutsche Bundesbank, central-bank cooperation might involve the demand for some German support operations and thus pressure to follow policies that might be costly or inflationary. Bundesbank President Karl Blessing consequently spoke out to German Chancellor Konrad Adenauer against any plan for a fund of EEC countries.[3]

The 1957 statement of the five EEC central banks that everything was well and that no innovation was needed seems to have been accepted until an event occurred which showed that there was really not much central-bank cooperation between Europeans. In March 1961, the Deutsche Mark and the Dutch guilder were revalued, after a long period of tensions in the markets, and after a great deal of discussion within the IMF about the appropriate response to the build-up of German surpluses, but after no particular consultation with Germany's fellow EEC members. All the negotiation was done in Washington. In consequence, some European leaders thought they should bring European discussions back home.

The EEC Commission published its Action Programme for the Second Phase of EEC on 24 October 1962, referring to the desirability of a general liberalisation of capital accounts, in accordance with the provisions of the Treaty of Rome. It concluded in a visionary way that made explicit the logical link between monetary union and fiscal union. That linkage, which also figured in the lead-up to the Maastricht Treaty and became a recurrent centre of the debate during the eurozone crisis, was actually stated with greater clarity and force than it would be in the 1990s discussions. There would be parallel councils or committees to coordinate or determine ('fix') fiscal policy as well as monetary policy, because both were seen as part of the management of demand:

> The creation of a monetary union could become the objective of the third phase of the Common Market. The Finance or Economics Ministers of the Community, assembled in Council, would decide on conditions that should be fixed at an opportune time: the overall size of national budgets, and of the Community budget, and the general conditions of financing of these budgets. The Council of Central Bank Governors would become the central organ of the banking system of a federal type. (EEC 1962)

It would begin to resemble what was later sometimes called a 'Eurofed'. This passage might be thought of as prophetic, in that the latter part of this suggestion was followed fairly precisely in the 1990s, but there was a major difference in that, by the end of the twentieth century, central banks placed a very substantial premium on devising legal guarantees of their institutional and operational independence.

The BIS had already hosted, since the 1960s, the regular Group of Ten (G10) central-bank governors' meetings. When the Committee of Governors was created by an EEC Council decision of 8 May 1964, the governors made sure that the Committee as a rule would meet in Basel – for convenience reasons, but surely also to signal their intent to remain independent from the EEC's political centre in Brussels. From 1964, the BIS provided (for a fee) the staffing for the CoG's initially very modest secretariat (though in the early 1990s the secretariat expanded rapidly). From the beginning, the location meant that the new body would play with the geometry of power or engineer what later came to be called 'variable geometry'. All the member countries were represented in the CoG (with Belgium representing Luxembourg as well), but as the CoG began to devise new monetary arrangements in the 1970s (in particular, the so-called

Snake arrangements), some member countries excluded themselves from the new forms of monetary cooperation, as they found the discipline too constraining. At the same time, the CoG devised association arrangements to work with non-EC members, notably Norway, Sweden and Switzerland (the Swiss agreement was never implemented). This development was welcomed by the EEC Commission as a contribution to an enhanced integration process: Denmark, Ireland and the United Kingdom all participated in the CoG well before they joined the EEC. The repercussions of the locational peculiarity and consequent flexibility and openness were felt for a long time. The Treaty of Maastricht, which laid down the timetable for monetary union, did not end this separation of European monetary institutions from the European Community or Union constitutionalisation. It found an end only in the provisions of the Lisbon Treaty, which came into force in December 2009 and which amended Article 9 of the EEC Treaty to include the European Central Bank (ECB) as an 'institution' of the European Union.

The CoG was not established as part of the original architecture of the EEC. Nor was it envisaged as the embryo of a future ECB, although that paradoxically is what it would become. It was created to provide a specifically European mechanism and voice in the discussion and resolution of global monetary issues. Indeed, at the beginning, the global and the regional were closely linked. And that linkage continued to be a constant feature. It was significant that its regular meetings took place in Basel, at the BIS, and thus even outside the territory of the EEC. The meetings were coordinated with other meetings in Basel, of the BIS governors and of the G10, so that there was always a link to broad global developments. And the BIS provided the secretariat of the CoG and administered payments as agent for the European Monetary Cooperation Fund (EMCF), created after the Werner Report and initially envisaged as a potential Federal Reserve System for Europe, and later for the European Monetary System (EMS). In addition, in the 1980s and 1990s, the BIS acted as agent for private bank European Currency Unit (ECU) clearing arrangements.

In his judicious account of the early history of BIS engagement with the European issue, Gianni Toniolo quotes a major EEC figure on the disappointment that not only was monetary union a non-topic but also no progress was made on 'the less ambitious goal of monetary policy harmonisation'. The latter verdict could indeed be extended to the work of the CoG right up to 1992. The contribution of the CoG was more mundane: 'to stimulate exchanges of view' on the differing policy and outcome stances of the various countries, to 'encourage consultations' between economic and financial leaders and to improve the comparability and timeliness of statistical collection. In retrospect it is clear that such work was essential to a realistic formulation of an approach based on targeting price stability (Toniolo 2005: 443). Other accounts make a similar point. The BIS official Gunter Baer, for instance, who as rapporteur for the Delors Committee worked closely with the CoG (and later became its secretary general), acknowledges that 'for those who expect monetary cooperation to result in a strategic interaction in policy making [...] the record of the Committee's achievements may be disappointing'. But the CoG did contribute to the establishment of economic and financial stability, and 'the process of mutual information and consultation and the intensive discussions in the Committee certainly enhanced the understanding of, and promoted a convergence of views on, important questions of principle', in particular the recognition that 'the attainment of price stability is the primary objective of monetary policy' (Baer 1994: 154–5). The Bank of England Governor Leslie O'Brien argued that the most important contribution of the BIS was 'I suppose ... the creation of an atmosphere of realism' (Toniolo 2005: 473).

What was the linkage between European initiatives and global debates? Were they complementary or rather alternatives? UK Prime Minister James Callaghan, a veteran of many British struggles with the IMF, put the problem in this way when he thought that an overall solution was preferable: 'I think there comes a clear question – do we try to build a world monetary system or are we going to have a European one?' The European Commission president, Roy Jenkins, replying to Callaghan, by contrast, stated: 'I think we might move to a substantially more coordinated European monetary position which could help to create a better world monetary position.'[4]

One more issue overshadowed the monetary debate. There was always an ambiguity in the story of monetary integration: was it designed primarily to deal with a technical issue – alternatively formulated as exchange rate volatility as a barrier to trade and thus to greater economic integration, or else as a quest for price stability – or was it part of a grand political plan, in which money was used to tie the European knot? Sometimes the monetary path just seemed politically and bureaucratically less fraught than, say, the task of coordinating European defence, with the hosts of national defence contractors and lobbyists obstructing progress. In 1950 Jacques Rueff, France's major mid-century thinker about money, coined a phrase that was subsequently often erroneously linked to the great architect of European integration Jean Monnet: *L'Europe se fera par la monnaie ou ne se fera pas* (Rueff 1978).[5] In the 1960s a theory of optimum currency areas was developed by US-based economists (Kenen 1969; McKinnon 1963; Mundell 1961); although they continued to be influential figures in the European debate, their theories were irrelevant to the final push to monetary integration in the 1990s (Bayoumi and Eichengreen 1993). The states that signed up to economic union had different expectations and hopes: some saw it as a way of building credibility and thus of reducing borrowing costs, while others focused on the constitutionalisation of a stable monetary regime. How could the divergent visions of the potential gains from monetary integration and central-bank cooperation be mutually reconciled?

1.2 Dealing with the German Current Account

The outbreak of the European debt crisis in 2010 called attention to what was actually a perennial issue: German current-account surpluses (see Graph 1.1). In each phase of the negotiation about European monetary integration, Germany's partners tried to devise an institutional mechanism to control German surpluses. The debate went back a long way. The French economist Raymond Barre, then vice president of the European Commission, for instance, argued in 1968 that Germany should take 'energetic measures for speedier growth and the stimulation of imports' as well as 'special action to inhibit the flow of speculative capital into Germany' (Ungerer 1997).

In the Bretton Woods era of fixed exchange rates and controlled capital markets, even relatively small deficits could not be financed and produced immediate pressure on the exchange markets. The deficit countries then had to apply fiscal brakes in a stop–go cycle. Germany's partners, notably France, were faced by the prospect of austerity and deflation in order to correct deficits. This alternative was unattractive to the French political elite, because it constrained growth and guaranteed electoral unpopularity. Their preferred policy alternative was thus German expansion, but this course was unpopular with a German public worried about the legacy of inflation and was opposed by the powerful and independent Bundesbank.

Solving the question of the German current account in the European setting at first appeared to require some sophisticated and ingenious political mechanism that would force French politicians to pursue more austerity than they would have liked and Germans less price orthodoxy than they thought they needed. A political mechanism, however, requires continual negotiation and public deliberation, which would have been painful given the policy preferences in the two countries (and in those countries that lined up with either of the Big Two). The increased attraction of monetary union was that it required no such drawn-out political process. The operation of an

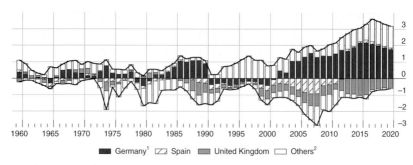

Graph 1.1 Sum of current-account balances of deficit and surplus countries (percentage of GDP; forecasts after 2017)
1. From 1991 the balance-of-payments statistics also include the external transactions of the former German Democratic Republic.
2. Belgium, Denmark, France, Greece, Ireland, Italy, Luxembourg, the Netherlands and Portugal.
Source: European Commission, AMECO database.

entirely automatic device would constrain political debate, initiative and policy choice.

Monetary union was thus conceptualised as a way of simplifying or depoliticising politics. This had been a feature of European arguments from the beginning: the German current account easily became the occasion of a blame game in which countries argued about who had the responsibility to adjust – the 'virtuous' creditor, where politicians presented the surplus as the outcome of good policy, or the 'spendthrift' debtor, which thought that it was the victim of a new mercantilism. Robert Triffin (1957) had shown how a problem could be reduced to its most basic level: 'The significance of monetary unification, like that of exchange stability in a free market, is that both exclude any resort to any other corrective techniques except those of internal fiscal and credit policies.'

The problem of current accounts grew bigger, the surpluses and deficits ever larger. The monetary union occurred after a drive to capital-market liberalisation and was intended to be the logical completion of that liberalisation. Current-account imbalances were apparently sustainable for much longer periods – though not for ever. The effects of movements in capital in allowing current-account imbalances to build up to a much greater extent, and ensuring that corrections, when they occurred, would be much more dramatic, were already noticeable in the late 1980s and early 1990s, before the move to monetary union. Indeed, those large build-ups in the imbalances were what convinced Europe's policymakers that a monetary union was the only way of avoiding the risk of periodic crises with currency realignments whose trade policy consequences threatened the survival of an integrated internal European market. The success of the early years of monetary union lies in the effective privatisation of current-account imbalances, so that the issue disappeared from the radar screen of policy debates. It would only reappear when the freezing-up of the banking system after 2008 required the substitution of public-sector claims for private claims: with that the old problem of the politicisation of current-account imbalances immediately resurfaced.

The escalation of the German current-account problem was also always linked to global debates about currency disorder. European monetary integration appeared urgent in the late 1960s, as the Bretton Woods regime disintegrated, again in the late 1970s, when US monetary policy was subject to big political pressures and the dollar collapsed, and finally – and with an apparently successful outcome – in the late 1980s, in the aftermath of a debate about global monetary stabilisation at the Plaza and Louvre meetings of the major industrial countries.

1.3 The Werner Initiative

In the late 1960s, as the Bretton Woods par value system was entering a period of strain, crisis and ultimately collapse, the first of the major sustained political initiatives aiming at the creation of a monetary union was launched by the EEC Commission. The result, usually referred to as the Werner Plan (after the prime minister of Luxembourg, Pierre Werner, who chaired the committee that produced the document), is frequently regarded as a damp squib. It was characteristic of many of the phases of European monetary integration in that the approach depended excessively on an unlikely congruence or simultaneity of multifarious aspects of the integration process. But, in fact, the suggestions made at this time were not dissimilar to those made in more apparently auspicious circumstances at the end of the 1980s and the beginning of the 1990s. Amy Verdun (2001), as a result, refers to Werner as being a 'remarkably similar blueprint' to that of Jacques Delors and the committee he chaired in 1988–9 that provided a basic draft of the mechanism required for European monetary union. Institutional innovation, in the form of a new institution, the European Monetary Cooperation Fund (EMCF), initially envisaged as a potential Federal Reserve System for Europe, was at the heart of the Werner proposals. The major difficulty lay in the actual implementation, which proved to circumscribe severely the operations of the EMCF (similar considerations would later prevent the emergence of a European Monetary Fund).

The Werner Plan originated with a report from European Commission vice president Raymond Barre, published on 12 February 1969 and focusing on the failure of Community mutual assistance mechanisms in the Italian crisis of 1964 and in the French difficulties of 1968. Barre's initiative was a response to the debacle of the Bonn G10 meeting in November 1968 and its intense political manoeuvring, when not only the differences between European countries but also their incapacity to coordinate on exchange rate issues had been revealed in a humiliating way. Barre's report analysed the way in which Community objectives could be frustrated by the action of large member states. It constituted one of the first expressions of the fear that Germany and its anti-inflationary policy priorities might dominate and distort European discussions.

Barre intended to establish a close link between economic policy and monetary cooperation and also discussed the possibility of coordinating cyclical fiscal policies. Short-term monetary-support operations and medium-term financial assistance would be linked with the convergence of medium-term economic objectives and coordination of short-term policies. The short-term assistance would be entirely automatic in the new proposal and hence would avoid a politicisation of the issue of European transfers. The thought ran in parallel lines to John Maynard Keynes's plans for automaticity in IMF lending in the negotiations leading up to the Bretton Woods settlement, an approach which the United States as the largest and most powerful creditor rejected (Skidelsky 2001; Steil 2013). Many projects, successful and unsuccessful, were launched in 1969: at the Paris Air Show, France and Germany announced that they would embark on a joint aircraft project, Airbus; and a Franco-British cooperation, Concorde, went on a test flight. Was the European monetary project more like Airbus or more like Concorde?

The veteran Jean Monnet then persuaded the political leaders, German chancellor Willy Brandt and French president Georges Pompidou, to take up the issues raised by Barre. Monnet presented a paper to Brandt which stated that 'Germany could take a peaceful, constructive and generous initiative which would overlay – I might even say efface – the memories of the past'. Brandt was aware that a bold European initiative on monetary integration was viewed with great scepticism by his advisers. In particular, the German Foreign Office had been critical of the idea of producing economic convergence through monetary policy. He thought that only a high political initiative could break through the 'chicken and egg problem' created by alternate emphases on the primacy of monetary or economic integration (Wilkens 1999, 2005; Zimmermann 2001). But there were some exceptions to the German bureaucratic critique, and in the German Economics Ministry the Europe department headed by Hans Tietmeyer had produced at the end of October a memorandum including a *Stufenplan* (Plan by Stages) for the European Economic and Monetary Union (EMU). Tietmeyer's document envisaged that coherent economic policy could be achieved by a 'codex on cyclical good behaviour' (which has resemblances to the discussions of the 1990s of the Stability Pact), and also envisaged a Business Cycle Advisory Council and a European Central Banking Council (Tietmeyer 1996).

The outcome of the willingness of Brandt and Pompidou to come together was the appointment in March 1970 of a 'Committee of Presidents of Committees', chaired by Werner, in which the Monetary Committee, the EEC Committee of Central Bank Governors, the EEC Committee on Medium-Term Economic Policy, the Committee on Business Cycle Policy and the Budgetary Committee, as well as the Commission, were represented. The committee was divided between those who wanted to accelerate monetary integration (France, Luxembourg, Belgium, Italy and the Commission) and Germany, supported by the Netherlands, which argued the case for greater economic coherence as a prerequisite for closer monetary coordination. From the beginning, the members found that they could only come together around a theme of 'parallel' development of economic and monetary integration.

The final version of the Werner Report was presented on 27 October 1970. It came at a moment when the G10 was debating whether bands of fluctuation within the Bretton Woods system should be *widened*. Such a challenge required some European response:

The increasing interpenetration of the economies has entailed a weakening of autonomy for national economic policies. The control of economic policy has become all the more difficult because the loss of autonomy at the national level has not been compensated by the inauguration of Community policies. The inadequacies and disequilibrium that have occurred in the process of realization of the Common Market are thus thrown into relief.

The report's most striking feature was the sharp delineation of a final objective, of monetary union:

Economic and monetary union will make it possible to realize an area within which goods and services, people and capital will circulate freely and without competitive distortions, without thereby giving rise to structural or regional disequilibrium. [...] The implementation of such a union will effect a lasting improvement in welfare in the Community and will reinforce the contribution of the Community to economic and monetary equilibrium in the world.

The report also discussed the principal consequences of economic and monetary union in very broad terms, including the following points:

- the Community currencies will be assured of total and irreversible mutual convertibility free from fluctuations in rates and with immutable parity rates, or preferably they will be replaced by a sole Community currency;
- monetary policy in relation to the outside world will be within the jurisdiction of the Community;
- the essential features of the whole of the public budgets, and in particular variations in their volume, the size of balances and the methods of financing or utilising them, will be decided at the Community level;
- a systematic and continuous consultation between the social partners will be ensured at the Community level.

In retrospect, the discussions around the Werner Plan seem to have been rapidly overtaken by events. It took over a year just to achieve a consensus on reducing the intra-Community marginal band from 1.50 to 1.20 per cent. The date of operation of the new system (15 June 1971) was agreed on 19 April 1971: but before the system could come into effect, Germany's response to global exchange turbulence (and specifically, substantial short-term capital outflows into the Deutsche Mark) blew up the whole system. German Economics Minister Karl Schiller tried to persuade other EEC governments of the virtues of a joint float but failed, and on 10 May 1971 Germany embarked on a unilateral float, even though both the Bundesbank president and the majority of the Central Bank Council were still opposed to such a move. The German float was only the beginning of a process that led to the end of the post-war exchange rate regime (the Bretton Woods system) with US President Richard Nixon's announcement on 15 August 1971 that he would close the gold window and impose an extraordinary import surcharge.

1.4 The European Monetary System

In 1978, the European monetary regime was remade, again against a backdrop of a blockage in the international discussion of monetary reform. The major initiative came from French President Valéry Giscard d'Estaing and German Chancellor Helmut Schmidt. Their high-level debates were charged with lofty geopolitical thoughts, and the new monetary arrangements were frequently seen as a challenge to the role of the dollar, which they believed was being deliberately depreciated (in a so-called malign neglect) against other currencies in order to obtain trade advantages.

The eventual outcome of the intense negotiations of 1978, the EMS, is often regarded as a transformative step on a progressive path to monetary integration (Ludlow 1982). Members of the new EMS exchange rate mechanism (ERM) were obliged to intervene without limits at the 2.25 per cent fluctuation margins either side of a central parity calculated bilaterally on the basis of a central rate around a basket currency (the ECU), which was to be 'at the centre of the EMS' (so that there would be no national currency like the Deutsche Mark as the basis of the peg). Central rates could be adjusted 'subject to mutual agreement by a common procedure which will comprise all countries participating in the exchange-rate mechanism and the Commission'. A divergence indicator of 75 per cent of the maximum spread of each currency would, when attained, allow the identification of the country which was diverging and then trigger corrective action (Mourlon-Druol 2012). As had been the case from the start of the EMCF in 1972, the BIS continued to perform its functions as agent under the aegis of the EMS: managing the swap operations by which the participating central banks made 20 per cent of their reserves available to the EMCF in the form of ECUs and maintaining the accounts through which the EMCF operated its short-term monetary support and very short-term financing interventions.

The most significant feature of the agreement was something that it did not contain: the promise the Bundesbank extracted from Chancellor Schmidt that it might be released from the intervention requirements if monetary stability were to be threatened. The document, usually known as the 'Emminger letter', made it clear that the Bundesbank's Central Bank Council had agreed 'under the precondition that the government and central bank agree on the legal basis and also on the future possibility of opting out in specific circumstances'.[6] Schmidt checked the memorandum with the letter 'r' for *richtig*, 'correct', and returned it to the Bundesbank, which kept it secret – its existence only became widely known in the September 1992 speculative attack on the EMS.

The EMS represents a major success in bringing down European inflation rates, but de facto the fundamental mechanism of this disinflation process was an anchoring of currencies on the Deutsche Mark. It thus in practice looked very different to the design of 1978. Its history falls into two phases: in the first, to 1987, there were relatively frequent exchange rate realignments (Gros and Thygesen 1998). After 1987, however, it began to resemble more the practice of the Bretton Woods regime, with a great reluctance of countries to realign their rates and a corresponding risk of creating incentives for speculative attacks, especially as restrictions on capital movements were lifted. It was not so much a perception of failure of the EMS that prompted a rethinking in the late 1980s, when the mechanism looked uniquely successful, but a global challenge.

1.5 The Delors Initiative and the Maastricht Treaty

When the dollar was soaring in the mid-1980s, when American manufacturing was threatened and when there appeared to be the possibility of a protectionist backlash, the finance ministers of the major industrial countries pushed for exchange rate agreement. The G7 finance ministers' Louvre meeting in 1987 agreed to lock exchange rates into a system of target zones (Funabashi 1988).

In practice, nothing came of that global plan, but then Edouard Balladur, the French finance minister who had largely been responsible for the Louvre proposal, came up with a tighter European scheme. When German Foreign Minister Hans-Dietrich Genscher appeared sympathetic, Europe's central bankers were asked by the president of the European Commission, Jacques Delors, to prepare a timetable and a plan for currency union. The Delors Committee met between September 1988 and April 1989 at the BIS in Basel and produced its report at a moment when no one in Western Europe seriously thought that a profound geopolitical transformation such as the collapse of the Soviet bloc and of communist ideology could be at all likely (the fall of the Berlin Wall in November 1989 was a surprise to almost everyone, and certainly to the European governments). Gunter Baer, a BIS official, as rapporteur drew up the report; the second rapporteur, Tommaso Padoa-Schioppa, had been a past Director-General of Monetary Affairs in the Commission, was Vice-Director General of the Bank of Italy from 1984 to 1997 and a regular presence in Basel, and was a key intellectual influence on Delors's thinking about the consequences of capital liberalisation and the need for a new institutional framework. These two men brought the world view of the BIS into the work of the Delors Committee.

The positive outcome of the Delors Committee was a surprise in that the most powerful central banker in the Committee, Bundesbank President Karl Otto Pöhl, was generally believed to be opposed to any project for enhanced monetary cooperation, and the Eurosceptic UK government tried to keep the British member of the Committee working with Pöhl in order to frustrate such cooperation. Since the report required unanimity in order to be convincing or effective, it thus seemed more or less certain at the outset that the project would not lead to the visionary result intended by Jacques Delors.

The eventual success of his plan invites a comparison of the effectiveness of different Commission presidents and officials: the initiative of Raymond Barre at the end of the 1960s only disappointed and led to bitter disillusion; Commission President Roy Jenkins in the late 1970s produced over-bold proposals that in the end were held to be unrealistic and were sidelined by Giscard and Schmidt. Delors produced just the right mixture of vision and practical sense: the vision of a bold move to realise the idea of 'Union' and the pragmatic acknowledgement that only the central bankers could really remove the obstacles that lay in the way (especially the political and institutional obstacles that lay in Germany and in the particular position of the Bundesbank). Dismissing the central bankers as fundamentally obstructive, as the European Commission had done in the late 1970s, would only create an institutional impasse. Binding them in opened the way to a process of innovation.

The Delors Report clearly laid out the path to monetary union, defined as 'a currency area in which policies are managed jointly with a view to attaining common macroeconomic objectives'. But the Committee also added the rider:

The adoption of a single currency, while not strictly necessary for the creation of a monetary union, might be seen for economic as well as psychological and political reasons as a natural and desirable further development of the monetary union. A single currency would clearly demonstrate the irreversibility of the move to monetary union, considerably facilitate the monetary management of the Community and avoid the transactions costs of converting currencies.

It provided for a three-stage process, in which Stage One simply expanded existing cooperative arrangements to which even the Eurosceptic government of Margaret Thatcher could have no objection.

In Stage Two, a new European System of Central Banks (ESCB) would manage the transition from the combination of monetary policies of national central banks to a common monetary policy. In Stage Three, exchange rates would be locked finally and irrevocably. The ESCB would pool reserves and manage interventions with regard to third currencies. 'With the establishment of the European System of Central Banks the Community would also have created an institution through which it could participate in all aspects of international monetary coordination' (Section 38). Delors emphasised that the monetary integration would need to be accompanied by a consolidation of the single market and competition policy, as well as by an evaluation and adaptation of regional policies (Section 56).

The central banks continued to play the dominant role in designing the new institutions. It is not surprising that they opted for a strong form of central-bank independence, with a primary mandate for the new European central bank in the maintenance of price stability. The process reflected the outcome of a tussle between southern Europeans who wanted to control German monetary policy and Germans who wanted to make European monetary policy in line with a German vision of *Ordnungspolitik* (Brunnermeier, James and Landau 2016). The BIS commented in its 1992 Annual Report that 'to concede that the EMS has been an effective anti-inflationary instrument while seeking ways of softening its constraints may seem somewhat paradoxical' (BIS AR 1992: 124).

The design of the Maastricht Treaty, which enshrined the conclusions of the Delors Report in the political decision to move towards EMU, eventually clearly reflected German preferences for limits on government fiscal activism. Article 104 prohibited overdraft facilities from the central bank to governments (monetary financing); it was later taken over as Article 123 of the 2007 Lisbon Treaty (Treaty on the Functioning of the European Union, TFEU). Article 104a prohibited privileged access to financial institutions (Article 124 TFEU), and Article 104b (Article 125 TFEU), the 'no bailout' clause, stated: 'The Community shall not be liable for or assume the commitments of central governments, regional, local or other public authorities, other bodies governed by public law, or public undertakings of any Member State, without prejudice to mutual financial guarantees for the joint execution of a specific project.' In practice, however, a consensus soon developed that government bonds would not be subject to a risk of default, and thus were not treated by financial markets as the equivalent of corporate bonds (Prati and Schinasi 1997).

The German character of monetary union became clearer in the aftermath of Maastricht and of the major currency crises that shook the EMS in 1992–3 and almost destroyed the integration project. The EMS was only rescued at the last moment in July 1993, with the suggestion by the UK Chancellor of the Exchequer Kenneth Clarke of moving to much wider exchange rate bands. The crises of 1992–3 highlighted the centrality of the German position, as the Bundesbank suspended interventions in the French franc, and other currencies, on the argument that the extensive use of Deutsche Mark for intervention would threaten German domestic monetary stability (at this moment the 1978 Emminger letter was used as the shield for Bundesbank actions).

The ERM experience was a game changer in thinking about monetary policy and exchange rates. Before the speculative attacks on the lira, the pound, the peseta and the escudo of September 1992, the way economists thought about currency crises was largely in terms of responses to bad and unsustainable fiscal policies. The responses of markets had been modelled by Paul Krugman in what was later termed the 'first-generation' currency crisis model (Krugman 1979). The 'second generation' came when expectations about self-sustaining attacks were built in, most prominently in the model developed by Maurice Obstfeld. Such expectations could be applied very effectively to the European crisis. Willem Buiter, Giancarlo Corsetti and Paolo Pesenti explained the origins in terms of a 'disinflation game' with a centre (Germany) committed to stable prices and a periphery where markets had diverging expectations about the extent and the political tolerability of the output cost that would be involved in keeping inflation down and the exchange rate stable (Buiter, Corsetti and Pesenti 1998; Jeanne 2000; Obstfeld 1994; Obstfeld 1996). To economic historians, that interpretation looked very like the traumatic 1931 crisis, when rumours of a naval mutiny at the Scottish base of Invergordon triggered a run on the pound, with the Bank of England being unable to stage a defence with higher interest rates, as that would make the pain of austerity worse. There existed multiple equilibria: markets would believe in the permanence of one exchange rate fix until a momentum developed to push to a different equilibrium. The crisis could thus be entirely explained in terms of the calculations of George Soros. By the time of the 1997–8 Asian crisis, where a similar pattern of radically revised exchange rate expectations drove a domino effect of one country after another collapsing, the 'second-generation' interpretation became canonical, and Asian leaders demonised Soros. Putting the theory and the history together led to the inescapable conclusion that the intermediate solution of a fixed and adjustable peg was unsustainable and that in consequence there were only two realistic and stable options, corner solutions, either a publicly announced, credible and time-consistent monetary policy or monetary unification with only one central bank for a large currency area. By the late 1990s, it was easy to see that the United Kingdom was going on the first route and continental Europe on the second (Eichengreen 2000). After 2016, that choice began to be referred to as an earlier version of Brexit (as was 1931, and perhaps also the 1532 legislation of the Henrician Reformation). The Asian crisis had seemed to demonstrate to both the Europeans and UK policymakers that their decision was the correct or economically literate choice.

At the time, in the immediate aftermath of the EMS crises, the BIS Annual Report reflected on how Europe was likely to proceed. It emphasised the political element of the European response:

One (non-economic) background factor was the strength of the commitment, at the political level, to the Maastricht process. At the core of the European Community, a strong political commitment has always been the fundamental, powerful and beneficent binding force, and one which has to be interpreted in the light of the history of the first half of this century. But the concrete manifestation of this political will has tended to concentrate for most of the time not on political union, but rather on economic cooperation and institutions (and with undoubted economic benefits). This has been the case all the way from the European Coal and Steel Community, through the EMS and, finally, to the agreement on the Maastricht Treaty on European Union reached by the twelve Heads of State and Government in December 1991. (BIS AR 1993: 191)

The 1992 Annual Report had been much more hesitant about the Maastricht process, and some European central bankers, and also BIS General Manager Alexandre Lamfalussy, were upset about the rather critical sentences that had been inserted by the (German) chief economist (Economic Adviser) Horst Bockelmann:

The Treaty represents agreement on the bare bones of economic and monetary union and many important matters have yet to be decided. Strangely, the fact of having reached this basic consensus does not seem to have made it any easier to resolve the remaining issues. Those governments that were committed to achieving agreement on the principle were not unhappy about the lack of public debate in their countries prior to the Maastricht Summit and did little or nothing to stimulate it. Having managed to spring the programme on a largely unprepared public they are now faced with debate and dissension very late in the day. This has cast some doubt on the prospects for implementation. (BIS AR 1992: 8)

The implementation in fact occurred on quite German lines. Frankfurt was chosen as the location of the European Monetary Institute (EMI, the predecessor institution that would prepare the work of the ECB) in October 1993, and the name 'euro' was agreed in 1995 (as 'ECU' was thought to sound too French). Lamfalussy moved from his position at the BIS to become the first head of the EMI. At the same time, German Finance Minister Theo Waigel pushed for a Stability Pact that would enforce the Maastricht deficit and debt levels. It became clear that convergence would not be complete by 1997, the first possible date under the Maastricht Treaty for the final stage of monetary union, but then attention focused on making the alternative date (1 January 1999) a reality, with the physical introduction of a new money coming some years later (2001). In practice, although the old physical notes continued to circulate after 1999, the Deutsche Mark, francs and so on were already then legally only units of a completely new currency.

1.6 Planning for Monetary Union

The planning for monetary union was at the same time sober and meticulous, but also involved two potentially devastating flaws. In the debates of the central bankers' group that Delors chaired in 1988–9, before the fall of the Berlin Wall, two really critical issues were highlighted – and they were the ones that really mattered. Neither was adequately resolved in the 1990s, and the monetary union was thus left incomplete.

The first concerned the fiscal discipline needed for currency union. An explicit discussion took place as to whether the capital market by itself was enough to discipline borrowers, and a consensus emerged that market discipline would not be adequate and that a system of rules was needed. The influential Belgian economist and BIS General Manager Lamfalussy, a member of the Delors Committee, brought up cases from the United States and Canada as well as from Europe, where cities and regions were insufficiently disciplined. Lamfalussy drew out the debate about whether market forces were enough to ensure fiscal convergence. The minutes of the December 1988 meeting of the Delors Committee record his suggestion that 'the idea, not shared by him, that market discipline was sufficient to bring about fiscal convergence should be considered in the report'. Bundesbank President Karl Otto Pöhl said that 'the report should be clear in stating that [monetary union] required a substantial increase in the resources devoted to transfers'.[7]

Lamfalussy went on to develop his proposal for an alternative to market discipline into a suggestion for the creation of a centre for macrofiscal coordination, which would allow Europe to make a significant contribution to global financial stability. The new institution would work on the following binding regulations:

1. Establishment of limits on national budgetary deficits and rules governing their financing; these binding limitations should be recognised by changes in national legislation in accordance with provisions agreed in the treaty.
2. A one-time consolidation of budgetary positions in those countries that lie outside the limits stipulated under (1).
3. Annual coordination of budgetary policies (within the framework of setting the Community's macroeconomic policy mix), leaving the possibility of temporarily waiving the limits stipulated under (1).

4. Harsh procedures aimed at exerting peer pressure on countries that in the course of executing their budgets deviate from the agreed objectives; this would involve, for example, special meetings.[8]

In a memorandum written for the Delors Committee in response to a paper by Claudio Borio of the BIS on the fiscal arrangements of federal states, Lamfalussy noted:

With widely divergent 'propensities to run deficits' prevailing in the various European countries, I doubt whether we could count in the foreseeable future on a convergence within a European EMU similar to that observed in most contemporary federal systems. Nor do I believe that it would be wise to rely principally on the free functioning of financial markets to iron out the differences in fiscal behaviour between member countries: (a) the interest premium to be paid by a high-deficit member country would be unlikely to be very large, since market participants would tend to act on the assumption that the EMU solidarity would prevent the 'bankruptcy' of the deficit country; and (b) to the extent that there was a premium, I doubt whether it would be large enough to reduce significantly the deficit country's propensity to borrow. There is therefore a serious risk that, in the absence of constraining policy coordination, major differences in fiscal behaviour would persist within a European EMU. This would be one contrast between most contemporary federal systems and a European EMU. [...] Such a situation would appear even less tolerable once the EMU was regarded as part and parcel of the world economy, with a clear obligation to cooperate with the United States and Japan in an attempt to preserve (or restore) an acceptable pattern of external balances and to achieve exchange rate stabilization. To have the smallest chance of reaching these objectives, all cooperating partners need flexibility in the fiscal/monetary policy mix – as we have so often told the United States. In short, it would seem to me very strange if we did not insist on the need to make appropriate arrangements that would allow the gradual emergence, and the full operation once the EMU is completed, of a Community-wide macroeconomic fiscal policy that would be the natural complement to the common monetary policy of the Community.[9]

This clear statement that a monetary union also requires some measure of fiscal union seems apposite and intellectually compelling – and has indeed been borne out in the difficulties encountered in the eurozone in 2009 and since.

Jacques Delors during the meetings of the Committee appropriately raised the prospect of a two- (or even multi-) speed Europe, in which one or two countries might need a 'different kind of marriage contract'[10] (James 2012). There is a tendency for fiscal policy to be procyclical, particularly when the cycles are driven by property booms, in that enhanced fiscal revenue from real estate exuberance prompts politicians to think that the increase in their resources is permanent. But the procyclical fiscal element may be magnified in a currency union.

The need for fiscal discipline arising from spillover effects of large borrowing requirements is a European issue, but it is clearly not one confined to Europe alone. In emerging markets, this problem was identified after the 1997–8 Asian crisis, and the problem of major fiscal strains became primarily one of the industrial world – and especially of the United States. An appropriate response would involve some democratically legitimated mechanism for limiting the debt build-up, as in the Swiss debt brake (*Schuldenbremse*), which was supported by 85 per cent of voters in a referendum (2001).

The debt and deficit criteria built into the Maastricht Treaty in fact proved to be at the centre of most of the debate in the 1990s. Germany insisted again and again on a strict interpretation of the Treaty: German Finance Minister Theo Waigel repeated that 3.0 meant 3.0 with an insistence that led the French press to dub him 'Monsieur 3.0'. But in practice, some bending of the rules took place. First was the problem of Belgium, with a debt level that looked sustainable but exceeded 60 per cent of GDP (it was 130 per cent in 1997), but Belgium was in a currency union with Luxembourg, which qualified unambiguously, and Brussels was also the seat of the vital European institutions. Then, since Italy's debt level, at 120 per cent of GDP, was lower than that of Belgium, it was hard to exclude Italy. From the point of view of the high-debt countries, such as Italy, the great political attraction of membership in the currency union was the added credibility that would reduce interest rates and thus bring an immediate fiscal saving. The downside was a loss of exchange rate flexibility, but many Italian policymakers and businessmen recognised that the cycles of inflation and devaluation that had characterised the 1970s and 1980s did nothing to increase productivity or output growth.[11]

The original concept of a Stability Pact to perpetuate the eligibility criteria after the final stage of monetary union was cosmetically watered down to take account of French concerns about growth as a Stability and Growth Pact (SGP). A fatal blow came when France and Germany ignored the SGP and had it suspended in November 2003 as a counter to a – as it proved spurious – threat of recession. In 2005, the Pact was considerably reworked and in the process became more complex and less transparent; in hindsight, it also did too little to push fiscal consolidation in a boom phase and made the subsequent crisis years consequently harder and more painful.

The second flaw in the European plans identified by the central bankers as they prepared monetary union was much more serious. In the original version of a plan for a central bank that would run a monetary union, the central bank would have overall supervisory and regulatory powers. That demand met strong resistance, above all from the Bundesbank, which worried that a role in maintaining financial stability might undermine the future central bank's ability to focus on price stability as the primary goal of monetary policy. There was also bureaucratic resistance to a European solution from the existing national regulators.

Just before the establishment of the Delors Committee, a subcommittee of the CoG was established to deal with bank supervision. This new body was chaired by Brian Quinn, the chief banking supervisor for the Bank of England.[12] The initiative had come from Huib Muller of the Netherlands Bank, who was also chairman of the Basel Committee on Banking Supervision, and Tommaso Padio-Schioppa, the chairman of the Banking Advisory Committee to the EC Commission (and who would later follow Muller as chair of the Basel Committee). They argued that there was a satisfactory framework for drawing up legislative proposals on banking supervision in the Community but no adequate way of drawing up policies on prudential supervision. Muller had written to the central-bank governors to outline the basis of the proposal for vesting supervisory policy matters in a European monetary authority:

However, there was agreement that the existing arrangements for the formula-tion of policy in the area of prudential supervision were not structured in such a way as to take full account of contemporaneous developments in the structure of the financial system in Community countries. In particular, the group noted the issues raised by the growing interdependence in recent years between the banking systems of different countries and between the banking system and other financial markets. These close links, assisted by product innovation and technical developments, are creating risks for banks and for the financial system that pose challenging questions for the central banks, which have special responsibilities for dealing with disturbances in financial markets. All EC central banks already have a direct or indirect involvement in the supervision of banks in their countries. The group agreed that progress toward economic and monetary union would be very likely to increase the degree of interdependence between national banking systems in the Community and would strengthen the need for central bank involvement in the prudential supervision of banks and other closely related financial Institutions. [. . .] Senior representatives of EC central banks therefore propose to meet regularly in the future to discuss such matters at the time of the meetings of the Banking Advisory Committee. If agreeable to the Committee of EC Governors, the group would take the form of a subcommittee of the Committee of EC Governors, who would receive reports about its deliberations.[13]

Muller's memorandum specifically identified the novel policy problem posed by the development of transnational banking groups with ownership located in more than one EC member country.

In the CoG, Wim Duisenberg, the Dutch central banker who would eventually become the first president of the ECB, forcefully stated the view that banking supervision needed to occur at the European level.[14] Such a move would deal with a very powerful objection to global attempts by the Basel Committee to evolve what became the 'Core Principles of Banking Supervision': Quinn, who was also a veteran member of the Basel Committee, repeatedly worried that global rules evolved by a committee of central bankers might lack 'democratic legitimacy' (Goodhart 2011: 551). Might Europe be a more viable umbrella for banking supervision? There was, however, considerable opposition to the CoG's developing a major competence for Europe in this field. The president of the German Credit Supervisory Office (Bundesaufsichtsamt für das Kreditwesen) wrote to Pöhl in early 1989 protesting attempts to Europeanise banking supervision, which he saw as parallel to the initiatives of the G10 and of the Basel Committee on Banking Supervision as potentially reducing the competitiveness of German banking. At the same time, Hans Tietmeyer (who was still at the Finance Ministry but would join the Bundesbank in 1990) argued that banking supervision was a responsibility of finance ministers, and not of central banks, and that the German ministry should be represented in CoG discussions of this issue. Pöhl tried to respond to these domestic German critiques by pointing out that any decision would need to be taken by governments and parliaments and that such a moment of choice lay in the distant future. There was similar opposition from France's Banking Commission, which urged the governor of the Bank of France to exercise 'vigilance' because Brian Quinn was believed to favour the transfer of supervisory and regulatory authority to the ECB.[15]

In February 1990, at the EC Monetary Committee meeting in Brussels, there was complete agreement that the different national rules regarding bank regulation should be left in place.[16] Delors was unwilling to force the pace on this issue and stated that the EC Commission approached the issue of banking supervision with an 'open mind': the ESCB should simply 'participate in the coordination of national policies but would not have a monopoly on those policies'.[17]

On 29 June 1990, in the CoG alternates' meeting, Andrew Crockett of the Bank of England proposed that 'a further objective of the ESCB will be to preserve the integrity of the financial system'. Tietmeyer objected that this outcome should be considered a 'task' rather than an 'objective'. At the governors' meeting to discuss such a goal, the wording was softened, mostly in response to the German position. It was agreed that 'any suggestion that the system should undertake rescue operations in favour of individual banks should be avoided', though there might be a need to deal with (rather vaguely defined) 'sudden developments' in financial markets. The wording changed, so that 'preserve' became 'support' and 'integrity' became 'stability'. That phrasing seemed to preclude any responsibility to act as a classic central-bank lender of last resort. In the end, the 'tasks' of Article 3 were watered down to the much less far-reaching and less ambitious goal 'to promote the smooth operation of the payment system'.[18]

In October 1990, when the alternates discussed the CoG's Banking Supervision Subcommittee proposals on draft articles for the central-bank statute, Tietmeyer restated the sceptical position of the Bundesbank, which was consistently worried about the moral-hazard implications of central-bank involvement in supervision. If the central bank took on the responsibility of regulating, it would also deliver an implicit commitment to rescue banks should there be bad developments that it had overlooked. Tietmeyer provided a neat encapsulation of the German philosophy of regulation: 'This did not mean from the view of the Board of the Deutsche Bundesbank that the ECB should not support the stability of the financial system, but that it should never be written down; this would be moral hazard.'[19] The Luxembourg non-paper of 10 May 1991 spoke instead of the central bank participating in 'the coordination and execution of policies relating to the prudential control and stability of the financial system'.

In June 1991 the Intergovernmental Conference (IGC) seemed possibly to exclude any financial-sector supervisory role of the ESCB and the ECB, contrary to the governors' draft statute. There was only a last-hope get-out clause, as a Spanish commentary on the ECB Statute noted:

The relevant provisions were introduced into the Statute with three considerations in mind: first, the System, even though operating strictly at the macroeconomic level, will have a broad oversight of developments in financial markets and institutions and therefore should possess a detailed working knowledge which would be of value to the exercise of supervisory functions. Secondly, there is a legitimate interest on the part of the system in the maintenance of sound and stable financial markets. Thirdly, legislative changes in regulatory provisions may have important technical consequences for the conduct of monetary policy. [...] However, the Statute recognizes the evolutionary character of financial markets and the concurrent need to adapt prudential supervision. For this reason Article 25.2 offers the possibility of designating the ECB as a competent supervisory authority, for example, if it were necessary and desirable to formulate and implement a Community-wide supervisory policy for pan-EC financial conglomerates. Such a task could be undertaken by the ECB only if it were designated as the competent supervisory authority through secondary Community legislation.[20]

There was an opportunity to discuss a concrete example of the problem in September 1991, after the collapse of the Bank of Credit and Commerce International (BCCI) (Goodhart 2011: 392–5). Before that, bank failures and their consequences looked like such a remote possibility that the highly sensitive issues involved had not been really discussed since the 1974 Herstatt case, when the failure of a small German bank had raised the problem of international counterparty risk. The director of the Luxembourg Monetary Institute, Pierre Jaans, explained that the BCCI was legally based in Luxembourg and in the Cayman Islands but had extensive operations in London, the Middle East, the Far East and Africa. As a result, the BCCI banking group could not be fitted into the philosophy of supervision on a consolidated basis that had been developed since the 1970s. The Bank of England Governor Robert ('Robin') Leigh-Pemberton asked whether a repetition of such a collapse was possible. It clearly was, although the systemic issues involved in large-scale banking crises only really became apparent in 2007–8. For the moment, the BCCI looked idiosyncratically unique and banking in general reassuringly solid. Moreover, the BCCI affair also contributed to the erosion of any impetus to include a broader mandate for securing financial stability, because it brought considerable criticism of Brian Quinn, the Bank of England director who had taken over Huib Muller's international role of pushing for more international coordination of banking supervision and regulation. Thus, far from strengthening the case for a sustained and coordinated European approach to the issues of a newly vigorous international banking system, the BCCI collapse actually weakened the demand for action.

Thus, the governors' draft referred to the possibility that the ECB would take over banking supervision and regulation functions, but by the time this proposal was included in the Maastricht Treaty provisions on monetary policy (Article 105, Section 6), it was accompanied by so many provisos that it looked as if the hurdles to effective European banking supervision could not be set higher (Kenen 1995: 33). The intrusion of politics had therefore resulted in a fundamental flaw in the new European monetary order.

The ECB was thus never given overall supervisory and regulatory powers, and until the outbreak of the financial crisis in 2007–8 almost no one in positions of responsibility thought that was a problem. The critique remained largely academic.

After Maastricht, the BIS largely disengaged from the EMU project, as it turned into a more global institution.[21] The BIS had played a useful role in the European monetary unification process as a discreet meeting venue,

providing logistical and intellectual input through the CoG secretariat and
technical assistance in operating the EMS. Now that the political decision
had been taken to start implementing European monetary union, these
functions naturally had to be taken over by a new independent institution
operating within EU territory, the EMI. The physical move of the EMI –
with its staff now numbering close to fifty – from Basel to Frankfurt in
1993–94 was in that sense the end of an era. The BIS's function as agent of
the EMCF and, somewhat later, as agent for the private ECU clearing also
ceased. The institution in its public pronouncements deliberately held back
on what at least some of its staff perceived as important deficiencies or
absent features of the euro project, generally treating the eurozone as
a single jurisdiction in its Annual Reports.

1.7 Current Accounts Solved?

As the single European currency was realised, did the current account,
which had been *the* issue in European economic policymaking of the pre-
Maastricht period, matter any more? There was some discussion of this
issue before the global financial crisis of 2008, but it was inconclusive. Both
the BIS and the IMF provided diagnoses of the European dilemma that in
retrospect seem perspicacious but which did not grapple adequately with
how the domestic reforms that implicitly were needed to make the
European system robust might be implemented. The BIS Annual Report
in 1999 concluded:

While policy was set to reflect overall economic developments in the euro area,
the process of convergence has led to a situation in which interest rates have
fallen the furthest in Ireland, Italy, Spain and Portugal, where inflation rates
remain relatively high. The implications of the observed regional differences in
inflation rates in the euro area should, however, not be overemphasised.
Although differences in inflation rates may threaten the sustainability of the
exchange rate commitment in a system of fixed but adjustable rates, they have
no comparable implications in a single currency regime. Moreover, the importance of the diversity in regional inflation rates is further limited to the extent that
they reflect differences in the demand for, and the rate of increase in prices of,
non-traded goods. On the other hand, with nominal exchange rate changes no
longer possible, adjustment to any past relative price movements is shifted
entirely to labour and goods markets. Promoting domestic wage and price
flexibility in response to declines in competitiveness within the euro area has
thus become all the more important. (BIS AR 1999: 68)

A 1998 IMF Executive Board paper also thought about the circumstances
in which a member of the monetary union might potentially draw on IMF

resources. The main focus of the paper concerned the fact that the usual way of judging balance-of-payments needs, a shortage of international reserves, would not apply to a union in which members had given up some part of their reserves to the union central bank. It also reflected on how large and stable countries might operate with low levels of reserves. But the authors then went on to think about the possible problems that might arise and traced the possibility of strains either to fiscal needs or to a breakdown of financing (what the paper termed a 'liquidity squeeze'). The opening started by observing that the Fund's interventions must begin with an argument about the balance of payments: 'A member must represent a balance of payments need to make use of the Fund's general resources.' There might be a debt overhang: 'As for balance of payments need in the context of a request by a member for the use of Fund resources, it has often been possible, for members of these other monetary unions, to deduce such a need from the existence of arrears and/or debt rescheduling.'

But a monetary union was not like a standard country issuing its own currency: 'The variable that often plays a crucial role in financing external payments imbalances in countries that have their own currency – international reserves – is usually either completely absent or at least constrained.'

The critical moment would come in a liquidity squeeze, and the document in this respect reads prophetically:

Balance of payments surpluses or deficits could, however, arise in individual members of the monetary union in the event that the union-wide financial system became segmented. For a union like EMU, of course, this would be extremely unlikely. For instance, if country-specific risks triggered a liquidity squeeze and thus pressures on interest rates in an individual union member, the union central bank or the national authorities (within the confines of their limited authority) might be prompted to take official action, if they perceive a risk of harm to the prosperity of the individual member and/or of the union as a whole. In order to alleviate interest rate pressures, the national authorities could in principle choose to engage in official external borrowing, seek debt relief, accumulate external arrears, or induce other residents to incur liabilities abroad.

There might be support through the union: 'It is also conceivable that the union central bank would intervene in the money or credit markets of the member, supplying liquidity or credit to residents (in the form of open market operations or other lending). In the case of EMU, prospective participants have been explicit in ruling out any such intentional intervention.' There was still the possibility of intervention through the payments system, TARGET and then TARGET2:

The provision of liquidity to a part of the union-wide financial system that has become segmented from the rest could also, however, be a byproduct of the central bank's continued provision of liquidity to the union-wide financial system, as the most aggressive and hence successful bidders for such liquidity would be the banks of the distressed country. In both cases, the relevant operations by the union-wide central bank could be regarded as operations inducing residents of an individual member country to borrow abroad, thereby providing accommodating transactions financing an imbalance in that member's external balance.

This paragraph spells out the essential system of the build-up of liabilities in the European settlement system. But it did not go into the issue of what would happen if the liabilities were not regularly settled in a manner analogous to that of the Federal Reserve's Interdistrict Settlement Account.[22]

In fact, the major problems of the eurozone in the Global Financial Crisis were not initially about current-account imbalances (as expressed in net flows) but rather the large gross flows between financial institutions in the eurozone, which represented a vulnerability when panic set in and once national regulators tried to restrict financial flows. That part of the crisis proved to be a vindication of the BIS focus on gross rather than net cross-border movements of capital.[23]

The crisis more generally raised the question of the limits of technocratic policy frameworks. Were not all the major problems of Europe fundamentally political?

1.8 The Primacy of Politics

The Maastricht process was also a result of a major political imperative following from the collapse of the Warsaw Pact and of the Soviet Union, and from the way that German unification in 1990 altered the political balance of power. French President François Mitterrand was outraged by Chancellor Helmut Kohl's Ten-Point Plan for German unity and told the Germans that there was a risk of falling back to the world of 1913 – in other words to the Great Power conflicts that had led to the First World War. Kohl gave in to French pressure and agreed at a meeting in Strasbourg on 5 December 1989 to concrete plans to hold an IGC that would prepare for a European Union (Kohl would initially have preferred to defer the IGC). French diplomatic historians refer to this as a French success, which ensured that German unity was embedded firmly in a European process (Bozo 2009: 130–1). Three days later, at one of the critical meetings to discuss the shape of the post–Cold War world, Helmut Kohl told US

Secretary of State James Baker that Germany would be obliged as a condition for French consent to unification to give up its currency and that the move was opposed by the powerful Bundesbank and would 'hurt German interests'. But nevertheless Kohl saw the move as necessary since 'Germany needs friends' in Europe (Sarotte 2011: 85). In consequence, and referring to this conversation, many Germans – especially German conservatives – have seen the euro as from the beginning a concession to France, ceding monetary control from a powerful Bundesbank that in practice in the EMS dictated the conditions of European monetary policy, to a European central bank, in which the German influence would be watered down, and the German vote equal to that of very small member states such as Malta (later, with the expansion of the monetary union, a rotating voting mechanism meant that at some moments the German representative did not even have a vote). Some interpreters have seen this incident as a new version of the betrayal theory that poisoned German democracy in the 1920s with the view that Germany had not been legitimately defeated in the First World War but that German interests had been 'stabbed in the back' by domestic politicians. Kohl was responsible in this view for a key abdication of German interests (Hanke 1998).

Interpreting Kohl's statement is not easy, and it should probably not be taken at face value. Kohl wanted to impress on the US administration the sacrifice that Germany was undertaking. Some influential Germans, including the President of the Bundesbank Helmut Schlesinger, believed that the independence of the Bundesbank, which they regarded as central to Germany's political economy, could always be revoked by the German parliament and that embodying the 'German' features of central-bank independence in a treaty would give a much more secure guarantee that policy would be set in the right way. French diplomatic historians have also demonstrated the fallaciousness of the view that Mitterrand demanded the sacrifice of the Deutsche Mark as the price for German unity. The technical discussion of monetary union in the Delors Committee had been concluded in April 1989, at a time when no one in any influential position in the West expected any quick end to the Cold War

In the wake of the 2007–8 financial crisis, when the combination of a bank crisis and a sovereign debt crisis in the eurozone led to doubts about the economic rationale of integration, primarily political theories about the fundamental drivers of the process began to flourish. There are two versions of the political story. Both focus obsessively on the politics of the German role in driving monetary union, so that it again appears that solving the German question is central to the future of Europe. Both are mirror images of each other: in one Germany appears as uniquely virtuous and in the other as terribly vicious.

In the first view – the virtuous German story – the currency union was a high-minded European political project that ignored economic realities. It was needed to stop the recurrence of war between France and Germany. Proponents of the euro project, such as the veteran German Foreign Minister Hans-Dietrich Genscher, but also opponents, such as the economist Martin Feldstein (2012), have touted this theory. But it is implausible. Americans are perfectly aware that they have not had a war with Canada or Mexico recently (although in the long past there were indeed such conflicts) and that they don't need a currency union to improve relations with neighbours. On the other hand, Americans are aware that civil wars can occur in malfunctioning currency unions (in the mid-nineteenth century, at exactly the time Napoleon III was dreaming of world monetary union), and Ireland too has its own terrible twentieth-century experience of the damage done by civil war.

Then there is the vicious view of the origins of the euro, a conspiracy theory about a deep-seated German masterplan. Some of its earliest proponents were British, such as the former UK Chancellor of the Exchequer Denis Healey (1989), but now it is circulating widely, above all in southern and peripheral Europe. Since Germany had lower rates of wage inflation than France and much lower rates than the Mediterranean countries, a locked currency would guarantee increased export surpluses, at the price of misery elsewhere. A German grasp for European economic primacy would succeed at the end of the twentieth century and in the new millennium where a similar German military plan had failed one century earlier. For the critics, Germany's currency manipulation was a mercantilist strategy of securing permanent trade and current-account surpluses that would give Germany a commanding control of resources.

This view seems as absurd as the first myth about peace and money. If this is what the Germans were aiming at, wouldn't other countries be able to get some whiff of the nefarious plot? And more importantly, if this were really a strategy it is a pretty short-sighted one (not really that much better than the disastrous Schlieffen Plan of 1914 to defeat both France and Russia at the same time). Plunging one's neighbours into national bankruptcy is not a good way of building any kind of stable prosperity.

It has become fashionable to say that the moves of the early 1990s were undertaken in a mood of carelessness (*Sorglosigkeit*), in Otmar Issing's phrase (2012), or that Chancellor Kohl was neglectful (*leichtsinnig*), according to Hans Peter Schwarz's monumental recent biography (2012).

Kohl promised a political union: on 6 November 1991, he told an ecstatically applauding German parliament that 'one cannot repeat it often enough: political union is the indispensable counterpart of the economic and monetary union'. But when the governments negotiated a few weeks later in Maastricht, there were very concrete plans for the monetary union, and for the political union – none at all. The reality is that reassuring Europeans in the aftermath of 1990 that the continent would be peaceful did require a dramatic gesture. The most obvious and reassuring step might have been to create a common European army, but there were no plans for that; the defence ministries and national procurement strategies that aimed at providing a kind of industrial policy would block any such move. But the central bankers had developed in 1988–89, before there was any chance of German unity, a coherent plan that would represent a dramatic gesture of Europeanness: the creation of a common money. So that plan was at the heart of the IGC of Maastricht.

The legacy of Kohl and Mitterrand was a tremendous political investment in the euro. At the beginning of the euro crisis, in 2010, justifying the German contribution of 123 billion euros to the Greek rescue package, Chancellor Angela Merkel told the German parliament that the crisis posed an 'existential challenge' for Europe and that if the euro failed, Europe would fail.[24] Meeting that challenge would require, in Merkel's view, a new 'stability culture' (a favourite concept of traditional Germans), a reform of the global financial architecture, and a resolute uncovering of the flaws of the European Union. It was a matter of maintaining and sustaining the 'European idea'. She explicitly, however, rejected any move to a 'transfer union', and that position remained a key part of German politics.

The consequence of this initial stance was that there was a massive capital of political credibility in the monetary union that surprised many market participants who speculated on a collapse of the kind that hedge funds and others had inflicted on the EMS in 1992–3. That political capital came as a long-term consequence of the early 1990s crises and of the lessons learnt then. Some of the key participants in critical moments of the euro crisis had indeed also been in central positions in the early 1990s. Michel Sapin was France's Minister of Finance from 1992 to 1993, when he briefly proposed treating speculators as the French Revolution had dealt with *agioteurs*, and again from 2014 to 2017. Wolfgang Schäuble, the German finance minister from 2009 to 2017, had been the leader of the Christian Democratic group in the German parliament from 1991 to 2000. Mario Draghi was at the centre of the Italian lira crisis in 1992 as Director of the Treasury, and in the euro crisis was Governor of the Bank of Italy from 2005 to 2011 and then President of the ECB. They all learnt about how an absolute political commitment might take the rug from under the 'speculators'. On the other side, David Cameron had been caught on camera standing behind the Chancellor of the Exchequer as the failure of the British European policy was announced and learnt a lesson about European failure. From the European perspective, the struggle was often seen as one that pitted politics against markets. There is an irony in that the euro survived the period when many saw a break-up as imminent and inevitable, between the summer of 2011 and the summer of 2012, but in the longer run the preservation of the euro increased the strains on the political system and led to a widespread questioning of the European Union and its role.

The origins of the euro in a German-French compromise had another consequence for the capacity of Europe to respond to a major crisis. A concern with fiscal discipline and strict fiscal limits meant that all the European firepower against the crisis lay in the construction of a monetary policy big bazooka. Monetary action was the only game in town: but it was one about which Germans also felt highly uncomfortable.

Europe's move to monetary integration with a common currency (the euro) was a quite unique process and is often held up as a model for monetary cooperation in other parts of the world: in the Gulf region, where there are periodic discussions of monetary unification, as well as in Asia and Latin America, where movements towards greater monetary integration also have some support but encounter a plethora of difficulties. Nevertheless, at the latest by the financial crisis of 2007–8, it became clear that there were substantial design flaws in the concept of the EMU. As Patrick Honohan (2012) put it, 'release 1.0 of the euro was under-designed, and robust only to moderate shocks'.

What was the design flaw? It is often claimed – especially but not only by American economists – that the travails of the euro, as well as the history of past monetary unions (Bordo and Jonung 2003), show that it is impossible to have a monetary union in the absence of a political union, which establishes a common political process for determining the distribution of fiscal costs. Paul de Grauwe (2012) stated the case quite simply: 'The Euro is a currency without a country. To make it sustainable a European country has to be created.' Successive ECB presidents, rhetorically at least, seemed to endorse this advice. Accepting the Charlemagne Prize in Aachen, Jean-Claude Trichet (2011) said: 'In a long term historical perspective, Europe – which has invented the concept and the word of democracy – is called to complete the design of what it already calls a "Union".' Mario Draghi (2012) has been even more dramatic, demanding the collective commitment of all governments to reform the governance of the euro area. This means completing economic and monetary union along four key pillars: (i) a financial union with a single supervisor at its heart, to re-unify the banking system; (ii) a fiscal union with enforceable rules to restore fiscal capacity; (iii) an economic union that fosters sustained growth and employment; and (iv) a political union, where the exercise of shared sovereignty is rooted in political legitimacy.

This advice seems appallingly radical to many, since almost every politician denies that there is any real possibility of creating something resembling a European state, and almost every citizen recoils at the prospect. The fact that the discussion to which Draghi contributed had been going on for decades suggests that there were no very easy solutions.

In responding to the debt crisis, Europe moved quite quickly to create a range of new institutions: in May 2010, the European Financial Stability Facility (EFSF) and the European Financial Stabilisation Mechanism (EFSM), with a combined volume of up to 500 billion euros. In 2011, the initially temporary EFSF was transformed into a permanent European Stability Mechanism that was eventually to morph into a European Monetary Fund. The European Banking Authority (EBA) was established on 1 January 2011 as part of the European System of Financial Supervision (ESFS). Most critically, the ECB was given responsibility for banking supervision in 2012, and there was an agreement to set up a Single Resolution Mechanism, which started to operate in 2016. Without that institutional framework, Draghi's famous 'whatever it takes' promise would have been vain. But the banking union is still incomplete. The resolution framework looked spectacularly successful in Spain, with the winding-up of Banco Popular Español, but the case of two smaller banks in northeastern Italy raised the question of how systematically the framework would be applied. The issue of deposit insurance also remained unresolved.

The obvious flaws of the monetary union, the problem of fiscal rules and of financial supervision, needed a political fix. The BIS as a locus of 'realism', to take up Leslie O'Brien's phrase, had to accommodate itself to a politically driven process that extended the idea of central-bank cooperation to its ultimate conclusion – monetary integration – in the aftermath of a profoundly disruptive series of crises in the early 1990s that brought home the realities of capital mobility and the inadequacies of existing solutions. The view adopted, that this move necessarily required more labour and product market flexibility, was logical, but it was not clear how or why the political drive to make that change would sustain itself in the absence of an explicit political commitment to realising more dimensions of what was implied by the concept 'European Union'.

The BIS, in fulfilment of its mission as a mechanism for central-bank cooperation, was a major provider of the logistical infrastructure that made possible and thinkable the drive for monetary union. Its umbrella allowed the EPU, the CoG, the EMCF, the CoG's Banking Supervision Subcommittee and initially even the EMI, the precursor of the ECB, to operate smoothly and silently outside the political limelight. If central banks became more and more prominent in the late twentieth century, that process in itself was an eloquent testimony to the effectiveness of the BIS operations. The BIS did not do large-scale politics – that had to come from governments; what it did in a constrained technical domain, however, allowed politics to realise, in the financial and economic sphere, key elements of the dream of European integration. It didn't comment or interpret the dreams, and that meant too that it couldn't really tackle the nightmares.

Notes

1. BoE G1/1, 28 July 1929, Sir Charles Addis to Frederick Leith-Ross.
2. On the internationalisation of the BIS at the end of the twentieth century, see Chapter 2 (Catherine Schenk) of this volume.
3. Historical Archive of Deutsche Bundesbank, HADB, 4 November 1958 ZBR and 11 November 1958 ZBR.
4. UK National Archives, NA, PREM 16/1615, Couzens note for Wicks, 31 March 1978; PREM 16/1641, Prime Minister's conversation with Mr Roy Jenkins, 31 March 1978.
5. A fair translation would be 'Europe will be created through the currency, or it will not be created at all.'
6. HADB, B330/26258, 16 November 1978, Emminger to Schmidt, Betr. Stellungnahme des Zentralbankrats zum künftigen EWS.
7. ECB Archive, CoG, Fourth meeting of Delors Committee, 13 December 1998, minutes.
8. CoG, 4 January 1989, Macrofiscal functions performed by the Centre for Economic Policy Coordination.
9. CoG, 31 January 1989, Lamfalussy note.
10. CoG, Second Delors committee meeting, 10 October 1988, transcript.
11. Moreover, later work, i.a. by the BIS Economic Adviser Stephen Cecchetti, found that government debt levels above a threshold of 85 per cent of GDP usually constitute a drag on growth (Cecchetti, Mohanty and Zampolli 2011).
12. CoG Secretariat, 9 February 1990, Note for the Attention of President Pöhl; also HADB, B330/24111.
13. CoG, Huib Muller, 7 December 1988: Note for EC Governors, Prudential Supervision of Banks in the European Community.
14. CoG, Meeting 243, 13 March 1990, Basel.
15. HADB, B330/018462, 26 January 1989, Wolfgang Kuntz to Pöhl; 20 February 1989, Tietmeyer to Pöhl; 23 February 1989, Pöhl to Kuntze; BdF, 1489200205/118, 5 May 1992, Commission bancaire: Note pour le Gouverneur.

16. HADB, B330/24112, 22 February 1990, Report on Monetary Policy Committee.

17. CoG, Meeting 243, 13 March 1990.

18. CoG, Committee of Alternates, 29 June 1990; See also C. van den Berg, *The Making of the Statute of the European System of Central Banks,* 67.

19. CoG, Committee of Alternates, 16 October 1990.

20. CoG, 28 June 1991, Banco de España, Comparison between the Governors' and the Presidency's Non-Paper. Draft Statutes of the ESCB; 16 July 1991, Explanatory Note.

21. On the globalisation of the BIS after the move of the EMI from Basel to Frankfurt, see chapter 2 (Catherine Schenk) of this volume.

22. IMF, *EMU and the Fund – Use of Fund Resources and Use of Euros in the Fund's Operational Budget* (EBS/98/132).

23. The BIS focus on gross financial flows first came to the fore in C. Borio and P. Disyatat, Global imbalances and the financial crisis: link or no link?, *BIS Working Papers,* No. 346, May 2011. See also: C. Borio, H. James and H. S. Shin, The international monetary and financial system: a capital account historical perspective, *BIS Working Papers,* No. 457, August 2014.

24. See www.bundestag.de/dokumente/textarchiv/2010/29826227_kw20_de_stabilisier-ungsmechanismus-201760

2

The Governance of the Bank for International Settlements, 1973–2020

Catherine R. Schenk

The changes in the structure, organisation and governance of the Bank for International Settlements (BIS) from the 1970s to the early twenty-first century were profoundly affected by international political change as well as the shifting pattern of global banking. The end of the Cold War and the rise of Asia rebalanced the global economy. At the same time, these decades witnessed the explosion of international financial activity, rapid financial innovation and changes to the role and influence of central banks. The challenges posed by the transformation of international finance became even more profoundly important in the wake of the global financial crisis of 2007–8. But the structure and operations of the BIS also responded to internal pressures, especially changes in leadership and vision, and were constrained by the Bank's formal Statutes from its founding in 1930. This chapter will explore how these external and internal pressures manifested themselves in the structures and governance of the BIS. First, however, a few words on the unusual nature of the BIS.

The BIS came from an earlier generation of international financial institutions (IFIs) than the Bretton Woods institutions like the International Monetary Fund (IMF) and World Bank. By the 1970s it had emerged as an awkward entity, somewhere between commercial bank and international policy institution. It operated on a profit-making basis through its Banking Department, and its shares were held mainly but not exclusively by public or quasi-public bodies. Its key committees were devoted to sharing best practice, discussing policy, monitoring the market and devising benchmarks or standards for regulation and supervision. In times of international crisis, the BIS was often a participant alongside the IMF in providing short-term credit, but on the other hand its operations have always been confidential and commercially based and it did not have the same level of public accountability as a governmental or quasi-governmental organisation. Since the 1960s key monetary and financial policy discussions at the BIS took place within the framework of the Group of Ten (G10) of leading industrialised countries that emerged from the IMF's General Arrangements to Borrow (GAB). But it took the BIS until 1994 to adapt its formal governance to this reality, by ensuring that all G10 central-bank Governors were part of the BIS Board of Directors. Therefore, there was – and still is – a continual tension between discretion, market operations and customer service on the one hand and public service, policy coordination and diffusion of standard-setting on the other. This has left the Bank open to challenges about its transparency (e.g. LeBor 2013).

By the 1990s, the functions and governance of the major IFIs were under attack, partly because of the persistence of inequalities in income between countries and partly because the global system these IFIs were designed to protect collapsed with the end of the pegged exchange rate system (Gore 2000; Ocampo 2017; Woods 2000). The BIS had a narrower remit to provide banking services and to promote cooperation among central banks primarily in Europe and with the United States, so it mostly escaped public attention during these debates. It also avoided political influence by constraining its membership to central banks and its governance to central bankers rather than finance ministers. This effect was amplified by the growing orthodoxy that central banks should be independent of governments. This benign environment meant that the formal governance of the Bank remained largely unchanged for almost seventy years, although it did not completely escape the challenges of legitimacy and authority.

The modern conception of governance describes the way power is exerted in the management of an organisation and became linked closely to formal structures in the debate over corporate governance in the 1990s. Key determinants of 'good' governance include interlinked characteristics of legitimacy, authority and effectiveness (Stoker 1998; Williamson 1996). Legitimacy can be gained through inclusivity in representation and transparency, and from a track record of effectiveness. Authority, in turn, draws on expertise proven through a record of success. Effective governance requires efficient and timely decision-making as well as traction to translate decisions into action. This constellation creates tensions between inclusivity and efficiency. The governance of the BIS was particularly challenging because the Board believed the effectiveness of its core mandate for cooperation relied on the exclusive 'club-like' atmosphere that had grown over the first fifty years of its operations. On the other hand, with financial globalisation, traction was required to disseminate its benchmark standards and the Bank's legitimacy was challenged by its narrow leadership and exclusive membership.

In terms of economic diplomacy, the BIS was trapped between region-alism and multilateralism: until the mid-1990s governance was regional while the target of the Bank's policy was more widely multilateral. During the period under review, the leadership resisted becoming truly multi-lateral in terms of a (close to) universal membership, as is the case for the IMF, World Bank or United Nations. Instead, new members were added with limited powers of decision-making and without diluting the privileges of founding members. The 1990s orthodoxy of central-bank independence and the increased focus of the Bank's activities on the diffusion of precau-tionary regulatory standards to enhance systemic financial stability further legitimised this approach. Retaining the Bank's distinctive governance was also made easier from 1999, when the Financial Stability Forum (FSF) coordinated the Bank's expertise with those of other IFIs and embedded the Bank into a wider network of agencies and institutions.

Another reason to restrict the governance of the Bank was the value placed on trust, which allowed frank and open discussions behind closed doors. The privacy of discussions allowed the exchange of privileged information. But as the Board and management debated and delayed over expanding the breadth of its governance, the scale and scope of the global financial system changed dramatically. In 2007, it was clear that this 'club' model had failed. Rather than protecting the system, the echo chamber of the G10 Governors failed to rectify the market frailties that ultimately led to the global financial crisis. The source of the crisis was not in the emerging-market economies that were lobbying for entry into the BIS throughout the 1990s but within the G10; mismanagement in US mortgage markets and the European sovereign-debt market spilled over into the rest of the world. The Bank faced losing its authority and legiti-macy unless it adapted to the new global economic structure.

Since its creation in 1930, the BIS has had three levels of governance: its members, the Board of Directors and the management. The BIS has always been mainly owned by its member central banks through shareholding, although in its early days some of the shares issued to the central banks of Belgium, France and the United States were sold publicly. By 2000, 14 per cent of the shares were in the portfolios of about 4,400 private investors with no voting rights who received regular dividends. The Bank acquired these shares back through compulsory purchase in 2001. Since then the shares are exclusively owned by member central banks. The Board of Directors is the decision-making body and was drawn from the Governors of the founding central banks, except the US Federal Reserve Board, which did not take up its seat until 1994. The Board elected a Chair, who appointed the President of the Bank. In practice, since 1948, these two offices were held by the same person. The five founding central banks (those of Belgium, France, Germany, Italy and the United Kingdom) each had two Directors on the Board, who then elected a further three representatives from among the other member central banks (since the early 1930s these had always been the Governors of the central banks of the Netherlands, Sweden and Switzerland). The General Manager was appointed by the Board and had important influence over the direction of the Bank and its day-to-day operations but could not force through major changes without the agreement of the Board. The General Manager chaired the Executive Committee, which brought together department heads and other senior managers to discuss the management of the Bank's activities. From 1995 a separate Finance Committee had a strategic role in determining the risk strategy in the banking operations side of the Bank. The governance therefore had remained largely unchanged in the forty years to 1973.

At the same time, it is important to make a distinction between the governance structure, including membership, on the one hand, and the BIS's customer base, on the other. The BIS serves a broad community of central banks, not only those that are shareholding members. This is done partly through its banking services. Currently, the BIS has a banking relationship with some 190 central banks and international organisations. Its cooperative activities also involve a broader community, including meetings at the BIS and of the standard-setting bodies and international secretariats hosted by the Bank, as well as the collection and dissemination of statistics and research. Over time, these banking and cooperative activities have widened their geographic reach beyond the shareholding membership. Meanwhile, the Bank's governance has faced new challenges as the Bretton Woods system ended and international banking markets have become more integrated.

First we look at the BIS's governance arrangements in the first two decades after the collapse of the Bretton Woods system. Throughout this period the G10 remained the main focal point of meetings and governance at the BIS. The second section looks at the gradual but very significant expansion of BIS membership after 1994, which turned the Bank into a truly global organisation. Section 2.3 deals with the difficult and slow reform of the Bank's highest governance body – the BIS Board of Directors. This process was greatly speeded up as the result of the new realities created by the 2007–8 financial crisis. This is the topic of Section 2.4. Section 2.5 summarises and concludes.

2.1 1973–1994: Focus on the G10

For the first twenty years after the end of the Bretton Woods system, the BIS remained largely unchanged. It did play a role in the main international economic events of this period, including providing bridge funding during the 1980s sovereign-debt crisis and helping with technical advice and banking services to the central banks of the post-communist states after the end of the Cold War. But these were changes in the Bank's operations that did not profoundly affect its organisation or governance. Throughout this period, the G10 that had emerged in the early 1960s as the main driver for international monetary reform was also a key focus for international cooperation within the BIS (Borio, Toniolo and Clement 2008; Schenk 2010). From the start, the BIS had a complex relationship with this grouping, since the G10 Governors met at the monthly meetings in Basel, but not all members of the G10 were represented on the BIS Board. Importantly, the US Federal Reserve, the Bank of Canada and the Bank of Japan were not Board members. Instead, Sunday-night dinners of G10 Governors at the monthly meeting weekends became the main forum for cooperation during these decades, although this was not part of the original Statutes. While the dinners were relatively informal, they often had a chosen topic or agenda. The meetings were not formally minuted, although reports of what was discussed filtered back to member central banks. They thus allowed the Governors to discuss major issues in the international system as well as confidential details about their own national economies and banking systems. This discreet and frank exchange of information was the foundation of the international cooperation fostered at the Bank.

From the time of the collapse of the pegged exchange rate system in 1973 to the arrival of Andrew Crockett as General Manager in 1994, the transformation of the international banking and monetary system preoccupied the BIS management and its operations. This was the era of the rise of influence and prominence of the key committees of the BIS: the Basel Committee on Banking Supervision (BCBS), the Euro-currency Standing Committee (ECSC), the Gold and Foreign Exchange Committee and the Committee on Payment and Settlement Systems (CPSS). These committees, particularly the Basel Committee, became the most visible parts of the BIS for outside observers and the market. The BIS supplied the secretariats, but the members and chairs of the committees themselves were mostly drawn from staff of the G10 central banks. The committees thus brought together the key technical staff responsible for their area of expertise at regular meetings to

Table 2.1 *The BIS between 1973 and 1993 – Board of Directors and member central banks*

Composition of the BIS Board of Directors (number of Directors in parentheses)

National Bank of Belgium (2)	Deutsche Bundesbank (2)	Bank of England (2)	Sveriges Riksbank (1) Swiss National Bank (1)
Bank of France (2)	Bank of Italy (2)	Netherlands Bank (1)	

Shareholding central banks (with year of accession)

National Bank of Belgium (1930)	Central Bank of the Republic of Austria (1930)	Bank of Estonia (1930)	Central Bank of the Republic of Turkey (1951)
Bank of France (1930)	Bulgarian National Bank (1930)	Bank of Latvia (1930)	Bank of Spain (1960)
Deutsche Bundesbank (1930)	Danmarks Nationalbank (1930)	Bank of Lithuania (1931)	Bank of Canada (1970)
Bank of Italy (1930)	Bank of Finland (1930)	Central Bank of Norway (1931)	Bank of Japan (1930, 1970)[2]
Bank of England (1930)	Bank of Greece (1930)	National Bank of Yugoslavia (1931)[3]	Reserve Bank of Australia (1970)
Federal Reserve System USA (1930)[1]	Magyar Nemzeti Bank (1930)	Central Bank of Iceland (1950)	South African Reserve Bank (1971)
Netherlands Bank (1930)	Narodowy Bank Polski (1930)	Central Bank of Ireland (1950)	Czech National Bank (1930, 1993)[4]
Sveriges Riksbank (1930)	National Bank of Romania (1930)	Bank of Portugal (1951)	National Bank of Slovakia (1930, 1993)[4]
Swiss National Bank (1930)			

1 The Federal Reserve System did not itself take up any BIS shares but chose to offer the issue assigned to it for public subscription.

2 The Bank of Japan had been one of the BIS's founder members in 1930, although it was not itself allowed to hold BIS shares back then (these were held by a consortium of Japanese private banks instead). As a result of the 1952 San Francisco Peace Treaty, Japan renounced all rights linked to its participation in the 1930 Young Plan, including BIS membership. The Bank of Japan became a BIS member again in 1970.

3 The membership of the National Bank of Yugoslavia was in abeyance from 1991 to 1992 as a result of the civil war and dissolution of the Yugoslav Republic. The legal succession of the National Bank of Yugoslavia as BIS member central bank was resolved in 1997–2009, with the central banks of Croatia, Macedonia, Slovenia, Bosnia-Herzegovina and Serbia all becoming BIS member central banks.

4 The Czechoslovak National Bank was a BIS member central bank from 1930. In 1993, it was legally succeeded as BIS member central bank by both the Czech National Bank and the National Bank of Slovakia.

develop practical solutions in response to calls from the G10 Governors. They also monitored developments in each jurisdiction and shared best practice. BIS staff contributed in important ways to shape the agenda and pace of their business, but the committees took their direction from, and reported back to, the G10 Governors. The committee structure thus reinforced the G10 Governors' leadership role in driving the agenda for the BIS policy areas, as distinct from the Board, which was still exclusively European until 1994.

The BCBS has the highest public profile. From 1973 the new exchange rate system mixed floating rates for the US dollar, Japanese yen and Deutsche Mark with pegged rates among European currencies and pegs to the floating key currencies among a range of developing and emerging economies. This system introduced new risks to international banking, from volatile exchange rates and interest rates that erupted in a 'silent crisis' in 1974 when several small international banks collapsed and others were undermined by fraud and liquidity losses (Schenk 2014). The most famous was the collapse of Herstatt Bank, which was deemed insolvent and closed by German regulators in June 1974 while its US correspondent banks in New York were still open for business, leaving uncovered exposures. This episode is widely credited with spurring the launch of the BCBS in 1974. In fact, the collapse of the lesser-known Israel-British Bank (IBB) in London and a rogue-trading scandal at the Lloyds Bank branch in Lugano that same summer more closely reflected the Basel Committee's early business. The IBB collapse highlighted a lack of agreement about which central bank was responsible as lender of last resort for international subsidiaries. The Lloyds scandal revealed the risks inherent in the division of responsibility between host and home authorities for supervising international bank offices. At the end of 1974, these episodes prompted the Governors of the G10 central banks to launch the Basel Committee to consider developing an 'early warning' system to help central banks anticipate bank failures, but this initiative was abandoned at the first meeting of the Committee on the grounds that no new system was needed to supplement national supervisory authorities (Schenk 2014). Instead, the Committee focused on allocating responsibility for supervising international banks between home and host authorities, following up work that had begun among European central bankers in their Groupe de Contact (Goodhart 2011: 96–100). The first attempt was the Basel Concordat of 1975, which set out general guidelines, but noted that 'it is not possible to draw up clear-cut rules for determining exactly where the responsibility for supervision can best be placed in any particular situation'. Different solutions were recommended for different forms of international representation (branches, subsidiaries and joint ventures) and also for different indicators (liquidity, solvency and foreign exchange position). An important concern was that no individual central bank was willing to become de facto lender of last resort to the international banking system. Instead, the Concordat emphasised that cross-border sharing of information was vital to close supervisory gaps effectively.

After the first Concordat, the Basel Committee turned to setting capital-adequacy standards, an issue which became particularly acute after the sovereign-debt crisis of 1982, which downgraded the assets of many banks internationally. During the 1970s banks in most financial centres had taken part in syndicated loans to governments in Latin America and other developing economies that were many times the nominal value of individual bank capital. The threat that these loans would lose their value, leading to bank insolvency that could prove contagious across borders, prompted greater urgency to setting standards for risk-based minimum capital requirements. Staff of the IMF, for example, had already warned its Executive Board in September 1974 of a potential sovereign-debt crisis if the pace of lending continued. The pace of lending receded in 1975, but the G10 central-bank Governors remained uneasy, and by 1977 country risk and maturity transformation were being discussed in the Basel Committee. In 1980 the G10 Governors publicly expressed their concern about capital adequacy, liquidity and concentration of risks. A key obstacle was the lack of consistent data, which was taken up by a special working group, although this made little progress before the sovereign-debt crisis struck in August 1982. Likewise, the Basel Committee's efforts to agree to principles on capital adequacy for international lending were mired in lengthy questionnaires sent to member central banks and technical discussions that dragged on through 1981 to 1984 (Goodhart 2011: 146–60). The lengthy process of achieving consensus and coping with objections by banks became symptomatic of the Basel Committee's deliberations. In the end, a bilateral agreement between the Bank of England and the Federal Reserve increased the pressure on other members of the Committee, and the first Basel Accord on minimum capital requirements was finally released in July 1988.

Meanwhile, the sovereign-debt crisis had also highlighted failures in supervision of international banking, and the 1975 Concordat was updated in 1983 to reflect the need to monitor the consolidated business of international banks, which put more onus on home supervisors. This approach to viewing the breadth of a bank's activities also anticipated the complications from the mergers-and-acquisitions boom in international banking that began in the mid-1980s. The Basel Accord was reviewed in the wake of the Asian financial crisis of 1997. The revision of some aspects of the Accord was agreed in 1999. A new Basel II framework was finally adopted in 2004–2005, but it was just in the process of being implemented when the global financial crisis struck a few years later. The global financial crisis exposed a series of gaps and weaknesses that were addressed in Basel III, the first version of which was published in 2011 and which was finalised in 2017. The Basel Capital Accords have focused attention on a minimum threshold of adequate reserves and encouraged banks to develop more sophisticated risk-assessment tools.[1] In 1998, the Basel Committee and the BIS jointly created the Financial Stability Institute (FSI) with a mandate to reach out to and assist supervisors around the world in improving and strengthening their financial systems, that is through information-sharing and training.[2] But as Stefan Ingves, the Chair of the Basel Committee, remarked in 2018, 'banking crises are inevitable' and the business of the standards is to 'mitigate their likelihood and impact' (Ingves 2018).

Although not as well known outside the BIS as the BCBS, the Eurocurrency Standing Committee (ECSC) was a vital arena for international cooperation among G10 central bankers. The need to monitor the globalisation of international payments, particularly through the Eurodollar market, prompted the G10 central-bank Governors to establish the ECSC in 1971. The creation of the Basel Committee three years later introduced overlapping between more macroeconomic systemic overview for the ECSC as against the microprudential policy remit of the Basel Committee. Through the 1973–1974 oil crisis the Eurodollar market allowed OPEC dollar surpluses to be channelled through the European banking system to oil importers. But, as seen earlier, the huge accumulation of bank lending to governments prompted disquiet in many areas. One of the key difficulties was the lack of precise data on the amount and direction of international bank lending, and this became a main stream of activity for the ECSC, which laboured to collect consistent data from G10 central banks. Data on the Eurocurrency market were published in the BIS Annual Report, and from 1983 more data on sovereign borrowing in particular were circulated in a joint initiative between the BIS, the OECD and the IMF. Unfortunately, this proved to be too little, too late. The Mexican government threatened to suspend service of its debts in August 1982, prompting other countries to follow and drawing the international banking community into a sovereign-debt crisis. During the 1990s, the focus of the ECSC shifted to systemic stability issues and in 1999 it was renamed the Committee on the Global Financial System to reflect its wider remit (Borio and Toniolo 2008: 49–68).

The tensions over the remits of the Committees were starkly exposed in the run-up to the 1982 sovereign-debt crisis. In 1979 the ECSC, chaired by the BIS Economic Adviser Alexandre Lamfalussy, tried to push for more progress on country-risk analysis and ensuring banks had adequate reserves in the case of default or restructuring.[3] But it faced resistance from the Basel Committee under Peter Cooke (Chair 1977–1988), which felt the topic encroached on its own remit of microprudential supervision. The Basel Committee's view was that supervisors' duties were to ensure that banks themselves had appropriate methods in place rather than mandating a particular approach to country risk. In the end, the BCBS sent out general guidance on country risk in June 1982, a mere two months before the sovereign-debt crisis struck in August (Goodhart 2011: 137–40).

The potential impact of the information and communication technology revolution on banking systems prompted the G10 Governors to establish a Group of Computer Experts in 1969, from which the Group of Experts on Payment Systems was separated out in 1980. Compared with the Basel Committee, this group kept a fairly low profile and was mainly restricted to technical issues. Nevertheless, the architecture for international payments was a vital area of cooperation. Its first Chair (1980–1982) was George Blunden from the Bank of England, who had also been the inaugural chair of the Basel Committee from 1975 to 1977. In 1989 the G10 Governors shifted the work of the Group to an ad hoc Committee on Interbank Netting Systems, which was then widened to the Committee on Payment and Settlement Systems in 1990 (since 2014 named Committee on Payments and Market Infrastructures (CPMI)).

Finally, the Gold and Foreign Exchange Committee had been established in 1962 to monitor the global gold market and manage the Gold Pool (Toniolo 2005: 375–81; also Annex 2). It also became the venue for discussions of other ways to support the international monetary system both during and after the Bretton Woods era, including through central-bank swaps (McCauley and Schenk 2020). The Committee started as a European-US body reflecting the membership of the Gold Pool, but the discussions quickly widened beyond monitoring the Gold Pool to questions of managing the international monetary system through foreign exchange intervention. Meeting usually monthly, the Committee became a venue to share intervention strategies and how central bankers viewed the future of exchange markets in a timely manner. Thus, it was through this Committee that much of the discussion of the support for sterling was arranged, culminating in the last Basel sterling agreement of 1977. In 2002 it was renamed the Markets Committee.

Beyond the gatherings of G10 central-bank Governors with their formal and informal agenda, these G10-governed Committees became the conduit for the important technical cooperation and exchange of information and best practice that was the focus of the BIS's activities during the 1970s and 1980s. Through their activities the Bank established itself as a useful venue for central-bank staff to meet, produce industry guidance and coordinate their activities. Of particular importance for the public and the banking industry was the development of the common standards through the Basel Committee, but the operations of the other committees cemented G10 central-banking relationships in a way that was more important than the Board's deliberations. This was especially the case because the G10 committees included the US Federal Reserve and the Bank of Japan at a time when the dollar and the yen formed two of the key poles of the global monetary system. Japanese banks were among the largest (and least capitalised) in the world, and therefore integrating them into systemic-stability discussions and data sharing was crucial. Within the existing governance of the BIS, the narrow Board membership, which excluded Japan and the United States, meant that these committees had to arise from the G10 central-bank group rather than the BIS Board itself. The functional committees received their directions from and reported to the G10 Governors, who then reported on their work through press statements. Already from the 1970s, therefore, the legacy of the BIS's governance structure, with its Eurocentric bias, was becoming an increasingly awkward foundation for the Bank's mission.

As noted earlier, the second part of the Bank's mission is to provide banking services to its customers, which are not only its member central banks but the broader central-banking community. Beyond the service aspect, the BIS's banking business is important for two main reasons. First, it provides the BIS and the central-bank community with additional resources that can be used if needed to initiate or contribute to bilateral or multilateral financial arrangements supporting the international monetary and financial system. Second, it is the profit earned through this banking activity that allows the BIS to finance itself and fund all its cooperative activities. In the banking area, too, the BIS's outreach witnessed a steady expansion in the 1970s and 1980s beyond its traditional European constituency. From its origins the Bank accepted deposits of central-bank reserves, mainly at short term, and from the 1970s the balance sheet expanded as the nominal value of global reserves increased and opportunities for the Bank to deposit its funds in the Eurodollar market created a lucrative business. The BIS was able to reinvest the reserves of central banks into the Eurodollar market at a margin. The central banks thus accessed the Eurodollar market without the counter-party risk of directly depositing with commercial banks. Graph A.1 in Annex 3 to this book shows the growth of the Bank's balance sheet from 1980 to 2003. The international financial arrangements in which the BIS played an active role in this period – such as the sterling support arrangements, the recycling of petrodollars and the credit operations in the context of the 1980s sovereign-debt crisis – drew an ever larger number of central banks into the orbit of the BIS banking services, many of them from outside Europe and not members of the BIS. Nevertheless, over time, the Bank held a declining share of global foreign exchange reserves, partly because it needed to be compliant with its own capital requirements from the late 1980s and partly because global foreign exchange reserves grew so quickly from the 1990s onwards and could not be absorbed in the Bank. Even so, by the early 2000s central-bank deposits at the BIS still represented some 5–6 per cent of global foreign exchange reserves. In order to be more attractive to its customers, the Banking Department developed longer-term tradable instruments that generated higher returns to customers without reducing their liquidity. From the early 1990s, the Bank issued tradable instruments with tenors of up to one year. These funds were then hedged by purchasing assets of similar maturities. Towards the end of the 1990s, new medium-term instruments (MTIs) were offered with maturities of up to ten years, also tradable with the BIS. These instruments proved popular with central banks because they offered a return higher than highly rated sovereign bonds of equivalent tenor, while at the same time being liquid through the ability to trade them with the BIS, which was an exceptionally high-quality counterparty. The risk of the BIS defaulting or collapsing was extremely remote compared with commercial banks or other private-sector providers. From the end of the 1990s the Bank also began managing portfolios for central banks on a fee-paid basis, and this required the hiring of new staff familiar with portfolio management and new compliance procedures. This business was off the balance sheet of the Bank itself and tended to be dominated by fixed-income products rather than the more lucrative equities and derivatives trading undertaken in the private sector. In these ways, the Bank sought to make itself useful and relevant for all central banks – not just its members – as well as generating a return for its shareholding members, while retaining its reputation for managing risk conservatively.

2.2 1994–2003: Expanding the Membership

Despite some evolution in the 1970s and 1980s, the BIS that existed by the early 1990s might easily have been from an earlier era. But a new vision for the Bank was set to disrupt this cosy environment with the appointment of Andrew Crockett as General Manager. Crockett came from the Bank of England, where he was Executive Director after a career at the IMF. When he arrived at the BIS in 1994, it was an institution that had changed little despite dramatic shifts in the global economy and political framework. The so-called East Asian economic miracles of the 1980s, huge increases in global financial flows and the end of the Cold War had left the governance of the Bank largely untouched. It remained an essentially European club of wealthy countries with the world's largest economy, the United States, an essential though formally peripheral participant. The collapse of the Soviet Union in 1990, and the disintegration of Yugoslavia and Czechoslovakia that followed, created new states that swiftly became part of the international institutions such as the World Bank Group and the IMF. These IFIs had a universal and inclusive mandate, to which the BIS never aspired. On the other hand, the European members were moving towards economic and monetary union, with an ultimate goal of a single central bank, and so their cooperation forum was shifting away from the BIS to regional frameworks.[4] This became very apparent when in 1994 the Committee of Governors of the EU central banks, which had met at the BIS since 1964, transformed into the European Monetary Institute (EMI). On this occasion, the EMI physically moved from Basel to Frankfurt. Alexandre Lamfalussy, Crockett's predecessor as BIS General Manager, also moved from Basel to Frankfurt as the EMI's first President.

The notion of adjusting the membership of the Bank to reflect the changes in the global system since the 1970s was especially challenging because membership was selective but the criteria for membership were vague. Moreover, the discretion of its operations and reliance on consensus meant that trust and common interest were considered essential to the Bank's effectiveness. Greater diversity could threaten its operations, but at the same time it ran the risk of seeming irrelevant as the next wave of globalisation took hold.

One of the first changes was to bring the rest of the G10 onto the Board. Thus, the central banks of Japan, Canada and the United States joined the Board of Directors in 1994. This move seemed to make sense at the time and had three important outcomes. Firstly, it finally brought the US Federal Reserve Board and the New York Federal Reserve Bank more firmly and formally into the governance (and accountability) of the Bank. Secondly, it extended the Board beyond its European founding members by adding three central banks from the Americas and East Asia. Thirdly, it reinforced the BIS into the framework of G10 meetings of governments, finance ministers and central-bank Governors that met at IMF/World Bank meetings.[5] But, rather than the Board, it was the Bank's membership that became the main focus of reform for Crockett.

Of thirty-three members in 1994 (see Table 2.1), only six were from outside Europe and only three could be considered emerging-market economies. The transformation under Crockett was certainly striking – he arrived at a predominantly European institution and left it much more global. But the process took a decade and was highly contested. The first strategy was to increase the membership, and three rounds of expansion were held starting in 1996. Table 2.2 shows the expansion in membership, which added seventeen non-European central banks with Russia and the European Central Bank (ECB) by the end of Crockett's term in 2003 (or shortly thereafter).

Table 2.2 *New members, 1996–2011: date invited (in parentheses, date when shares subscribed if different from date of invitation)*

9 September 1996	8 November 1999	30 June 2003	26 June 2011
Banco Central do Brasil (1997)	Banco Central de la República Argentina (2000)	Bank of Algeria	Central Bank of Colombia
People's Bank of China	European Central Bank	Central Bank of Chile	Central Bank of Luxembourg
Hong Kong Monetary Authority	Bank Indonesia (2003)	Bank of Israel	Central Reserve Bank of Peru
Reserve Bank of India	Bank Negara Malaysia	Reserve Bank of New Zealand	Central Bank of the United Arab Emirates
Bank of Korea (1997)	Bank of Thailand (2000)	Central Bank of the Philippines	
Banco de México			
Central Bank of the Russian Federation			
Saudi Arabian Monetary Agency			
Monetary Authority of Singapore			

After these additions, the next enlargement, bringing in four more central banks, took place eight years later in 2011.

Among his first acts, at the end of February 1994 Crockett asked his staff for guidance on how the outstanding 'third tranche' of shares in the Bank could be used to bring in new members.[6] He was open to suggestions of which countries, the number of shares they could buy and the pace of either admitting a group all at once or one member at a time. At this point eight central banks had made applications or sent enquiries in letter form since 1972 and a further nineteen less formal discussions had taken place. In 1993 and 1994 alone, the pace had accelerated, with four written requests and nine others. The end of the Cold War in 1989 led several central banks from newly independent Central and Eastern European countries to enquire, but the list also included several countries in Asia and the Middle East. With a pent-up demand for membership, the terms and criteria became important considerations.

According to the Bank's Statutes, membership was established by subscribing to shares in the Bank and voting rights were attached to the shares in proportion to the total issue. But there was no consistency on how many shares a member was offered.[7] In the original Statutes the criterion for membership was that the national currency needed to satisfy 'the practical requirements of the gold or gold exchange standard', but, in practice, the original membership was even more circumscribed and included only European central banks plus Japan (1930–1952) and the 'dormant' membership of the United States. On the other hand, the Statutes also required the Board to consider 'the desirability of associating with the Bank the largest possible number of central banks that make a substantial contribution to international monetary cooperation and to the Bank's activities'.[8] This text had been introduced to the Statues in 1969 at the time of the accession of the central banks of Canada, Australia and South Africa in 1970, as discussed in Toniolo (2005).

At the time, a distinction was made between the five European founding central banks (and the United States) and the three non-founder central banks that were included in the Board of Directors.[9] The founding banks benefited from having two Board members and their shares formed almost 59 per cent of the votes at the General Meeting of members. They also had the statutory right to subscribe to 55 per cent of any new issue of shares, to secure their continued majority even if the membership was expanded. But this also constrained the number of new members that could be accommodated within the existing authorised capital. The total authorised capital was 600,000 shares, of which 473,125 had been issued and 5,435 were earmarked for the Federal Reserve System, leaving 121,440. But only 45 per cent of these could be offered to new members if the founding members took up their option to subscribe. The outcome of this complicated arithmetic was that there was only room for six new members with 8,000 shares each, or 15 if the founding members did not take up their subscription option. Crockett had opened a Pandora's box that his predecessors had shied away from.

Bank staff assessed various ways to establish an objective quantitative set of criteria for membership, but this proved difficult to fit with the existing membership and political considerations. Calculations were made using weighted averages of GDP, reserves, average international payments and receipts, international financial transactions and their variability. While not providing consistent outcomes, the various weightings and variables identified Singapore, South Korea, Mexico, Brazil and China among the group with the strongest presence in the international economy. But there were also issues about the extent of financial and political stability among this group, or other characteristics such as OECD membership, that might promote the case for other prospective members. Despite these problems, the Bank's Monetary and Economic Department (MED) recommended that 'it is not in the interest of the BIS to be seen as a static institution in a changing world. Therefore, a limited expansion of its shareholders seems fully warranted.'[10] Meanwhile, the Banking Department applied other metrics related to the BIS's banking activities, such as the amount of borrowing or depositing of reserves, that identified Argentina, Brazil and India as front runners.[11] The two methods combined identified four Latin American and four Asian countries.[12] Clearly, the criteria were likely to be subjective rather than merely quantitative, but these efforts demonstrate an intention to identify future members on some even playing field.

In July 1994, Crockett told the Chair of the Federal Reserve, Alan Greenspan, and Swedish central-bank Governor Urban Bäckström that he was likely to recommend that the Board consider potential members against three criteria: size, quality of economic management and relationship with the BIS. This formula had identified Mexico, South Korea, India and Saudi Arabia as likely candidates in a first round, with the possibility of others joining later.[13] The Board meeting in September 1994, however, recommended further delay. The Board agreed on the principle of expansion, but some Board members thought that the timing was too soon after the recent enlargement of the Board to the full G10. Instead, the Board wanted to take time to reflect on the future role of the BIS and how the expansion in shareholding would be managed. They encouraged management to look for other ways to strengthen relationships with non-members.[14]

Just at the time of these discussions in Basel, Bernie Fraser, Governor of the Reserve Bank of Australia, gave a lecture to the 24th Conference of Economists in Australia suggesting a new Asian institution modelled on the BIS but separate from it, to promote regional central-bank cooperation (Fraser 1995). The motivation was explicitly that the BIS was too narrowly governed with thirteen out of seventeen Board members from Europe.[15] Fraser expected that a formal study group of the Executives' Meeting of East Asia and Pacific Central Banks (EMEAP) would begin to consider an 'Asian BIS' in mid-1996.[16] This prompted a quick reaction from Crockett, who organised a small Board sub-committee.[17] Crockett also drew on conversations with colleagues in the Bank of Japan, who had shown interest in Fraser's proposals but were more cautious than others in the region. Part of the incentive from their point of view was concern about the impact of a future regional financial crisis, which might not attract as much support as Mexico had in 1994 from the United States in particular.[18] The potential of a rival institution threatened the BIS's legitimacy and authority.

2.2.1 First Membership Expansion, 1996

In November 1995, the Board set up a formal Sub-Committee to consider how the BIS could 'become a more useful and attractive forum for cooperation' for non-member central banks. The Sub-Committee followed a very conservative line: 'existing central bank cooperation arrangements were not a matter of concern to the BIS' and 'efforts to make the BIS a more useful and effective forum should be regarded as the BIS' own initiative and not as a response to Fraser's speech'.[19] The definition of the G10, which matched the current Board membership, was based on the IMF's GAB, which was then under review. But the Sub-Committee noted that the enlargement of the GAB should not itself be reflected in BIS governance. Instead, they proposed a new Global Group of at least twenty-five participants 'starting with exchange of information and, once confidence has been established, moving on to discussion of policy-related matters'. Choosing the members of this group would be kept separate from the question of enlarging the membership of the BIS itself and 'should not form part of the report to the Board' of the Sub-Committee's deliberations.[20] This process thus spawned a separate, but almost as controversial, process of selection criteria for the BIS's wider engagement beyond its membership. In January 1996, Governor Verplaetse of Belgium, then Chair of the Board, and Gunter Baer, the BIS Secretary General, visited the one Asian member of the Board of Governors,

Governor Matsushita of the Bank of Japan, to ask for his views. Matsushita agreed with Fraser that the EMEAP was the most important regional discussion forum and also noted that there was evidence of progress in cooperation through the bilateral repo agreements signed in November among six Asian central banks.[21] He welcomed the Global Group idea but stressed that it needed to be bolstered by involving senior staff from the region in BIS committees and expert groups.

The Sub-Committee's report to the Board in March 1996 reasserted that the "'club" atmosphere' created by selective participation had 'proved to be conducive to fruitful discussions and the development of trust'. Moreover, the G10 group was 'at the heart of Bank activities' and its integrity 'must be preserved'.[22] Nevertheless, globalisation and greater risks from cross-border capital flows confirmed a need for wider cooperation. The BIS had already taken steps in this direction through inviting a wide range of member Governors to monthly meetings in Basel as well as arranging ad hoc meetings on particular themes with emerging-market central bankers. The report included the Global Group proposal but thought that it was excessively risky to the integrity of the G10 framework and that, once created, it would not be possible to change the members or curtail it, even if it did not 'function satisfactorily'.[23] Instead, they recommended expanding BIS membership cautiously by selling small amounts of shares to a limited number of new members, which would not challenge the G10 dominance or guarantee a right to take part in any meetings beyond the Annual General Meeting and shareholders' meetings, but it would demonstrate 'a visible move forward'. A key advantage was that it was 'flexible' in that the Board could manage the degree of involvement of these new members.

At their Sunday-night dinner in March 1996, the G10 Governors unanimously rejected the Global Group proposal.[24] On the question of whether to go so far as to issue new shares rather than just continue ad hoc invitations to participate, Nagashima of the Bank of Japan argued that unless membership was offered there would be increased impetus for a separate 'Asian BIS'. By this time, several more countries had made written and oral requests to be considered for membership.[25] President Duisenberg suggested issuing 100,000 shares to admit twelve new members as well as 25,000 shares to the non-founder Board members to bring their total holdings up to 16,000, which was closer to the amount held by each founding member.[26] This would only be possible if the founding members renounced their right to subscribe 55 per cent of any new shares and thereby lost their majority of votes. The discussion was partly prompted by the prospect of the ECB and the advent of the single currency, which might collect the shares of the participating countries. Under the proposals, the eurozone could end up with up to 32 per cent of the votes. The Board would also need to consider whether the national central banks in the eurozone should continue their membership of the BIS separately.

When the G10 Governors discussed the proposals at dinner at the end of July 1996, there was still no full agreement except that something needed to be done.[27] On the other hand, it was also clear that there was unlikely to be any other proposal that would have greater support than issuing a small number of shares to a few new members. After a 'difficult, though generally amicable' discussion the Governors agreed to the recommendations of the Sub-Committee report, although five Governors expressed only 'lukewarm support'. Concerns included the dilution of European founder members and the 'two-wave' gradualist approach rather than a one-off expansion. 'Trichet struck a chord when he said that expansion would help the BIS to resist the challenge of the IMF in the area of banking supervision.'[28] Crockett wasted no time in making progress.

In late July 1996, Crockett visited the Governors of nine central banks to which the Board intended to offer membership and received positive responses from all. Of the nine central banks chosen in this round of expansion, seven were from the largest economies in their regions, and Hong Kong and Singapore were important financial centres. The Board decided that central banks would be offered 3,000 shares each (rather than the 8,000 initially envisaged) except for the Hong Kong Monetary Authority (HKMA), which would be offered only 1,000 shares, on the grounds that Hong Kong's hand-over from British to Chinese rule was imminent.[29] Several central banks would have liked to have the opportunity to buy more shares, and Hong Kong protested that the smaller offer might 'suggest a lack of confidence in the HKMA's future as an independent central bank'. The list of proposed new members was put to the Board at its meeting on 9 September 1996 and approved. These members would be offered 3,000 shares each.[30]

After some discussion, the founder members agreed not to subscribe to their full allocation of 55 per cent of the new shares. The creation of the ECB was expected to require a change in the Statutes in any case to accommodate European interests. Instead the founder members agreed to subscribe a total of 17,000 shares (around 70 per cent of their entitlement), but to give them back to the Bank to be cancelled. This allowed the issue of new shares for the Japanese, Dutch, Swiss and Swedish central banks to bring their holdings up to 16,000 shares each, without requiring a fresh release of a tranche of the Bank's capital. The power of the G10 vis-à-vis the broader membership was thereby enhanced.[31]

The selection of new members was designed to be as uncontroversial as possible while reflecting Crockett's agenda of expanding the geographical reach of the BIS's governance. After the largest country in each region had joined, the Bank intended to embark on a second round of selecting other central banks 'somewhat later'.[32] Of particular importance was the invitation to the People's Bank of China (PBoC) and the HKMA. The HKMA had been created only three years earlier in April 1993, and its accession to the BIS predated the return of the colony of Hong Kong to China in July 1997. But the 'one country, two systems' framework was already well established by the Basic Law, which ensured that Hong Kong would continue to operate its own distinct currency after it became a Special Administrative Region of China. The lawyers wondered whether the HKMA met the definition of central bank and whether Hong Kong could be considered a 'country' under the Statutes (although not a state).[33] Crockett took a strong view that if it was the will of the Board, then the interpretation of the Statutes should be made to fit with this desire, especially since no definition of 'bank' or 'country' was included in the Statutes.[34] This was an issue that had particular resonance as the Bank began to consider how it would deal with a single European currency and single central bank for several founding members, as General Counsel Mario Giovanoli pointed out. Crockett noted that 'on the question of EMU [EU Economic and Monetary Union], I agree that we will have to start looking soon at the implications. But I'd prefer not to "frighten the horses" by telling them the HKMA case requires them to decide on the much bigger issue of the status of National Central Banks in Europe following EMU.'[35] Joseph Yam of the HKMA wrote to the Governors of the founding members' central banks to argue the case for uniform treatment in the offer of shares to Hong Kong.[36] Hong Kong participated independently in other international institutions and had been an active participant in a range of BIS activities. The timing was obviously critical as Hong Kong approached the handover to China, and there was the potential threat to confidence in the HKMA's future if it were revealed that it had been offered one-third as many shares as other new members. Yam was fully supported by Dai Xianglong, Governor of the PBoC.[37] At its meeting on 9 September 1996, the Board agreed to offer 3,000 shares to the HKMA, on the basis that the Bank's Statutes established that these shares could not be transferred automatically to the PBoC at a later date if Hong Kong ceased to be an independent monetary area. They would have to be cancelled.

The PBoC was also controversial, but for other reasons. It had been reformed substantially in the 1990s, and this was set to continue in the 2000s, but it still remained controlled by the Chinese state. At the time when it was considered for membership, the Chinese banking system was much more concentrated in exclusively state-owned banks and had large amounts of non-performing loans associated with lending to state-owned enterprises. China also operated strict exchange controls on the renminbi that restricted its convertibility and its use internationally, until it was liberalised for current-account transactions in December 1996. Bringing these two members into the BIS was therefore a bold decision, which partly anticipated the future importance of China in the global monetary system.

Expanding the membership without changing the governance (e.g. reforming the Board and the role played by the G10) prompted BIS management to consider how to engage the new members into the operational and strategic direction of the Bank. Crockett suggested a standing committee of Governors from emerging markets that could meet annually in Basel and perhaps also in a host central bank.[38] Staff from these members could also be included in working groups below the level of Governor. These discussions eventually heralded the creation of the Global Economy Meeting (GEM) in 1998, discussed in the following section.

The private shareholdings presented another challenge. Management began to consider whether it was still appropriate for the Bank to have privately held shares, but at this point a repurchase operation would be long drawn-out and perhaps too ambitious to take on at the same time as the enlargement. Nevertheless, Crockett asked for further investigation of how the BIS had dealt with the voluntary repurchase during the mid-1970s when some private shareholders had been bought out.[39] The peculiar relic of private shareholders was finally addressed in 2000–1. As noted earlier, approximately 14 per cent of the BIS's shares originally issued to the central banks of the United States, Belgium and France were held privately and traded in Paris and Zurich. All shares were only 25 per cent paid up, and when they were first issued in the 1930s the central banks had the option of selling these shares or paying up 25 per cent of their full quota. In the end Belgium and France chose to sell part of their allotment in the market and the Federal Reserve sold its total allocation. By 2000 the market was illiquid and the privately held proportion had been diluted by the expansion of membership since 1996. Perhaps most importantly, private shareholding was felt to be no longer compatible with the explicitly public mission of the Bank of promoting global monetary and financial stability. The Board finally approved the acquisition of the private shares at its meeting in December 2000, and shareholders were offered CHF 16,000 per share. The price had been determined by JP Morgan and Arthur Andersen and represented a premium of 95 per cent on the American shares, 105 per cent on the price of the Belgian issue and 155 per cent over the closing price for the French issue. The cost of the share buy-back altogether amounted to CHF 1,162,368,000, borne out of the Bank's own resources. At the start of January 2001, the Statutes of the BIS were changed to exclude private shareholders. The terms of the share buy-back prompted a suit from three claimants that their shares had been undervalued, in a case that ended up before a special tribunal established at the Permanent Court of Arbitration in The Hague. The prediction that this would be a challenging and lengthy process proved accurate. In September 2003, the Court ruled that the BIS should pay plaintiffs an additional compensation of CHF 9,052.90 per share (on top of the CHF 16,000 per share they had received initially). The Bank then voluntarily extended this additional payment to all former private shareholders.

2.2.2 Second Membership Expansion, 1999

Nine months after the first enlargement under Crockett's tenure, the Asian financial crisis struck abruptly in July 1997 with the collapse of the Thai baht. At the same time, Hong Kong was handed over to China as a Special Administrative Region. The fears expressed at the time of the 1996 discussions about the need for support in a crisis were realised as Asian countries such as Thailand and South Korea were forced to borrow from the IMF. Central-bank swaps played some part in alleviating the impact of the crisis, and the BIS proved valuable to the region through its members and non-members. But the BIS remained on the defensive as Asian and Latin American central banks began to intensify their regional cooperation. Organisations such as the Asia-Pacific Economic Cooperation (APEC, founded in 1989) and the South East Asian Central Banks (SEACEN, formed in 1966) hosted annual central-bank or central-bank and finance-ministry meetings. From 1996 the Governors of the eleven EMEAP central banks began meeting annually and created three working/study groups that mirrored those in the BIS: for financial markets development, central-banking operations and banking supervision. In response to these other agencies and the Asian financial crisis of 1997, the BIS began a new Global Economy Meeting (GEM) from 1998. This allowed these members to have more discussion than was possible at the All Governors' Meeting hosted at the BIS during the Board meeting weekends. In the early 2000s the GEM was seen as a key venue for non-G10 members to discuss the outlook for the global economy along with their G10 peers at the monthly meetings. The Bank also sought to associate regional groupings more directly with

the work of the Board of Directors. In March 2001 it created an Asian
Consultative Council (ACC), which brought together the Governors of
member central banks in the Asia-Pacific region.[40] Fraser's successor as
Governor of the Reserve Bank of Australia, Ian MacFarlane, was selected as
the ACC's first Chair. An analogous Consultative Council for the Americas
(CCA) would be created in 2008. Thus, the BIS's strategy to respond to the
evident demand for non-G10 central-banking cooperation was to engage
more members directly.

The second round of enlargement in 1999 was designed to bring in the
new European Central Bank, which raised some difficulties. The Board and
membership continued to be dominated by European founding members,
and adding a new European voting member would only increase this
imbalance. Moreover, the ECB was poised to take over a range of central-
banking activities from the member national central banks that were the
core business of the BIS, including monetary policy and ultimately supervision. But the national central banks continued to manage separate
foreign exchange reserves and retained national supervisory powers at
least in the interim, until legislation and frameworks could be designed
to collect the supervision of European banks within the ECB. In the end,
the Single Supervisory System took many years (and a major financial
crisis) to develop and reserves were not completely pooled in the ECB.
This left some rationale for the individual national central banks in Europe
to retain their place and voting power on the Board.

Between the first and second rounds of enlargement, the emerging-
market financial crises seemed to confirm the importance of engaging
a wider range of members into the BIS's operations and policymaking
forums. The Bank was heavily involved in the resolution of the East Asian
financial crisis through providing bridge lending, but it was also clear that
its efforts to promote systemic stability had failed. A working group of the
Basel Committee determined in June 1999 that the Asian crisis had important implications for the supervision of G10 banks, particularly in the
measurement and weighting of country risk in the BIS Capital Accord.[41]
The emerging-market crises also prompted the creation of the G20 group
of finance ministers and central-bank Governors that began to meet in
1999. The Bank was thus part of a wider trend of inclusion of emerging-
market countries in the governance of the global economy. At the same
time as the ECB, three members from Southeast Asia that had been deeply
affected by the crisis were invited to join: Thailand, Malaysia and
Indonesia.[42] The final addition in this round was Argentina as the leading
candidate from South America.

The clear evidence of globalisation of financial markets as well as the risks of systemic contagion prompted the G7 finance ministers and central-bank Governors to commission Hans Tietmeyer, President of the Deutsche Bundesbank, to consider how to enhance international cooperation among supervisory authorities and IFIs. Tietmeyer's 1999 report drew attention to 'the dichotomy of fragmented supervisory structures and increasingly integrated markets'. Bridging this gap had been the very basis for the founding and deliberations of the Basel Committee twenty-five years earlier in 1974 and so might be considered an implicit criticism of the BIS framework (Tietmeyer 1999). He identified three aspects:

[F]irstly, overcoming the separate treatment of micro-prudential and macro-prudential issues; secondly, bringing together the major international institutions and key national authorities involved in financial sector stability; and thirdly, integrating emerging markets more closely in this process.

The report noted that the IMF and the World Bank (IBRD) were the main global IFIs. Tietmeyer described the BIS as providing 'analytical, statistical and secretariat support for various official groupings working to strengthen the global financial system', which was rather passive compared with the OECD, which he described as 'participat[ing] in the process of macroeconomic and financial surveillance'. The Basel Committee was 'an important rule-setting body in the field of banking supervision' alongside the International Organization of Securities Commissions (IOSCO) for securities and futures markets and the International Association of Insurance Supervisors (IAIS) for insurance. The BIS also hosted the two main groups of central-bank experts 'concerned with market infrastructure and functioning': the Committee on Payment and Settlement Systems and the Committee on the Global Financial System. His proposal for a Financial Stability Forum (FSF) to bring together these national, international and sectoral institutions was endorsed by the G7 at its meeting in Bonn in February 1999. Andrew Crockett took the role of Chair at its inauguration, firmly anchoring the new organisation into the BIS by also providing a secretariat in Basel.

2.2.3 Third Membership Expansion, 2003

The terrorist attack on the World Trade Center towers in New York City on 11 September 2001 imparted an abrupt shock to international banking markets as well as destabilising global security. New York banks were suddenly out of communication. Many European banks which had relied on the custody services of the Federal Reserve Bank of New York found themselves unable to access their securities to engage in repos, and there was a scramble for dollars in Europe. Central banks there approached the BIS, which called around to American banks that were still operating and borrowed billions of dollars to lend to European commercial banks. The BIS Banking Department offered a US dollar facility to central banks to hold the system together until, late in the evening on Wednesday 12 September, a $50 billion Fed–ECB swap was arranged to provide a route for dollar liquidity for European banks. The 9/11 tragedy and the wars that followed changed the compliance infrastructure as legal sanctions were applied to try to prevent the financing of global terrorism. This gave an added impetus to cooperation and communication among the widest possible range of jurisdictions in international banking. It also confirmed both the importance of the globalisation of the BIS and the usefulness of its trusted presence as an intermediary between central banks and the market in a crisis.

Nevertheless, the next stage of membership enlargement was somewhat more difficult to arrange. The first round had been protracted but had succeeded by identifying the largest economies in their respective regions. The second round reflected the experience of the East Asian financial crisis and the need to bring Argentina in as the largest Latin American economy not yet a BIS member. Moving further could require different criteria to be developed, which had more marked political implications. At the same time, there was a mounting backlog of about twenty requests to join. On a practical basis, the larger membership also posed issues for the effectiveness of both the informal and formal meetings of member Governors at the monthly gatherings. The goal was that all members would be invited to participate in at least one meeting during these monthly gatherings. In practice all member Governors were invited to an All Governors' Meeting that reviewed the outcomes of the more exclusive committees and the Board for the full constituency.[43] If the membership grew too large, this process would become even more unwieldy and could threaten the informal but discreet nature of the meetings that were considered by the Board to be crucial to the Bank's effectiveness in fostering cooperation.

At their dinner in August 2001, the G10 Governors agreed to create a Sub-Committee to consider applications chaired by Jean-Claude Trichet and including Bill McDonough and Nout Wellink.[44] The group met three times between July and November 2001 and completed their report in March 2002.[45] They recommended continuing to admit a few new members at a time based on the criteria set out in the enlargement of 1996, that is ranking by economic size and financial market depth. The alternative was to stop considering new members altogether, but this might discourage non-members from cooperating with the BIS framework. There was a balance to be reached between ensuring engagement and compliance in the application of standards such as those of the Basel Committee and keeping the membership exclusive enough to retain the confidentiality and informality that was the foundation of the Bank's effectiveness in delivering cooperation. A third alternative, of open membership, would 'remove the element of discretion' but would fundamentally change the character of the Bank.[46] The Sub-Committee 'reaffirmed that the informal nature of BIS meetings, their frankness and small size were conducive to fostering mutual trust and confidence among participants and made meetings the principal vehicle for cooperation among central banks', and so they stressed that the expansion of membership should be limited and gradual.[47] As it was, they thought that the Board should consider limiting the attendance at the All Governors' Meetings to preserve the 'club' atmosphere.[48] Finally, the Sub-Committee considered the role and structure of the Board but decided that this should be kept within the remit of the G10 for the moment and should be separated from the issue of enlarging the shareholding membership. The outcome of these deliberations was, therefore, a conservative and cautious endorsement of the status quo even while there was recognition of the changing international character of the BIS. When it considered the recommendations, however, the Board was even more cautious and decided not to extend further invitations for the time being. The weight of opinion fell on the retention of the status quo rather than greater inclusiveness.

Just a few months later, Crockett made another effort to open the discussion on changes to the structure of the BIS. His paper for discussion at the informal dinner of G10 central-bank Governors on 12 May 2002 sought guidance on how the BIS should respond to the rapidly changing international environment, in particular the globalisation of financial activity.[49] Over the previous few years, the Bank had responded by increasing its contacts with other institutions that had a direct interest in promoting financial stability, especially by hosting the FSF and the IAIS, and planning to host the International Association of Deposit Insurers (IADI). But the Bank's own governance had not changed. Pressures for change concerned not only wider geographical representation but also how the BIS should engage with the proliferation of other agencies with which it shared the remit for international financial stability. The paper asked whether the BIS 'should aim to coordinate the work of the entire range of authorities concerned with financial stability', or to become a centre for collaboration for these authorities, and what longer-term changes in governance this might require. In particular, while Crockett was the first Chair of the FSF ('in a personal capacity'), there was no guarantee that the BIS General Manager would in future be the FSF Chair. If this link were broken, the paper suggested that the relationship between the BIS, central banks and the FSF might become more attenuated. At the same time, Crockett offered to reconsider the organisation of meetings of the BIS and its committees in response to the comments from Governors that the monthly meeting schedule was too crowded for crucial bilateral consultations, which were an important feature of the BIS. Some Governors had also complained about 'the uneven quality and value of the discussions at the 5:00pm meeting [All Governors' Meeting]', which would only be exacerbated by a future increase in membership.[50] The paper hinted that one way forward might be to consider 'a bipolar model' of meetings in Basel supplemented by regional meetings of relevant central banks. Another practical way to reduce the pressure of too many meetings was to reduce the number of BIS meeting weekends. This was implemented later in 2002, when the frequency of the BIS meeting weekends was changed from monthly to bimonthly.

However, at the July 2002 dinner, in reaction to Crockett's paper, the G10 Governors reasserted their conservative stance.[51] Chair of the Board Nout Wellink decided that the general issue of the Bank's role and future governance was too great to consider over dinner and asked the table instead to consider only the expansion of membership and the future of the All Governors' Meeting. On the latter, Governors asked the management to come back with proposals. The G10 Governors rejected the idea of expanding the membership in the short term, partly because several of the central banks that were likely to meet the established criteria were on a 'blacklist' of the Financial Action Task Force (FATF).[52] Crockett had wanted the expanded membership to be considered alongside broader issues about the role and mandate of the Bank. He was disappointed that there was still no consensus on the need for any changes to the dominance of the G10 Governors and 'a general reluctance to see change is needed, let alone a priority'.[53] Undeterred, Crockett revisited the membership question already in late 2002. This time he secured agreement from the Board to invite six further central banks to become BIS members. The process was not completed until June 2003, a few months after Crockett had left the BIS, when the central banks of Algeria, Chile, Indonesia, Israel, New Zealand and the Philippines became members. Incidentally, with the accession of the last two, all members of EMEAP were now also shareholding members of the BIS. With this, BIS membership reached fifty-six central banks (up from thirty-three when Crockett had joined the BIS in 1994) and would remain unchanged for the next eight years.

In addition to expanding the Bank's membership base, from early on Crockett had pressed ahead with increasing its regional presence in Asia and then the western hemisphere, with an emphasis on emerging-market engagement.

2.2.4 Representative Offices: Hong Kong and Mexico

While the membership and governance of the Bank were under discussion, another way to enhance the Bank's international scope was to open representative offices. This had both a functional and a presentational importance. The ability to provide banking services beyond the European time zone would increase the usefulness of the Bank's relations with its members. Such a strategy also made it easier to gather local intelligence on an ongoing basis in key markets, organise regional meetings and enhance the Bank's image as a non-exclusive organisation.

After the emerging-market financial crises, planning in the BIS advanced quickly to considering the purpose and costs of an Asian office. The purpose was to 'tighten relations with shareholding and non-shareholding Asian central banks', promote regional cooperation and serve as a 'first port of call on BIS matters' for interested parties in Asia. The office could promote banking relationships but would not itself engage in banking operations – at least not initially.[54] By the beginning of October 1997 there was a draft 'Action Plan' to visit Singapore and Hong Kong in November and seek Board agreement in early December.[55] By chance, the Annual Meetings of the Boards of Governors of the World Bank Group and the IMF were held in Hong Kong on 17–25 September 1997, which must have provided further opportunities to discuss the location before formal visits to both Singapore and Hong Kong in early November 1997. The letters to the HKMA and the Monetary Authority of Singapore (MAS) explained that the 'still rather preliminary thinking is to start with a small representative office', while 'keep[ing] open the option of expanding the office within a few years and to extend its functions to include banking operations'.[56] The main conditions included the need to ensure that the BIS, as an international organisation, had complete immunity from jurisdiction in the host country, free access for visitors and communications and immunities for staff. Banking operations should not be subject to financial or banking supervision, restrictions on counterparties or tax. The BIS delegations met with an enthusiastic reception in both territories, despite the financial turmoil still affecting the region.[57] The BIS was viewed as having a role to play in stabilising the situation through guidance, financial assistance and monitoring. At this point Hong Kong was considered much more expensive for staff and office space, and there were likely to be a few more legal 'snags', but the presence of China meant that it was a more strategic location than Singapore. At the end of November, the management recommended to the Board opening an Asian office in Hong Kong. The choice reflected three factors: Hong Kong's 'somewhat more convenient central position'; the existing close relationships and business contacts between the HKMA and the PBoC and the BIS and, not least, the more promising prospects for expanding banking activities out of Hong Kong.[58]

On Christmas Eve 1997, the BIS sent the HKMA a draft proposal for a host-country agreement.[59] There followed several months of negotiation with the HKMA, particularly over immunities, autonomy over the choice of the senior resident and staff, and allowing persons from any jurisdiction to visit the office. Differences in jurisdictional immunity in particular could open the BIS to legal suits related to its operations in Switzerland (where immunities were in force). The terms were particularly important to the BIS because this would set a precedent for any further representative office. On the Hong Kong side, the Host Country Agreement would be the first important bilateral treaty after the handover.[60] Housing, schools and staffing were raised as issues, but premises were identified in the Citibank building on Garden Road at the same address as the HKMA.[61] On 18 February 1998 Crockett announced that George Pickering was appointed Chief Representative designate for the BIS Asian office in an announcement that did not mention Hong Kong SAR.[62] The Host Country Agreement was finally initialled by both sides on 2 April 1998 in Beijing on terms 'very satisfactory for the Bank', followed by a signing ceremony in Basel on 11 May just before the Governors' dinner.[63] The formal local launch took place on 11 July 1998, almost exactly one year after the Asian financial crisis had struck the region and one year after the handover of the colony by the British to the Chinese. This was a potent symbol both of the Bank's recognition of the importance of Asia and of China as the most important emerging economy in the world.

In 2000 the Bank opened a dealing room in Hong Kong, marking an important operational change. This allowed the Bank to service its customers in the region more directly and extended the time period for the Bank's global trading. This innovation coincided with the rapid increase in foreign exchange reserves in central banks in East Asia, especially those of China,

Japan and South Korea. By 2005, close to half of the Bank's liabilities were to its customers in Asia.

In addition, the BIS expanded its asset management services to central banks in the region and beyond. At the request of EMEAP, an Asian Bond Fund was launched aimed at fostering regional cooperation in Asia and deepening Asia's capital markets. This initiative had grown from concerns over the resilience of Asia's capital markets at the time of the 1997–8 crisis. A first fund (ABF1) investing in a basket of liquid dollar-denominated bonds of major Asian economies was launched in June 2003 and had a size of approximately $1 billion. It was soon followed by a second fund (ABF2) of $2 billion, this time investing in domestic-currency bonds issued by sovereign and quasi-sovereign issuers in eight of the EMEAP markets. Moreover, in close cooperation with the PBoC, the BIS launched a local-currency (renminbi) government-bond fund which to date (2019) has attracted investments totalling nearly $5 billion from twenty-four central banks. The BIS Banking Department also provided technical advice when the renminbi was included as one of the component currencies of the SDR in 2016. In the same spirit, starting in 2006 the MED carried out an Asian research programme focused on policy issues faced by the central banks and supervisory authorities in the Asia-Pacific region. This programme was directly monitored by the ACC of regional central-bank Governors and led to the establishment of an Asian research network between the BIS and many Asian central banks. The functional services of the Bank thus reinforced the wider mission to promote international cooperation.

Opening an office in Latin America was already being discussed informally in 2000, and several countries were keen to host the office. In the end, Mexico was chosen as the lead candidate by the start of May 2001 and a site visit was arranged.[64] As in the case of the Asian regional office, the initiative took place at a time of regional financial turmoil, including financial crises in the two major economies, Brazil and Argentina. These emerging-market crises highlighted the importance of these economies for global financial stability and challenged the existing governance of the global economy. In September 1999 the G7 finance ministers invited their counterparts from eleven 'systemically important countries from regions around the world' to the first G20 meeting in Washington DC.[65] In November 2001 Jim O'Neill at Goldman Sachs grouped a sub-set of emerging economies together into the acronym BRICs, predicting that their growth rates and characteristics would become deeply influential in global economic and financial relations over the next decade.[66] Having the BIS represented in Asia and the Americas fitted well with the zeitgeist of the time.

The Host Country Agreement was signed between the BIS and the United Mexican States on 5 November 2001, but it took a further six months before it was finally ratified by the Mexican Senate.[67] Gregor Heinrich was appointed the first Chief Representative. As in the case of Hong Kong, there was already a regional central-bank network with ambitions to fulfil some of the BIS's mandate for central-bank cooperation, in this case CEMLA, which had several BIS members on its governing board.[68] The goals of the Mexico office were the same as in Hong Kong: strengthening relations with member and non-member central banks, fostering closer cooperation and exchange of information, and promoting banking relationships for the Head Office. The Representative Office for the Americas also helped with economic research and hosting meetings and activities in the region. The office opened in Torre Chapultepec, Mexico City, at the start of September 2002. Since its creation in 2008, the CCA, which comprises the Governors of the BIS member central banks in the Americas, helped to guide the activities of the BIS Office for the Americas, in particular its research programme. In contrast with the Hong Kong office, it was not initially planned to conduct BIS banking operations from Mexico. However, this changed in 2020 with the opening of a dealing room in the Office for the Americas, allowing the BIS Banking Department to offer its services across all major time zones of the world.

The opening of the BIS Representative Offices in 1997–2002, combined with the resolution of the buy-back of privately held shares in 2001, provided a new opportunity to reconsider the Bank's geographic reach and governance.

2.3 2002–2008: Board Reform

Crockett made considerable progress in widening the membership of the Bank during his tenure, but expanding the Board outside the G10 framework proved beyond even his exceptional negotiating skills. The lunch for G10 Governors in Mexico City in November 2002 provided an opportunity for Crockett to present his ideas to expand the Board. This time a business case as well as a principled case was made. Crockett's draft speaking notes pointed out that about 90 per cent of BIS deposits came from outside Europe and 80 per cent came from central banks which were not represented on the Board.[69] The banking business was thus dominated by non-Board member banks. Emerging markets were expected to continue to grow, especially in East Asia, and already dominated global population and foreign exchange reserves. European monetary union had made the anomaly of having thirteen out of seventeen Board Directors from Europe even more apparent, and non-Board members were likely to begin to form their own institutions if they could not gain involvement in the BIS's governance. He urged the Board to consider a medium- and longer-range strategy to consider what the governance of the Bank should look like in about ten years' time. In the short term, he suggested filling some vacant Board seats with the central-bank Governors from China, Brazil and the ECB, followed perhaps by South Africa.[70] A variant would be to follow a system of revolving regional representation, such as including the Chair of the ACC. The Bank's management thought that this was likely to be 'the most practical way of achieving non-G10 representation'. More radically, the banking business could continue to be governed by the existing Board while the central-bank-cooperation element of the remit was allocated to a separate, wider Board. One obstacle was that non-Board member countries dominated the bank's deposits, so they might object to being specifically excluded from this area of the Bank's business. Crockett recommended preserving the effectiveness of the G10 grouping by retaining the G10 dinner as an exclusive meeting. This was not a statutory group under the BIS but did have a rationale in terms of the IMF's GAB from the 1960s, which could justify excluding others. The topics discussed, however, might have to be truncated to avoid conflict with the Board agenda.

In the end, none of these proposals were approved, and Crockett's ambitions for reforming the governance of the BIS were only partially achieved. In July 2002 he announced his intention to step down at the end of March 2003. Nevertheless, the progress that Crockett was able to engineer was significant in responding to the changing characteristics of the global financial system and the reform of orthodox central-banking and financial-stability institutions. The widened membership under Crockett exerted an inexorable pressure to adapt the governance of the Bank despite the challenges this posed to the historic structures steering the Bank's direction.

Following, for the first time in BIS history, a competitive recruitment process, Malcolm Knight succeeded Andrew Crockett as General Manager of the BIS on 1 April 2003, moving from his post as Senior Deputy Governor of the Bank of Canada, having spent most of his career at the IMF. He was the first non-European General Manager, but he followed a less ambitious route for enhancing the global reach of the Bank through changes in governance. Knight devoted much of his energy to further deepening cooperation with existing member central banks, particularly those in Asia, and to improving the Bank's internal processes, particularly by strengthening the internal-audit and risk-management functions. In September 2003 he took part in the Board retreat to discuss the Bank's future, which had been recommended by Crockett in November 2002. But, rather than considering the ideal structure for the Bank in ten years' time, as Crockett had suggested, the meeting discussed the vision for the next five years only. On this basis, the Board agreed that after absorbing nineteen new members over the past seven years, no new members should be added for at least the next five years. Agreeing to pause would help to dampen expectations that the BIS would become universal in the near term. Moreover, the management noted that it could prove difficult to find the next tranche of eligible countries that were 'sufficiently systematically important and/or were based in a country of adequate corporate governance'.[71] The Board continued to be concerned to preserve the exclusive nature of membership, partly to distinguish itself from the IMF and to avoid the 'risk of political interference' in its work. Rather than extending membership, regional consultative councils would be used to engage a wider range of emerging-market central banks. The Asian Consultative Council that brought together regional central bankers was a success, and the Board agreed to work towards a similar body for Latin America and the Caribbean (as mentioned, the Consultative Council for the Americas was launched in 2008).

The temporary halt on adding new members was confirmed by the Board in its retreat of November 2005, on the grounds that 'bringing in additional countries would probably create more problems than benefits for the BIS, particularly in how it would distinguish itself from the IMF'.[72] The repeated references to the IMF are somewhat surprising, since the Fund had special functions in providing credit with conditionality, mainly to poorer and emerging-market countries, which is not in the BIS's remit, although both institutions promote international monetary and financial cooperation. The membership question would not be revisited until 2011 under Knight's successor as BIS General Manager, Jaime Caruana – and at the prompting of Board Chair Christian Noyer – when the central banks of Luxembourg (a significant international financial centre) and of Colombia, Peru and the United Arab Emirates became BIS shareholders.

With a further expansion of membership temporarily off the table, attention turned to changing the Board to better reflect the Bank's new membership. This proved much more controversial.

All agreed that bringing new members to the Board of Directors needed to be approached cautiously. The Bank's Statutes restricted the maximum number of seats on the Board to twenty-one, and at this point seventeen seats had already been taken up by the G10 central banks, so there was limited room for expansion.[73] Some Directors pointed out the risks of the exercise, since it challenged the existing homogeneity of outlook and interests of central-bank Governors that shared 'common values and a shared central banking philosophy' in a Board that 'was probably better prepared to govern the institution than a more heterogeneous group'. Having emerging-market central bankers on the Board could also weaken the 'influence and rationale of the G10 grouping'. On the other hand, some members thought the time had come to bring in up to three emerging-market Board members to represent key regions, such as Asia, Latin America, and Africa and the Middle East, to reflect the BIS's global mandate. The fourth seat could then be filled by the ECB. But the Board and its Chairperson would need to have an 'active role in selecting possible future members from emerging-market countries' rather than leaving it up to elections from regional consultative councils. There was in any case no sense of urgency; the management were tasked to bring alternatives to the Board in eighteen months.[74]

In May 2004, at the suggestion of Board Chair Wellink, the Bank hired a group of experts on corporate governance to review the Bank's Statutes. They reported in September 2004 with recommendations to change the Statutes to better reflect how the Board actually functioned and to clarify the relations between the Board and the management.[75] The emphasis was on maximising transparency and accountability and referenced the Basel Committee's own guidance on good governance for banking institutions from 1999, as well as the OECD's principles. The first suggestion was to eliminate the role of President, a post which had in any case been held by the Chair of the Board since 1948. The second was to expand the wording in the Statutes on the role of the Board from 'administration of the Bank' to deciding or approving 'the strategic policy direction of the Bank' and supervising the management (Article 26 of the BIS Statutes). These changes were adopted at an Extraordinary General Meeting in June 2005.

In the meantime, the management prompted changes to the Statutes that meant that the Board did not discuss issues related to the G10 per se at the Board meetings and, conversely, did not discuss managerial or 'house-keeping' issues at the G10 Governors' dinner. This separation cleared the way to involve non-G10 central-bank Governors on the Board in the future. In June 2005 the position of President was abolished.

With regard to the expansion of the Board, General Manager Knight and Board Chair Wellink recommended electing two or three central-bank Governors from emerging-market economies for a single three-year term and then rotating each member off, opening up a place for another.[76] The discussion among the management and at the retreat focused on how this would work for the PBoC, which was the obvious member to bring onto the Board considering China's role in the global monetary and financial system. By mid-2005 the PBoC had moved from a dollar-pegged exchange rate to a flexible rate referencing a basket of currencies, and had also resolved the non-performing loan problems in the country's banking system that had plagued the 1990s. Among the other candidates were Mexico (joining China in a first round), with India and Brazil replacing China and Mexico respectively after three years. The ECB was the other obvious candidate, but the management recommended that it should be elected to the Board only 'in a way that does not increase the total representation of the Eurozone on the Board'.[77] At the retreat, Governors discussed rotating some European members off the board. There was also discussion of the need for Board members to be politically independent from their home governments, which was not the case for the Governor of the PBoC. Once again, some members stressed the need to preserve 'the special and unique character of the BIS' through its 'open and intimate discussions'.[78] In the end, the Board could not agree on whether and how the rotation concept would work in practice. Once on the Board, it might be difficult to expect a central-bank Governor to step down after three years. The majority were still hesitant to break up the G10 framework by bringing the Governors of the PBoC and another emerging-market central bank to the Board immediately, but Knight warned that such a decision needed to take place soon or there was a risk of alienating these central banks from the BIS. Expectations of a breakthrough at this retreat were disappointed. The issue was referred to another ad hoc sub-committee of the Board, chaired by Jean-Pierre Roth, President of the Swiss National Bank.

The new Board sub-committee met at the two subsequent bimonthly meetings and submitted its proposals in early May 2006. Roth, who was Chair of the Board from 2006 to 2009, conceived of a route through the potential sensitivities over which central bankers would be invited. Since the BIS had representative offices in Mexico and Hong Kong, the Governors of the Bank of Mexico and PBoC would be appointed along with Jean-Claude Trichet as President of the ECB. The President of the ECB had joined the group of G10 Governors at their bimonthly meetings but had not joined the BIS Board. To overcome resistance to increasing the European domination of the Board, especially from the Japanese and American members, the Directors from the five European founder central banks agreed to take turns for one of their second Directors to come off the Board each year to make way for the ECB President.[79] These changes were adopted at the start of July 2006. The Board of the BIS itself was thereby widened to include one Asian and one Latin American member, but the meetings and dinners of G10 central-bank Governors, which were the locus of much of the strategic discussion and central-bank cooperation at the bimonthly meetings, continued to exclude emerging-market central banks. The global financial crisis, however, would soon forge a consensus that wider governance of the global economy was essential.

Under Governor Roth's period of office another important change to strengthen the governance of the BIS Board was implemented. The structure and mandates of the Board advisory committees were enhanced and their number increased to four: next to the Audit Committee, there was now an Administrative Committee (mainly dealing with oversight of the Bank's budget and human-resources policies) and a Banking and Risk Management Committee. Finally, a standing Nomination Committee was created to deal with all future senior-management appointments.

2.4 2008–2019: The Global Financial Crisis and Its Aftermath

The financial crises in the late 1990s were a wake-up call regarding the risks in emerging markets, but the advanced economies were mainly insulated from these crises. This led to some complacency: financial crisis seemed to be a symptom of less mature markets, mismanaged financial liberalisation and inappropriate international monetary policies. Ten years later, however, the global financial crisis reinforced the message that Crockett had been trying to deliver: in order to remain relevant and influential the BIS had to broaden its governance, and thereby also the scope of ideas and influences, beyond the historical European/US core group.

From the early 2000s, the BIS had repeatedly warned of mounting risks in the international financial system, but these warnings had gone largely unheeded. Now, as the crisis struck, the Bank found itself unexpectedly in something of a leadership crisis. In the summer of 2007, the markets had experienced a first shock with the collapse of Bear Stearns in July. A year later, in June 2008, Knight announced that he would resign and move to be Vice-Chair of Deutsche Bank Group from September, where he was to advise the Group on regulatory matters. This left the post of BIS General Manager open at a time the crisis reached its peak.[80] Under these challenging circumstances, Deputy General Manager Hervé Hannoun became Acting General Manager for nine months until Jaime Caruana (a former chair of the Basel Committee (2003–6) and former Governor of the Bank of Spain (2000–6)) came from the IMF to take up office from 1 April 2009.

Meanwhile, on 18 September 2008, Lehman Brothers collapsed, freezing global money markets, prompting a collapse in financial-asset prices and briefly halting international trade. The crisis, with its origins in transatlantic financial markets, challenged the existing governance of the global monetary and financial system. The reforms that ensued at the BIS reflected a rapidly growing conviction that widening the governance of the global economic and financial system had become urgent.

The immediate impact of the crisis on the Bank was dramatic. In the run-up to the crisis, the management of the MED had publicly warned about the increasingly risky environment, so the Bank's investment strategy remained cautious.[81] The Banking Department had invested in some highly rated securities, including covered bonds, but the bulk of its business continued to be accepting term placements from central banks and conducting maturity transformation. Nevertheless, the Bank suffered valuation losses on its assets in 2008, most of which were offset in the following years. The most dramatic impact of the crisis was the flood of funds coming in from central banks, which sought a secure safe haven for their foreign exchange reserves at a time of exceptional counterparty risk at other financial institutions. The reputation and reliability of the BIS made it a premier place to hold these reserves, but it created problems for the Banking Department, which had few ways to deploy the funds. The Bank's balance sheet had more than doubled between 2003 and 2008, primarily due to the growth in deposits received from central banks (see the balance-sheet data in Annex 3). The fastest increase was in deposits from Europe and Africa, which grew from about one-third to almost 45 per cent of the total. Already in July 2007, when the subprime mortgage crisis in the United States erupted, the Banking Department had drastically increased the BIS margin on its investment products in an attempt to discourage new placements and protect the Bank's profitability. Nonetheless, balance-sheet totals remained exceptionally high.

In October 2008, three weeks after the Lehman collapse, at the initiative of Acting General Manager Hervé Hannoun, the BIS took the dramatic step of rationing each central bank's new deposits to $100 million per day and allowed its tradable instruments to expire rather than renewing them, in order to reduce the size of the balance sheet. The suspension lasted for two months and led to a significant reduction in central-bank deposits with the BIS and a concomitant shift from medium- to short-term deposits. This signalled that the BIS was not prepared to be the 'deposit-taker' of last resort for the global banking system. The cautious stance continued for the remainder of the 2000s and beyond, through the European sovereign-debt crisis and the 2013 'taper tantrum', a strategy that helped the BIS to reduce risk while remaining profitable. In essence, it was a traditional, procyclical reaction of a risk-averse institution.[82]

Beyond the impact on the Bank's own balance sheet, the crisis finally created the consensus required to widen the governance framework. In November 2008, the G20 meeting included heads of state for the first time, and this wider constituency was confirmed as the key framework for discussion of the global financial system. The IMF and FSF were represented at that meeting, but the BIS was not included. The G20 leaders called on other organisations to widen their governance, with a particular emphasis on those like the BIS that set financial standards and benchmarks. The FSF turned into the Financial Stability Board (FSB) at the start of April 2009. Chaired by the Bank of Italy's Mario Draghi, it remained hosted at the BIS but expanded its remit significantly, increasing its membership immediately to twenty-four countries and territories, which promoted it to the key institutional gathering for IFIs, industry standard-setters and national monetary and financial authorities to respond to the financial crisis. The BIS's failure to widen its governance to adapt to globalisation in the decade leading up to the crisis meant that it did not reflect this more inclusive turn in global economic leadership. Nevertheless, the BIS was a core participant in the FSB deliberations and rushed to revise its new Basel capital-adequacy standards to acknowledge the revealed risks for financial institutions and banks.[83] The BCBS expanded its membership and invited representatives from Australia, Brazil, China, India, South Korea, Mexico and Russia in March 2009. The FSB began coordinating early-warning exercises, which had been one of the founding tasks of the Basel Committee in 1974 (Goodhart 2011).

Meanwhile, the November 2008 bimonthly Governors' meetings were held in São Paulo, Brazil, where a more fundamental discussion took place over the future role of the BIS in the rebuilding of the architecture of the international financial system. With its subtle public profile and limited breadth of governance, there was a risk that the BIS would be sidelined, and this created fresh momentum for change. In January 2009 the Board elected Guillermo Ortiz, Governor of the Bank of Mexico, as its first non-European Chair with effect from March 2009. It was also the first time that the Chair of the Board did not attend the G10 Governors' meetings and dinners. Ortiz almost immediately raised the issue of replacing the G10 Governors' meeting (including the Sunday-evening dinners) with a wider constituency. Board Secretary Hermann Greve then worked in parallel with the management to develop reforms, although the management initially remained reluctant to replace the G10. However, this soon changed. The BIS's new General Manager Jaime Caruana felt little nostalgia for the G10, coming as he did from the Bank of Spain, which like the Bank of Mexico was not a G10 member. During the Board discussion in early May 2009, most Governors agreed on the need to replace the G10 framework, although without losing the participation of any of the smaller members. The need was particularly acute in the context of the enhanced role of the FSB and the focus on G20 governance of the global economy. The legitimacy of the BIS as a key standard-setter and as the forum for central-bank cooperation was at stake. Still, the high value placed on informal and discreet discussions among central bankers, particularly at their closed Sunday-night dinners, remained undisputed.

In May 2009 the outbreak of swine flu in Mexico meant that Ortiz could not travel, so Tietmeyer (as Vice-Chair) presided over the Board and proposed that a small team – chaired by Ortiz and including General Manager Caruana – should develop options for adapting the governance of the BIS to the new realities of the global financial system. The group met five times before bringing their proposals to Board meetings in September and November 2009. The solution built on the existing Global Economy Meeting (GEM) of thirty central-bank members, which could take over some of the functions of the G10 group, such as the governance of BIS-based committees (e.g. setting membership and chairs for the CPMI, CGFS and MC). As of 1 January 2010, a new Economic Consultative Committee (ECC), including all the existing fifteen Board members plus Brazil and India (which had been considered earlier as candidates for Board membership), would be the new forum for informal central-bank cooperation, thereby replacing in particular the G10 Sunday-night dinner. The ECC also became an advisory body for the GEM. All Board-member Governors were included in the membership of both the ECC and GEM, the Chair of which was appointed by the Board.[84] In this way, the Directors established a governance framework that delegated the direct supervision of the Bank's cooperative activities to the ECC/GEM, while maintaining a strong link between the ECC/GEM and the Board, which remained ultimately responsible for all BIS institutional matters. The last Chair of the G10 Governors, ECB President Jean-Claude Trichet, called the reform 'revolutionary for the BIS'.[85] The G10 group, which had determined the governance of the BIS since the 1960s, effectively relinquished its governance over the BIS-based committees to the more globally representative GEM/ECC. A separate solution was worked out for the Basel Committee on Banking Supervision, because it also included non-central-bank supervisory authorities. Oversight of the BCBS would henceforth be exercised by the

Group of Governors and Heads of Supervision (GHOS), comprising all BCBS members (which by 2009 included all central banks and supervisory authorities of the G20).

The final stumbling block to making the governance of the BIS fully reflective of the changing shape of the global economy was Article 27 of the Statutes, which set out the terms of Board membership,[86] including the six ex-officio founding members of the Bank, allocated two seats each, plus nine vacant seats for further development (elected Board members). This had been the framework to add three more G10 Board members in 1994 (representing Canada, Japan and the United States) and two non-G10 members in 2006 (representing China and Mexico). But by 2008 there were still fourteen out of twenty members from Europe (despite the introduction of the euro in 1999). There was only one elected Director's seat out of nine left, but two members of the ECC were not members of the Board (India and Brazil). Towards the end of 2012, Ben Bernanke (Chair of the US Fed) suggested a new category of 'observer' to align with the current Statutes. Once again, a Board sub-committee drew up proposals, and in September 2013 the Board agreed to fill the last elected seat and introduce a new category of observer, which would rotate on a four-monthly basis among all the elected members of the Board. Thus, both India and Brazil could join the Board from December 2013, bringing the total to twenty-one participants – the statutory maximum – of which thirteen were European. However, following an intervention from Governors Kuroda from Japan and Zhou from China, this interim measure only gained full support on the understanding that Article 27 would be amended in the near future.

The puzzle was how to reduce the size of the Board to make it more manageable while at the same time expanding its geographical scope, protecting the bloc of the six founder members and ensuring that the United States had two members on the Board: one from the Federal Reserve Board and one from the Federal Reserve Bank of New York. Assisted by Hermann Greve, who as long-standing Board Secretary brought his experience as well as continuity to the reform process, Christian Noyer, then the Board Chair, worked out a solution which he put forward at the Board meeting in May 2015. The six ex-officio central banks would keep their seats, but would renounce the right to each appoint a second Director. Together, they would agree to appoint only one additional Director, which would by convention be the President of the Federal Reserve Bank of New York. By giving up their second seat, the founder central banks made it possible to increase the number of elected Directors – and thus do away with the 'observer' status – while at the same time allowing an overall reduction from twenty-one to eighteen Directors. The new maximum total of Directors (eighteen) would still not enable a two-thirds majority to vote against the founding members, who together retained seven votes. This ingenious solution was approved by the Board, but the timing was still delicate as the governments that in 1930 had signed the Convention establishing the BIS needed to be convinced at a time that the Fed, ECB and other central banks were politically exposed by engaging in controversial unconventional monetary policy. The process was expected to take some time. Board Secretary Greve and the BIS General Counsel Diego Devos began to draw up the final details, and the governments of the European founding members and the Swiss National Bank were consulted to ensure that they would not object. Under the leadership of Jens Weidmann, President of the Deutsche Bundesbank, who had become Chair of the BIS Board in November 2015, an Extraordinary General Meeting unanimously approved the scheme on 7 November 2016 to be implemented before the end of 2020.[87] In the end, approval from the relevant governments was forthcoming earlier than foreseen and the Article 27 amendments came into force at the start of 2019. In recognition of the importance of the Asia-Pacific region compared with its representation on the Board, the Governor of the Bank of Korea was elected as the additional member, bringing the total number of Directors to eighteen (of which half were not European). Importantly, all Directors were now ex-officio members of the ECC and the GEM, and the BIS embarked on a new stage of governance beyond the G10. That the BIS had by now become more global was further underlined by the appointment of Agustín Carstens, former Governor of the Bank of Mexico, first as Chair of the ECC and GEM in July 2013 and subsequently, in December 2017, as General Manager of the BIS in succession to Jaime Caruana.

2.5 Summary and Conclusions

While the post-1945 institutions such as the World Bank, the IMF and the United Nations stressed inclusivity of their membership (albeit in the context of the Cold War), the BIS sought to retain its 'club' atmosphere derived from an earlier era. This was justifiable during the Bretton Woods era because of the dominance of Europe and the United States in international banking and finance. Outside the Bank, in the 1960s the G10 became a prime locus for international monetary reform, and this spilled over to the BIS as the G10 central-bank Governors met in Basel to provide functional solutions to prop up the Bretton Woods monetary system. During the 1960s and 1970s the Bank institutionalised these solutions in more formal committees with G10 membership, and this increased the impact of the policy work and cooperation hosted at the Bank, but the governance of the Bank was unchanged. The informal Sunday-evening discussions among G10 central bankers at their monthly meetings remained the crucial format to share information and create consensus.

The lengthy and cautious process of reforming the governance of the Bank demonstrates the importance that the Directors placed on the discretion of their deliberations. Their belief in the effectiveness of privacy and informality contrasted with the growing challenge to the Bank's legitimacy and authority from the 1990s. On the other hand, the BIS never set out to be a universal institution nor a democratic expression of its members' interests. The purpose of the Bank was to foster international cooperation in the pursuit of monetary and financial stability, by hosting a forum for regular meetings between (small) groups of Governors and central-bank officials, by providing financial services to the central-bank community on a commercial basis and by undertaking research. The Bank focused on technocratic expertise, avoided overt political intervention and eschewed public attention. In response to the increasing pressure to become more inclusive, the strategy of the Bank's Board and management was to include a wider constituency through regional offices and consultative councils, engaging its members to protect the traction of its standard-setting through the GEM, and hosting and supporting other standard-setting bodies and the FSF/FSB, as well as disseminating its research on the global financial system. These were all ambitious and important initiatives, but the reluctance to amend the Statutes suggests how highly the G10 central banks prized their informal cooperation.

Over time, real changes to the Bank's governance were unavoidable given the momentous shifts in global economic and financial power. Under the leadership of Andrew Crockett during 1994–2003, the management pushed forward relentlessly to expand the membership of the BIS. In four stages, from 1996 to 2011, shareholding membership increased from thirty-three to sixty central banks, with all major emerging-market economies included. These sixty member central banks represent countries that together made up close to 95 per cent of global GDP at the end of the 2010s.[88] Thus, while BIS membership is not universal, from an economic and financial point of view it is certainly highly representative and relevant. The expansion of the BIS Board of Directors beyond its traditional European, and later G10, composition proved much more difficult. It took nearly twenty years – from the first informal discussions in 1999 until the implementation of the new statutory requirements (Article 27) in 2019 – until the Board's composition finally caught up with the governance of other key players in the international financial cooperation area. It was only after 2008, in the aftermath of the financial crisis, that the G20 and FSB intensified the pressure to expand the Bank's governance. An initially reluctant Board gradually became more accepting and ultimately even proactive in opening up to the new post-crisis realities. Even so, it took another ten years to adapt the Bank's Statutes.

The FSB chose the G20 as the optimal size of the governance of the global economy in the wake of the global financial crisis, but the sustainability of this size and shape has yet to be fully tested. It was relatively easy to achieve consensus and retain momentum in the immediate aftermath of the crisis, but as the interests of members diverged (e.g. via spillovers to emerging markets from ECB and Fed monetary policy) the effectiveness of this larger group has waned. Nevertheless, the Bank persisted with its own geographical expansion. The crucial task for the governance of the Bank is to retain and enhance its legitimacy and authority and its usefulness to its members and Board of Directors. The Bank's three main missions are promoting monetary and financial stability, providing banking services to the central-bank community at large and enhancing international cooperation among central banks. The research department and key committees fulfil the first mission, which has been broadened to include wider cooperation with other relevant agencies. The Banking Department fulfils the second operational task. The third mission, that of fostering international cooperation, is a more challenging goal. The Bank's traditional way to meet this challenge in the first decades after 1945 was through regular personal contact among a group of like-minded central-bank Governors who trusted in the discretion and frankness of their discussions. This peak-level cooperation has been supported and supplemented by the activities of formal committees and MED meetings. The future of this model depends on the willingness of extremely busy central-bank Governors to make frequent trips to Basel to meet in person, so the meetings and operations of the BIS must remain useful to the new wider group of Directors and their staffs. The history of the governance of the Bank during the era of globalisation suggests that its structure has proved resilient, if sometimes slow to respond in the face of dramatic changes in the political and economic configuration of the global financial system.

Notes

1. See Chapters 3 (Christopher Brummer) and 4 (Andrew Baker) of this volume on how the reforms after the 2007–8 financial crisis, and particularly the elaboration of Basel III, were influenced by work previously undertaken at the BIS.

2. One of its main tools is FSI Connect, a web-based information resource and learning tool that covers international financial regulatory standards and sound supervisory practices.
3. Significantly, for this purpose the ECSC in early 1979 created an ad hoc working party on possible approaches to constraining the growth of international bank lending. BISA, 1.3a(3)J. (Also, Clement and Maes 2016)
4. On the BIS's role in European monetary cooperation and unification from the 1960s, and the end of that role in the early 1990s, see Chapter 1 (Harold James) of this volume.
5. The G10 were identified in 1961 when these countries participated in the IMF's GAB; Switzerland was added in 1964. The BIS, European Commission and OECD were official observer institutions at G10 Ministers and Governors' meetings.
6. Memo by A. D. Crockett to Gros, Bockelmann, Giovanoli, 28 February 1994. BISA 7.18(31) ADC 216.1.
7. Although the standard was 8,000 shares per member, Iceland, Latvia and Lithuania held 1,000 shares each and Estonia 200 shares. The Czechoslovakian National Bank shares were divided 5,330 to the Czech Republic and 2,670 to Slovakia. The three non-founder central banks on the Board held 13,000 shares each. The founders (and the United States – in terms of voting rights) held considerably more.
8. BIS Statutes Article 8(3), Statutes of the Bank for International Settlements. See www.bis.org/about/statutes-en.pdf.
9. The founding banks were those of the United Kingdom, Germany, Italy, France and Belgium. The non-founding central banks represented on the BIS Board were those of the Netherlands, Sweden and Switzerland.
10. 'The use of quantitative indicators to assist decisions concerning the possible enlargement of BIS membership', Memo for Crockett, 27 May 1994. BISA 7.18(31) ADC 216.1.
11. Memo by John Lowen, Hugues Antheaume and Sybille Kraatz, 'Candidates for BIS Membership', 27 May 1994. BISA 7.18(31) ADC 216.1.
12. G. Noppen memo for Executive Committee Meeting, 30 May 1994. BISA 7.18(31) ADC 216.1.
13. Note for Record, A. Crockett, 25 July 1994. BISA 7.18(31), ADC 216.1.
14. Memo by Crockett, 'Line to take on the expansion of shareholding members', 23 September 1994. BISA 7.18(31), ADC 216.1.
15. Letter from Bernie Fraser to A. Crockett, 26 September 1995, enclosing the text of his speech. BISA 7.18(31), ADC 210.1.
16. Note for Record, 16 November 1995. BISA 7.18(31), ADC 210.1.
17. The committee was chaired by Alfons Verplaetse and included Bill McDonough and Jean-Claude Trichet. Gunter Baer was rapporteur. Note for Record, 10 October 1995. BISA 7.18(31), ADC 210.1.
18. Memo Z. Nakajima to Crockett, 26 October 1995. BISA 7.18(31), ADC 210.1.
19. Summary of main points of the Sub-Committee's Second Meeting on 10 December 1995 in Basel, BISA 7.18(31) ADC 215.1.
20. Ibid.
21. 'The views of the Bank of Japan on strengthening central bank cooperation in the framework of the BIS', 15 January 1996. BISA 7.18(31) ADC 215.1.

22. 'Report of the Sub-Committee of the Board on Enhancing Central Bank Cooperation at the BIS', 6 March 1996. BISA 7.18(31) ADC 215.1.
23. Ibid.
24. BIS Membership: further work for the Sub-Committee, 13 March 1996. BISA 7.18(31) ADC 215.1.
25. Letter to Hans Tietmeyer from A.D. Crockett, 12 February 1996. BISA 7.18(31), ADC 216.1. Russia was the only country to submit a formal letter.
26. Memo Actionnariat de la Banque, 20 March 1996. BIS Membership: further work for the Sub-Committee, 13 March 1996. BISA 7.18(31), ADC 216.1. The meeting was on 10 March 1996.
27. Email from Crockett to Icard, Baer, White, Gill, 7 August 1996, BISA 7.18(19) BAE 3.5.4.7.
28. Ibid.
29. Letter Crockett to Duisenberg, 2 August 1996. BISA 7.18(31), ADC 216.1.
30. With each share valued at 1,057.645 grams of fine gold, equivalent to about $13,141.
31. Extract of Board Meeting Minutes, 9 September 1996. BISA 7.18(19) BAE 3.5.4.2. As a result of these different operations, a total of 44,000 new BIS shares were subscribed, 27,000 of which went to the nine new shareholders and 17,000 to existing G10 members (the central banks of Japan, the Netherlands, Sweden and Switzerland).
32. Letter from Crockett to Pedro Pou, Banco Central de la República Argentina, 5 September 1996. BISA 7.18(31), ADC 216.1.
33. Memo by M. Giovanoli for Crockett 'Options for Granting BIS Membership to the HKMA', 31 May 1996 preliminary draft. BISA 7.18(31), ADC 216.2.
34. Memo by Crockett to Giovanoli, 20 May 1996. BISA 7.18(31), ADC 216.2.
35. Note from Crockett to Giovanoli, 3 June 1996. . BISA 7.18(31), ADC 216.2.
36. Letter Joseph Yam to Crockett, 7 August 1996. Encloses copy of letter to European central-bank governors. BISA 7.18(31), ADC 216.2.
37. Letter from Dai Xianglong, Governor of PBoC, to Crockett, 30 August 1996. BISA 7.18(31), ADC 216.2.
38. Note by Crockett to Icard, Baer, White, Gill, 6 September 1996. BISA 7.18(31), ADC 216.1.
39. Memo by Crockett to G. K. Simons, 25 July 1996. BISA 7.18(31), ADC 216.1.
40. The ACC also acted as the governance body overseeing the work and activities of the BIS Representative Office for Asia and the Pacific, set up in Hong Kong in 1998, about which we will see more later.
41. 'Supervisory Lessons to be drawn from the Asian Crisis', Working Group led by Rudi Bonte, Basel Committee on Banking Supervision Working Papers, No. 2, June 1999.
42. In the end, the Bank of Indonesia did not choose to devote scarce resources to take up its shares and delayed its membership until the next round of enlargement three and a half years later.
43. The All Governors' Meeting comprises the Governors of all BIS member central banks and is chaired by the Chair of the BIS Board. It convenes to discuss selected topics of general interest to its members.
44. Email from Crockett to Baer, Icard, Sleeper and White, 5 August 2001. BISA 7.18(31) ADC 21.1.

45. Report of the Sub-Committee of the Board on BIS membership and related issues, by GD Baer (Secretary), 8 March 2002. BISA 7.18(31). ADC 21.1.

46. Ibid.

47. Ibid.

48. Ibid.

49. 'Challenges facing the BIS: a note for discussion at the informal dinner of Governors', 10 May 2002. BISA 7.18(31) ADC 21.1.

50. These views were backed up by a comprehensive survey conducted among the BIS member central banks in 2002 about the services provided by the BIS. The report based on the survey was written by former Bank of Canada Governor Gordon Thyssen (2003).

51. Email from Crockett to Baer, Icard, Sleeper, White, 13 May 2002. BISA 7.18(31) ADC 21.1.

52. The FATF is an intergovernmental body founded in 1989 by the G7 heads of state to set standards and monitor compliance with rules against money laundering and (from 2001) financing of terrorism.

53. Email from Crockett to Baer, Icard, Sleeper, White, 13 May 2002. BISA 7.18(31) ADC 21.1.

54. Memo, Questions and Issues Arising in the Context of Establishing a BIS Office in Asia, 20 September 1997. BISA 7.18(31), ADC 210.1.

55. Draft Action Plan on preparing a Board decision on the Asia Office, 2 October 1997. BISA 7.18(31), ADC 210.1.

56. Letters from Gunter Baer to James H. Lau Jr HKMA and Leong Sing Chiong, MAS, 20 October 1997. BISA 7.18(31), ADC 210.1.

57. Back to Office Report, Baer and Mario Giovanoli, 10 November 1997. 20 October 1997. BISA 7.18(31), ADC 210.1.

58. Note for the Informal Board Meeting on 8 December 1997. 20 October 1997. BISA 7.18(31), ADC 210.1.

59. Telex to James Lau Jr. from Gunter Baer (Secretary General), 24 December 1997. 20 October 1997. BISA 7.18(31), ADC 210.1.

60. Memo to Crockett, Icard and Baer from Mario Giovanoli and Mark Milford, 8 February 1998. 20 October 1997. Back to Office Report by Baer to Crockett, 17 February 1998. BISA 7.18(31), ADC 210.1.

61. Memo from Paul Van den Bergh to Crockett, 10 February 1998. 20 October 1997. BISA 7.18(31), ADC 210.1.

62. Note to Members of Staff from Crockett, 18 February 1998. 20 October 1997. BISA 7.18(31), ADC 210.1.

63. Back to Office Report, Baer, Giovanoli, Pickering, Milford to Crockett, 6 April 1998. 20 October 1997. BISA 7.18(31), ADC 210.1.

64. Email Crockett to Baer, 4 May 2001. BISA 7.18(31), ADC 210.2.

65. The G20 included the G7 plus Argentina, Australia, Brazil, China, India, Mexico, Russia, Saudi Arabia, South Africa, Korea and Turkey, the IMF and World Bank.

66. BRICs included Brazil, Russia, India and China (O'Neill, 2001).

67. Letter Crockett to Jose Luis Bernal Rodriguez, Mexican ambassador to Switzerland, 6 May 2002. BISA 7.18(31), ADC 210.2.

68. The Center for Latin American Monetary Studies (CEMLA) was founded in 1952 to promote a better understanding of monetary and banking matters and policies in

Latin America and the Caribbean, and to provide regional central banks with training assistance and research. In that sense its mandate is less broad than that of, for instance, EMEAP in the East Asia-Pacific region, which is a forum for regular meetings of central-bank executives.

69. 'Draft speaking notes on BIS Governance: points to make G10 lunch, Mexico City, 10 November 2002', 7 November 2002. BISA 7.18(31) ADC 22. At this same meeting, Crockett also proposed inviting some more central banks to become shareholding members. This was approved and led to the membership of the central banks of Algeria, Chile, Indonesia, Israel, New Zealand and the Philippines in June 2003 (see above).

70. Crockett note for G10 Governors, 5 November 2002. BISA 7.18(31) ADC 22.

71. Draft Minutes, 'BIS Board Retreat: where should the Bank be five years from now?', Sunday 7 September 2003, Wasserschloss Inzlingen. BISA 7.18(19) BAE 3,5.

72. BIS Board of Directors' Retreat 6 November 2005, Hotel Bad Schauenburg, Liestal. 'Issue: Additional BIS shareholders?', BISA 7.18(37) KNI.

73. Comprising two Directors each for the five founder central banks (those of Belgium, France, Germany, Italy and the United Kingdom); two seats for the Federal Reserve System (the Chair of the Board of Governors of the Federal Reserve System and the President of the Federal Reserve Bank of New York); and one Director each for the central banks of Canada, Japan, the Netherlands, Sweden and Switzerland.

74. Draft Minutes, 'BIS Board Retreat: where should the Bank be five years from now?', Sunday 7 September 2003, Wasserschloss Inzlingen. BISA 7.18(19) BAE 3,5.

75. Review of the Governance of the Bank for International Settlements, 21 October 2004. The interim report was submitted in September 2004, the final report in November. The report was written by Klaus J. Hopt, Reinier H. Kraakman and Jean-Victor Louis. See www.bis.org/about/govreview.pdf

76. BIS Board of Directors' Retreat 6 November 2005, 'Issue: Extension of BIS Board membership', BISA 7.18 (37) KNI.

77. Ibid.

78. BIS Board of Directors' Retreat 6 November 2005, 'Note on the outcome of the retreat'. BISA 7.18 (37) KNI.

79. Interview with Hermann Greve, 12 September 2018.

80. BIS Economic Adviser and Head of the Monetary and Economic Department William White had left the Bank in June 2008 having reached compulsory retirement age. He was succeeded in July 2008 by the American economist Stephen G. Cecchetti.

81. See, for example, the warnings in the 2006 *Annual Report* (BIS AR 2006).

82. A point that did not go unnoticed (Pihlman and Van der Hoorn 2010). Robert McCauley and Jean-François Rigaudy of the BIS offered some defence, pointing out that the BIS has a fiduciary responsibility towards its central-bank shareholders and customers in protecting BIS credit quality and profitability (McCauley and Rigaudy 2011: 19–47).

83. More specifically on the role of the BIS in the post-crisis reforms from 2008 to 2009 onward, see Chapters 3 (Christopher Brummer) and 4 (Andrew Baker) of this volume.

84. Interview with Hermann Greve, 18 September 2018. Since the start of the ECC in 2010, this body and the broader GEM have shared the same Chairperson: Jean-

Claude Trichet of the ECB (from January 2010 until October 2011), Mervyn King of the Bank of England (from November 2011 until June 2013), Agustín Carstens of the Bank of Mexico (from July 2013 until November 2017), Mark Carney of the Bank of England (from December 2017 until January 2020). Carstens' appointment in July 2013 can be seen as evidence of the increasing involvement of the emerging-market economies in the BIS's governance.

85. BISA, Minutes of the BIS Board of Directors, Meeting of 7 September 2009.

86. BIS Statutes Article 27 was a so-called protected article. Changes required approval from the governments of the founder central banks, rather than just the Board itself.

87. Additional protections were added for the ex officio members, who together held 45 per cent of BIS capital, and so were more exposed to greater financial risk.

88. In January 2020, the BIS Board of Directors invited the central banks of Kuwait, Morocco and Vietnam to become BIS members, bringing the total number of members to sixty-three.

The BIS in Pictures, 1973–2020

When the BIS was created in 1930, it was decided that the Bank should be located in the city of Basel, Switzerland, because of its central location within Europe and because of Switzerland's neutrality. The BIS has retained its head office in Basel ever since, but also has set up two representative offices: one in the Hong Kong SAR (Representative Office for Asia and the Pacific, founded in 1998) and one in Mexico City (Representative Office for the Americas, founded in 2002).

This photographic section, reproducing pictures from the BIS archive collection, shows the BIS office buildings in Basel, Hong Kong and Mexico, as well as some of the meetings that take place at the BIS on a regular basis. It also features a gallery of the consecutive Chairs of the BIS Board of Directors and of the BIS General Managers from the early 1970s up to the start of 2020.

First BIS building, the Savoy Hôtel Univers, Basel, 1930–1977

BIS main building, Basel. The Bank moved into the "Tower" in 1977

Botta Building, Basel, which the BIS has occupied since 1998

Two International Finance Centre, Hong Kong SAR, where the BIS Asian Office is located

Opening Ceremony for the BIS Representative Office for Asia and the Pacific,
Hong Kong SAR, July 1998
From the left: Ma Yuzhen (Commissioner, Commissioner's Office of China's Foreign
Ministry in the Hong Kong SAR), Donald Tsang (Financial Secretary of the Hong Kong
SAR), Alfons Verplaetse (President and Chairman of the BIS Board of Directors), Dai
Xianglong (Governor, People's Bank of China), Joseph Yam (First Chief Executive of
the Hong Kong Monetary Authority), Andrew Crockett (BIS General Manager)

Torre Chapultepec, Mexico City, where the BIS Americas Office is located,
© Fideicomiso 325

Opening Ceremony for the BIS Representative Office for the Americas, Mexico City,
Mexico, November 2002
From the left: Gregor Heinrich (BIS Chief Representative for the Americas), Andrew
Crockett (BIS General Manager), Guillermo Ortiz (Governor of the Bank of Mexico)

BIS Annual General Meeting 1975, Basel

BIS Annual General Meeting 2018, Basel. On the podium, left to right: Hyun Song Shin (Economic Adviser and Head of Research), Claudio Borio (Head of Monetary and Economic Department), Peter Zöllner (Head of Banking Department), Agustín Carstens (General Manager), Jens Weidmann (Chairman of BIS Board of Directors; Deutsche Bundesbank, Frankfurt am Main), Luiz Awazu Pereira da Silva (Deputy General Manager), Monica Ellis (Secretary General), Diego Devos (General Counsel), Fernando Restoy (Chairman of Financial Stability Institute)

Global Economy Meeting, May 2019, Basel

BIS Board of Directors, with the BIS General Manager, May 2019. Standing, left to right: John C Williams (Federal Reserve Bank of New York, New York), Ignazio Visco (Bank of Italy, Rome), Shaktikanta Das (Reserve Bank of India, Mumbai), Jerome H Powell (Board of Governors of the Federal Reserve System, Washington DC), Mark Carney (Bank of England, London), Mario Draghi (European Central Bank, Frankfurt am Main), Stephen S Poloz (Bank of Canada, Ottawa), Stefan Ingves (Sveriges Riksbank, Stockholm), Juyeol Lee (Bank of Korea, Seoul), Pierre Wunsch (National Bank of Belgium, Brussels)
Seated, left to right: Alejandro Díaz de León (Bank of Mexico, Mexico City), François Villeroy de Galhau (Bank of France, Paris), Agustín Carstens (BIS General Manager), Jens Weidmann (Chairman; Deutsche Bundesbank, Frankfurt am Main), Yi Gang (People's Bank of China, Beijing), Klaas Knot (Netherlands Bank, Amsterdam), Thomas Jordan (Swiss National Bank, Zurich), Roberto Campos Neto (Central Bank of Brazil, Brasília). Not pictured: Haruhiko Kuroda (Bank of Japan, Tokyo)

BIS Management, May 2019. From left to right: Claudio Borio (Head of Monetary and Economic Department), Stijn Claessens (Deputy Head of Monetary and Economic Department), Monica Ellis (Secretary General), Hyun Song Shin (Economic Adviser and Head of Research), Bertrand Legros (Deputy Secretary General), Fernando Restoy (Chairman of Financial Stability Institute), Agustín Carstens (General Manager), Diego Devos (General Counsel), Luiz Awazu Pereira da Silva (Deputy General Manager), Jens Ulrich (Head of Risk Management), Peter Zöllner (Head of Banking Department), Jean-François Rigaudy (Deputy Head of Banking Department), Siddharth Tiwari (Chief Representative for Asia and the Pacific)

Jelle Zijlstra, President and Chairman of the BIS Board of Directors, Jul 1967–Dec 1981

Fritz Leutwiler, President and Chairman of the BIS Board of Directors, Jan 1982–Dec 1984

Jean Godeaux, President and Chairman of the BIS Board of Directors, Jan 1985–Dec 1987

Bengt Dennis, President and Chairman of the BIS Board of Directors, Jan 1991–Dec 1993

Willem Frederik Duisenberg, President and Chairman of the BIS Board of Directors,
Jan 1988–Dec 1990 and Jan 1994–Jun 1997

Alfons Verplaetse, President and Chairman of the BIS Board of Directors,
Jul 1997–Feb 1999

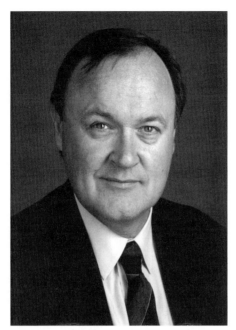

Urban Bäckström, President and Chairman of the BIS Board of Directors,
Mar 1999–Feb 2002

Arnout H E M Wellink, President and Chairman of the BIS Board of Directors,
Mar 2002–Feb 2006

Jean-Pierre Roth, Chairman of the BIS Board of Directors, Mar 2006–Feb 2009

Guillermo Ortiz, Chairman of the BIS Board of Directors, Mar 2009–Dec 2009

Christian Noyer, Chairman of the BIS Board of Directors, Mar 2010–Oct 2015

Jens Weidmann, Chairman of the BIS Board of Directors, Nov 2015–Present

René Larre, BIS General Manager, May 1971–Feb 1981

Günther Schleiminger, BIS General Manager, Mar 1981–Apr 1985

Alexandre Lamfalussy, BIS General Manager, May 1985–Dec 1993

Andrew Crockett, BIS General Manager, Jan 1994–Mar 2003

Malcolm D Knight, BIS General Manager, Apr 2003–Sep 2008

Hervé Hannoun, Acting BIS General Manager, Oct 2008–Mar 2009

Jaime Caruana, BIS General Manager, Apr 2009–Nov 2017

Agustín Carstens, BIS General Manager, Dec 2017–Present

3

A Theory of Everything

A Historically Grounded Understanding of Soft Law and the BIS

Chris Brummer

3.1 Introduction

The theorisation and study of soft law has advanced tremendously over the last fifteen years (Lipson 1991; Abbott and Duncan 2000; Guzman 2008; Shaffer and Pollack 2010; Slaughter and Zaring 2006). Overlooked and underestimated for decades, soft law is now widely recognised as a critical tool for financial regulators tasked with managing the global financial system. Among the varying insights of commentators and scholars, not only is soft law an at times high-profile and even solemn expression of intergovernmental commitments and norms, but it can also leverage reputational and market disciplines such that governments are, if not compelled, at least highly motivated to comply (Brummer 2014b: 145–8). In the process, the very concept of soft law has expanded to include, as I have argued, not only non-binding political accords but also information-sharing and enforcement agreements, codes of conduct, regulatory best practices and even high-level reports released by international organisations when endorsed and committed to by stakeholder regulatory agencies (Brummer 2014b: 119–24).

Yet despite this now formidable body of scholarship, little inquiry has been made into the institutional moorings supporting soft law beyond qualitative assessments evaluating varying features and their implications for legitimacy, compliance and international relations. Although scholars recognise the pivotal role played by standard-setting bodies in formulating policy, few if any have developed a historical account or theory as to why soft law as a regulatory tool would first appear in some institutional arrangements in the regulatory ecosystem as opposed to others (Goodhart 2011 is one notable exception).

On the occasion of the ninetieth anniversary of the Bank's creation, this chapter offers such an account with regard to the Bank for International Settlements (BIS). First, it argues that soft law's origins in financial regulation lay in the particular institutional evolution of the BIS *prior* to the articulation of bank capital standards. Institutional innovations tied with the Bank's navigation of the politics and economic particularities of the First World War reparations would enable the informality and expert-driven systems that would one day characterise today's modern 'Basel Process' of technocratic decision-making.[1] Furthermore, it shows how soft law, far from being an entirely radical break with the economic diplomacy of the times, was in fact merely the next step in an evolution of the Bank that in its deployment would not only enhance the credibility of non-binding understandings and accords in international economic diplomacy but also help to solidify and elevate the very stature of the BIS. It is indeed no coincidence that soft law would be deployed as a governance mechanism at the BIS, in particular as the international regulatory community turned to the challenge of prudential supervision – or that the BIS would conceive of soft law specifically to further urgent financial-market reforms in the post–Bretton Woods era.

In what follows, most of the focus is on the Basel Committee on Banking Supervision, the main regulatory standard-setting body operating under the aegis of the BIS.[2]

3.2 BIS Informality and the Origins of Financial Soft Law

The modern story of soft law and the global financial system is usually recognised as beginning in 1988, with the adoption by the Basel Committee on Banking Supervision of the Basel I Capital Accord, or 1997, with the creation of the Financial Stability Forum (FSF) in the aftermath of the Asian financial crisis.[3] Less well known, however, is that the groundwork for an informal system of norms and codes of conduct and financial standards had been laid far in advance and was in fact embedded in the very DNA of the BIS. This groundwork would not be so much substantive, but instead institutional, and provide the base-layer architecture for informal decision-making that would come to characterise Basel-based regulatory processes.

3.2.1 Reparations and Crisis Management

As persuasively recounted by Borio and Toniolo, the BIS's origins lay in a response to a challenge still perplexing international economics and international relations – the enforcement of sovereign-debt obligations. In the late 1920s, as part of a last-ditch effort to prevent France defaulting on its own war debt, central bankers and financiers sought an institutional framework for supporting the so-called commercialisation of German reparation payments that could free up cash for debt repayments (Borio and Toniolo 2006: 9). The idea was to move past an impasse on what was non-payment of German reparations obligations by transforming them into normal financial transactions where the German government would issue long-term bonds to international private banks and financial houses. Creditor countries wanted to receive upfront payments over the shortest time horizon possible, while Germany, as the obligor, sought the opposite – and most important, that a significant portion of the payments be reinvested in Germany, where hyperinflation was rampant and the currency had collapsed.

It was in this context that the BIS was envisioned to solve a quintessential 'hard law' compliance problem: how to make sure a country abides by the terms of a legally binding agreement (the repayment of its bonds) (Gelpern and Gulati 2010: v–vi). Macroeconomic conditions could change (and did change) dramatically as the Great Depression's malaise deepened. Moreover, as a debtor nation, Germany would have better information about economic conditions affecting debt payment than lenders, leading to information asymmetries during the course of the transaction (Toniolo 2005: 34). Authorities had to devise a flexible, responsive system that would deliver borrower information and some modicum of predictability as to future payments; at the same time, they needed a means for adjusting to new circumstances and collectively responding to any potential default, no small issue given the disparate views among allied countries as to the desired stringency of reparations terms.

The compliance puzzle was all the more intriguing – and challenging – given the fact that reparations were but the means to achieving the greater goal of re-establishing the international monetary system, which was based on the gold standard and its own concomitant 'macroeconomic' compliance dilemma.[4] In short, as a monetary regime, the gold standard depended on a state of affairs where central banks agreed to undertake the domestic policies necessary to maintain a sufficient supply of gold to support convertibility of their domestic currency into the precious metal. In its classical formulation, this meant the introduction of politically painful deflationary policies in times of economic stress and few restraints on trade or the flow of capital (Eichengreen 2008: 24). Yet throughout the period, there were no explicit rules as to how to operationalise such a commitment, much less how international responses should be coordinated where even a central bank's policy responses might prove insufficient to stave off capital flight.

Institutionally, the BIS would speak to this problem set by fulfilling not one but multiple roles as trustee, market participant and international organisation. As a trustee, it would serve as a central node for lowering information asymmetries and receiving and distributing reparation annuities; as a market participant, the Bank could issue its own securities in order to act as a source of liquidity for German bonds; and as an international organisation, the BIS could help countries come to a consensus about the sound management and operation of the gold standard and the obligations of participant countries (Toniolo 2005: 37).

The BIS would be endowed with extraordinary institutional features that, though formal, and subject to preset governance rules, would be premised on ad hoc and flexible policy development and response. On the one hand, the BIS was a bank structured as a limited-liability company, with a capital divided into 200,000 shares and distributed to central banks and key Japanese and US banking groups, who in turn were in principle free to release shares to the public. However, to maintain control among (primarily) official-sector interests, the BIS could decline to accept a transfer of shares to a new owner, and only originally participating central banks were entitled to vote (Toniolo 2005: 49).

At the same time, the BIS had all the characteristics of an international organisation, possessing a formal legal personality and endowed with many of the privileges and immunities normally conferred upon diplomatic entities and institutions.[5] In consequence, policy management and crisis response, while executed within the Bank's governance structure, could be relatively unrestricted and ad hoc; moreover, the BIS would be free to promote certain policy norms and develop 'the widest possible measure of common agreement on monetary theory, problems and practice', including agreement on the promotion of the 'international standard ... and how to maintain it' (Toniolo 2005: 2). No formal rule-making authority was afforded to the Bank, but the presumption was that suasion would be an effective force in corralling a relatively small community of central bankers.

3.2.2 The Great Depression and Policy Unmooring

At the time the BIS was first contemplated and initially launched in the late spring of 1930, the specific job of policy coordination was expected to be a relatively straightforward task. All initial members of the BIS were countries that evinced a philosophical agreement or commitment to the desirability of the gold standard, and thus once reparations and war-debt issues were sidelined, investment could resume and the international monetary system could achieve its full operations. By 1931, just months after the BIS's inauguration, consensus and credibility melted away as the Great Depression took hold, forcing many of the world's major economies off the gold standard over the following twenty-four months.

The abandonment of the gold standard, though envisaged as only temporary, would prove intellectually disastrous for the newly founded bank. For all its institutional flexibility and responsiveness, the BIS's operations were premised on an ideological assumption that a relatively strict adherence to the gold standard was the best – and only – guidepost for ad hoc policy action (Eichengreen 2008). Once this presumption was no longer operative, the Bank not only suffered a blow to its credibility, but it also lost what was at least implicitly one of its core duties – the maintenance of the gold standard and, by extension, the international monetary system – and associated tasks of norm-setting and consensus-building.

The BIS would, however, maintain its central role in overseeing, and ultimately ending, reparations paid by Germany to victorious allied states, and it is in this domain that one of the central institutions of soft-law production would appear: the Basel expert committees. As a financial crisis in Germany increasingly engulfed Europe, the BIS tasked a committee to 'inquire into the immediate further credit needs of Germany and to study the possibilities of converting a portion of short-term credits into long-term credits' (Toniolo 2005: 123). In contrast to modern Basel committees, however, most of the members hailed from the private sector, and represented large creditors (Toniolo 2005: 125).[6] Albert Wiggin, the then-chairman of the board of the Chase National Bank of New York, was elected chair. Through the committee, negotiations for a standstill agreement on German war debts would be accelerated, in what was up to that point in time a formidable accomplishment, made possible by a close-knit group of BIS banking and private-sector financial resources (Toniolo 2005: 123).

Soon thereafter, the German government would request the appointment of yet a second Basel committee to examine a wholesale re-evaluation of the Young Plan, which set forth many of Germany's post-war reparations obligations (Toniolo 2005: 128). The BIS obliged, and convened a committee headed by Alberto Beneduce, an Italian board member. Released shortly before Christmas in 1931, the recommendations of the Committee argued that intergovernmental reparations and war debts should be 'adjusted' to ensure peace and economic stability (LeBor 2013: 28). Six months later, in 1932, European governments convened in Lausanne to consider the recommendations, and acquiesced and eventually cancelled the payments.

3.3 The Bretton Woods Period

Although the end of Second World War would formally reinstate a dollar-based gold exchange standard, it would do little to immediately position the BIS at the centre of international diplomacy. The Bank's reputation had been tarnished by questions raised by its wartime receipt of gold transfers consisting of looted central-bank gold deposits and gold owned by persecuted Nazi victims (Toniolo 2005: 245–59). And with the creation of the International Monetary Fund (IMF) and the World Bank, two new financial institutions would be primarily tasked with the duties of crisis management, monetary oversight and economic development. Notably, these entities were international financial governmental institutions and not central-bank organisations.

Indeed, an international law of money would be memorialised in the IMF's Articles of Agreement, detailing various member-country obligations with regard to the convertibility of their currencies into gold or the US dollar. Among the most important provisions was Article IV(4)(a), which required signatories to collaborate with the Fund to promote exchange rate stability (Lowenfeld 2010). At the same time, a new hybrid system of monetary relations would be introduced whereby governments would still be permitted to impose controls on foreign exchange transactions and capital flows. Thus, while rules of the road would guide the conduct of governments and prohibit currency manipulation, countries would still continue to enjoy considerable control over their domestic macroeconomic policies (Brummer 2014a: 41).

With new commitments backed by the force of international law coming into place, some Bretton Woods negotiators, including Harry White, advocated the liquidation of the BIS, though calls for such action failed to garner the support of a super-majority of central-bank Governors (Bernholz 2009: 362). Nevertheless, the BIS's influence would continue to adapt, even while on the sidelines of the post-Bretton Woods financial system. For one, the BIS's economic views would evolve such that the gold-standard orthodoxy would itself be revised in ways that dovetailed increasingly with the Bretton Woods model of managed monetary relations (Bernholz 2009: 378). Moreover, the client list of the Bank would grow to include central banks from smaller countries in Europe beyond the founder institutions, reflecting what were increasingly competitive asset-management services offered to other central banks. Gold operations were an area where the Bank had accumulated extraordinary expertise in both the official and free markets. It operated on very narrow margins, endeavouring to secure from member central banks more advantageous terms than the official conditions of the Federal Reserve Board (Bernholz 2009: 370).

The Bank's positioning as a market actor with an expanding balance sheet and gold reserves, coupled with growing expertise, would render its Annual Reports increasingly influential (Bernholz 2009: 371). Larger revenues would allow the Bank to increase its research staff, as well as the range and rigour of its technical analysis. Thus, a long-standing belief in free trade, 'sound' money and international cooperation would increasingly inform larger policy conversations, and comprise implicit and explicit economic *standards* with which governments would, at a minimum, compare and contrast their own national policies.

By the 1960s, a large number of international monetary decisions originated either at or via the BIS. The Group of Ten (G10) became a leading forum for discussing international monetary matters as its members took on the role of financing the IMF's General Arrangements to Borrow. During this time, surveillance would arise through a small group, rather than at the IMF's board, with a sense that excluding non-G10 members (often debtor nations) would help the relevant policymakers address issues more consistently (Bossone 2008).[7] Correspondingly, the BIS would support a growing number of official and semi-official groups made up of G10 government and central-bank officials through secretariat services and analytical background work (Bossone 2008: 13). During this period, the BIS would help sponsor major innovations (and interventions), including the pooling of gold reserves to save the Bretton Woods system and defend the price of gold in the London gold market, as well as arrangements to defend the pound sterling (Toniolo 2005: 350–436).

3.4 The Prudential Turn

The departure of the United States from the gold standard in 1971 would usher in the conditions which would see the BIS – a multilateral organ that had developed informal forums for international monetary coordination alongside a deep expertise in payments – evolve into a pivotal player for macroprudential oversight.

The origins of such institutional growth were not auspicious. Post-war multilateralism, despite its broad-based institutional moorings, relied not only on US political and military support but also on the maintenance of certain trade and current-account surpluses. Once this was no longer possible, due in part to Vietnam War spending and growing social services obligations, the United States abandoned the gold standard – the governing monetary framework for the post-war period (Eichengreen 2011: 97, 121). Eventually others would follow and, in the process, catalyse dramatic shifts in international monetary policy.

The repercussions would be directly felt by multilateral institutions. For one, the IMF would find itself with its mission fundamentally questioned. The abandonment of the gold-dollar standard meant that its regulatory mandate to oversee and impose specific exchange rates was eliminated. The international law of money in effect established by the organisation's Articles of Agreement essentially dissolved, save a lasting prohibition on currency manipulation. Consequently, the IMF would be more fully converted into a surveillance tool. Many of the provisions for the Fund's Articles of Agreement would be rewritten, and a new Article IV (3) would – in lieu of requiring compliance with exchange rate rules – task members with providing the IMF with information necessary for carrying out surveillance and to consult with it when requested (Brummer 2014a: 46).

Meanwhile, the BIS would emerge within a half-decade of America's abandonment of the gold standard as a far more pivotal multilateral institution than in the past. Pragmatic as the Bretton Woods system was, it focused on the problems of its time, namely restoring global commerce through revived international monetary trade policy. Few efforts were launched to regulate or coordinate financial-market regulation. Cross-border capital flows at the time were limited and subject to the control and supervision of national regulatory authorities. IMF surveillance thus focused on classic macroeconomic problems like exchange rate stability and balance-of-payments crises.

The dissolution of the par system would, however, create new and unprecedented risks.[8] In order to create a true market for fiat currencies, controls on the cross-border movement of capital and investment were for the most part eliminated to enable floating prices. Besides potentially opening the floodgates to cross-border Ponzi schemes and accounting fraud, the ensuing financial globalisation enabled larger, and unregulated, flows of capital across borders that could enable asset bubbles and other forms of systemic risk with which authorities had limited experience in the preceding thirty years (Clement 2008: 6). Banks, once primarily domestic actors, would participate in increasingly far-flung transactional relationships and become comparatively more interdependent on one another.

Inklings of just what this meant would be seen as early as 1974 with the collapse of the now-infamous Herstatt bank in Cologne, Germany. Herstatt was the thirty-fifth largest bank in Germany, with total assets of just over 2 billion Deutsche Mark at the time, and was active in the foreign-exchange market. But in September 1973, Herstatt's foreign exchange business suffered losses four times the amount of its capital because of an unanticipated appreciation of the US dollar. When the German banking authority belatedly discovered the extent of the loss, and the insolvency of the bank, it withdrew the bank's licence and ordered it into liquidation.

The unanticipated move threw global markets into turmoil. Herstatt had entered into various foreign exchange transactions with banks around the world, including in the United States, which had already irrevocably paid Deutsche Mark through the German payment system expecting to be paid US dollars as a counter-currency through the US payment system. At the time Herstatt was closed, it was still morning in New York, and because of the time-zone differences, Herstatt ceased operations after US parties had paid, but before they could receive their US dollar payments in turn. The ensuing crisis was a drawing lesson for financial regulators in developed countries on potential risks of global banking markets and the value of enhanced supervisory coordination.

That said, the Herstatt debacle was not the first of its kind to illustrate the increasing interdependence of financial markets – or the special vulnerabilities of developed countries that hosted activities of large foreign banks (Mourlon-Druol 2015). Indeed, just months before Herstatt's collapse, the Franklin National Bank of New York, one of the twenty largest banks in the country, suffered massive losses in the foreign exchange markets and ever-riskier attempts to recoup them. Eventually, the Federal Reserve Bank, as with Herstatt, had been required to intervene, and kept the bank afloat with $2.8 billion in credits (Long Island Business News 2003).

The crises would highlight the increasing interconnectedness of banks and jurisdictions, as well as the need for new and better rules for global banking markets (Singer 2007: 39). They would also highlight the need for an international organ to quietly digest and study these changes, and develop multilateral tools for supervising banks whose overseas activities and transactions could end up imperilling domestic parent entities. Central-bank Governors from the G10 responded by establishing a committee to address the pressing need for new and better rules for global banking markets.

Housed at the BIS, the Standing Committee on Banking Regulations and Supervisory Practices (soon renamed the Basel Committee on Banking Supervision (BCBS)) would articulate aspirations far less ambitious than those of precedent expert committees at the Bank. Despite a desired interest expressed by the United Kingdom's Governor Gordon Richardson in an 'early warning system' so that regulators could take appropriate measures before a crisis began, the Basel Committee chairman George Blunden downplayed hopes of any initiative smacking of international regulatory harmonisation, and instead stated that the goal of committee members was 'to learn from each other and adapt the best features of each other's systems for inclusion in our own systems' (Singer 2007: 40).

From the start, information-sharing was robust and operationalised through the BIS's already established informal, technocratic club-like atmosphere. Within a year of the Basel Committee's launch, officials reached an agreement, the Concordat of 1975, that would hold parent banks responsible for the financial difficulties of foreign branches, thus absolving domestic central banks of lender-of-last-resort responsibilities (Singer 2007: 40; see also Goodhart 2011: 113[9]). Still, the Concordat was arguably not yet what one would come to expect of soft law, and would leave open key issues as to when a bank should be judged to be insolvent, and how banking crises should be managed. Few methodological interpretations were provided, and monitoring of any commitments was virtually non-existent.

Significantly, the central banks' policy response to the risk in payment systems highlighted by the Herstatt debacle ('Herstatt risk') also motivated early work of a Group of Experts on Payment Systems set up at the BIS in 1980. Much like that of the BCBS, this work was initially not focused on creating soft law in the form of international standards, but more on how to encourage efforts among central-bank payment-system operators to improve their systems and engage banks and bank supervisors to address settlement risk.[10]

3.5 The Emergence of Modern Financial Soft Law

With the Herstatt and Franklin National Bank collapses fresh in the memories of banking regulators, the Basel Committee was initially concerned with the threat of systemic risk arising from banks and payment systems in G10 countries (Alexander, Dhumale and Eatwell 2006: 41). But efforts to write international rules would not arise until members themselves established their own priorities – and leveraged the BIS as a platform to do so.[11]

Andrew Singer has persuasively documented how interest in such collaboration would begin to emerge in the United States in the late 1970s, as exchange rate volatility and anti-inflationary monetary policy by the Fed would combine to wreak havoc on the balance sheets of undercapitalised and loosely regulated banks (Singer 2007: 45). The rates of bank failures would, as a result, nearly triple, with thirteen bank failures in 1975, compared with an average of five banks annually for the prior five years (Singer 2007: 46). By 1981, US bank regulators released guidelines outlining formal capital-adequacy requirements for those institutions under their jurisdiction. Those efforts, however, failed to stem bank failures, especially given exposures to the Latin American sovereign-debt crisis. With forty banks entering insolvency in 1982, regulators were routinely prompted to hike capital requirements for institutions every several years (Goodhart 2011: 155).[12]

Similarly, the United Kingdom, reeling from bailouts of its own fringe banks, would introduce new supervisory practices for all deposit-taking institutions, along with capital requirements that would come to rival the strictness of those in the United States (Goodhart 2011: 165). Its prudential turn was, however, comparatively much starker than that of its Atlantic counterpart. Before 1979, there was essentially no formal regulatory apparatus for the prudential supervision of banks in the United Kingdom, with the Bank of England relying primarily on direct communications with bank managers relating to the proper way of conducting business (Goodhart 2011: 168). This relatively laissez-faire attitude would fall as the United Kingdom reeled from the secondary banking crisis of 1973–5, during which a spate of undercapitalised firms carrying on banking activities collapsed as the country's interest rates rose (Schenk 2014). The crisis – and subsequent rescue operations performed by the Bank of England – would trigger an era of enhanced supervisory reforms, including a published statement on bank capital adequacy for banks' lending activities in 1980 (Cooke 1982).

At the same time, the Bank of England would push at the BIS a greater interest in curbing international bank lending more generally. In a 1979 paper, 'The use of prudential measures in the international banking markets',[13] the Bank would outline an explicitly '"macro-prudential" approach' focusing on 'the market as a whole as distinct from an individual bank, and which may not be obvious at the micro-prudential level' (Maes 2011a: 277). Among its observations was that, while the growth of an individual bank's business might seem wholly acceptable from a microprudential standpoint, the overall rate of growth of international lending might be risky. Furthermore, the report observed that given the increasing international and complex chains of transactions and relationships banks might have with one another, they have limited information about leverage building up in markets. They could as a result become 'unduly complacent' about the funding risk, making them vulnerable to exogenous shocks (Maes 2011a: 278).

American and British regulators would learn of their mutual interest in enhancing prudential safeguards for banks under their jurisdictions during their regular meetings in Basel and through personal connections (Singer 2007: 59). Under the leadership of Fed chairman Paul Volcker and Bank of England Governor Robin Leigh-Pemberton, the two countries quickly devised a capital standard that met each of their regulatory and prudential objectives, and announced a bilateral agreement in January 1987. The deal included a shared, transatlantic definition of capital and a framework of risk-weighting based on five categories of assets (Singer 2007: 59; Goodhart 2011: 167–71).

Faced with the prospect of international banks leaving their countries for more lightly regulated jurisdictions, and in particular Japan, UK and US regulators pursued direct talks with the Japanese authorities and other G10 countries to garner international support for the capital standard (Singer 2007: 60). The object of the talks, as Gerald Corrigan, head of the New York Federal Reserve, would state, was to 'mov[e] Japanese bank capital standards into closer alignment with emerging international standards' (quoted in Kane 1994: 106). US and UK regulators emphasised that the bilateral accord was meant to be a stepping stone for the Basel Committee to promulgate multilateral capital standards based largely on the Anglo-American formula. Behind the talks was the prospect of excluding Japanese banks from US and UK markets should Japan not adopt stricter policies (Singer 2007: 60; Goodhart 2011: 550).

Ultimately, a new accord would be released – though with significant concessions on the part of both countries to accommodate some of the stronger preferences of the G10 countries, including Japan. Notably, most concessions related to the very definition of capital, arguably the most contentious matter for debate, with negotiators appeasing France by allowing subordinated debt to count as supplementary Tier 2 capital, and appeasing Japan by allowing a portion of unrealised capital gains on securities to be included in the capital base (Singer 2007: 61).

The Basel Accord was a political and regulatory watershed – and an institutional one as well. Of all the world's multilateral organs, agencies and forums, it was the informal, clubbish and highly technocratic Basel Committee that would emerge as the point of contact for international rule-making on a highly contentious, politically high-stake, economic-centric topic. And the output of the negotiations would be a regulatory product the BIS had relied on for decades: informal, non-binding codes of conduct, or soft law.

That said, the Basel Accord, like the Concordat before it, was not embedded in a fully mature regulatory ecosystem. For one, it lacked an institutionalised means by which adherence to its standards could be monitored. Japanese banks, facing the potential ire of the United States and the United Kingdom, were under significant pressure to conform. But there was no surveillance system to confirm whether or not changes were indeed implemented. Instead, the United States and Europe would have to determine ex ante which jurisdictions to assess closely. Additionally, and just as important, there was no means or mechanism for institutionalising any kind of 'compliance pull' such that the international regulatory community writ large would find sufficient incentives to conform with the new standards. Instead, the Basel system reflected the traditional committee systems embraced early in BIS history of clubbish networks of the most powerful states.

The relative absence of such coercion was, as Charles Goodhart persuasively argues, one of design. From the start, the Basel Committee's recommendations were, after all, primarily intended as tools for its members as regulators and supervisors (Goodhart 2011). As a result, there was rarely any specification of incentives and sanctions for abiding with or ignoring them (Goodhart 2011). For this very reason, transparency itself was very much viewed in a sceptical light insofar as it could, according to some officials, 'convey the impression' that central banks vying for approval from the body were 'participating in some qualifying process' (Eichengreen 2008).

The Basel Committee's largely inward-looking, G10 focus would change dramatically in the 1990s, which saw greater financial liberalisation and, most importantly, new risks tied to emerging markets. Starting in the early 1990s, first with Mexico,[14] and then later elsewhere in Latin America and Asia,[15] emerging markets began to open the door to international markets – and capital – as part of broader reforms geared to modernising the financial system. Yet market liberalisation was not accompanied by commensurate financial regulation, creating increasingly apparent global risks. As foreign investors poured money into newly opened economies, cavalier domestic banks loaded up on speculative real-estate and capital-market investments, and failed to maintain sufficient capital for bets gone awry. And with increasingly mobile capital, investors were able to move their money in and out of economies very quickly.

These risks would materialise most spectacularly in Southeast Asia, where initial speculative attacks on the Thai baht would trigger a chain reaction of currency devaluations requiring the IMF to provide over $100 billion in short-term loans for not only Thailand, but also regional neighbours like Indonesia, South Korea and even Hong Kong.

The global repercussions would reach investors in ways few expected. In 1998, Long-Term Capital Management (LTCM), an American hedge fund, collapsed as the impact of the Asian financial crisis spread to Russia and Russia stopped payments on its debt. At the time, LTCM was holding a significant, massively leveraged position in Russian government bonds. Ultimately, the Federal Reserve Bank of New York intervened given the fund's interconnectedness with other financial institutions, and the enormous write-offs LTCM's creditors would incur if it failed to repay them. It spearheaded a consortium consisting of some of LTCM's largest creditors, who together created a $3.65 billion loan fund, enabling LTCM to wait out the market turbulence and conduct an orderly liquidation two years later.

Ultimately, the Mexican, Asian and Russian financial crises would trigger unprecedented efforts to upgrade international regulatory cooperation. One of the main objectives was the publication of best practices by sectoral standard-setting bodies that could be implemented by emerging-market countries to prevent financial crises. The Basel Committee would be the first to do so, and released its Core Principles for Effective Banking Supervision in 1997, and later an accompanying methodology to serve as a benchmark for countries to assess the quality of their supervisory systems. Shortly thereafter, IOSCO embarked on its first-ever stream of public standard-setting, and released in 1998 its Objectives and Principles of Securities Regulation to provide a blueprint for US-style capital-market oversight (Jordan 2014: 35).[16] The Basel-based Committee on Payment and Settlement Systems (CPSS) would additionally establish a Task Force on Payment System Principles and Practices in May 1998 to consider what principles should govern the design and operation of payment systems in all countries, and released its Core Principles for Systemically Important Payment Systems in 2000. Other codes would be added as well, including standards established by private or quasi-private standard-setting bodies in accounting and auditing professions.

To get coordination off the ground, the G7 finance ministers and central-bank governors tasked Hans Tietmeyer, the President of the German Bundesbank, to consult international bodies on potential 'arrangements for cooperation and coordination between various international financial regulatory and supervisory bodies ... and to put to [them] expeditiously recommendations for any new structures and arrangements that may be required' (Tietmeyer 1999: 5).

Tietmeyer's subsequent report would highlight, above all, the need for coordinating the efforts of members of the international regulatory community to both identify and respond to risks. Notably, both processes would depend on inclusiveness in the standard-setting process, as well as surveillance of member countries and market participants alike:

Strengthening financial systems will demand a systematic approach to ensuring that gaps in international standards or codes of conduct are identified and effectively filled. This calls for intensified cooperation and coordination between the national authorities, international regulatory bodies and the IFIs [the IMF and World Bank] charged with monitoring and fostering implementation. In particular, national authorities and the regulatory groupings need to ensure that the process of developing standards benefits from the wide-ranging information obtained by the IFIs in their surveillance and assistance activities in individual countries. Greater involvement in these processes of the emerging market economies to which those standards would apply is needed to augment their commitment to implementing them.

A significant challenge for the international community in the years ahead will be to foster and monitor the worldwide implementation of accepted best practices and, in particular, of compliance with the Core Principles issued by both BCBS and IOSCO, and those being developed by other international groupings. The IFIs, using their established procedures for consultations, will need to assist countries in strengthening their financial systems. The information and expertise available to national authorities and international supervisory groupings can enhance the effectiveness of the IFIs in these tasks and vice versa.

National and international regulatory authorities must also develop procedures to ensure that market participants pay heed to the standards that have been developed in managing and pricing the risks they incur with respect to their counterparties. Strengthened procedures will be needed to coordinate and promote efficiency in this effort, as well as to avoid overlaps between the IFIs, and also with the rule-making capacities of the international supervisory bodies. (Tietmeyer 1999: 5)

To prevent gaps and regulatory lacunae, Tietmeyer called for convening a Financial Stability Forum (FSF) to prevent rules and best practices from being developed in isolation, supported by the BIS, which would provide advice and analysis. Additionally, BIS-based groupings of central-bank experts concerned with market infrastructure and functioning like the CPSS and the Committee on the Global Financial System (CGFS) would work alongside the BCBS and IOSCO to create a comprehensive set of rules for the global financial system.

The implementation of the international codes and standards would meanwhile take shape along a number of dimensions. First, the IMF's post-gold-standard Article IV provisions requiring members to provide the fund with information necessary for carrying out surveillance enabled the Fund to carry out limited reviews of members' financial systems each year.

Moreover, a new Financial Sector Assessment Program (FSAP) was launched to evaluate how the rules operated on the ground in countries at the domestic level. Intended to be more muscular, intrusive and rigorous, the FSAP would call on experts from the IMF in the case of developed countries, and the IMF and World Bank in the case of developing countries (along with external experts and regulators from powerful jurisdictions), to identify vulnerabilities in financial systems on a country-by-country basis with a view to preventing financial crises before they can arise. Ultimately twelve international standards would be issued in the process of benchmarking or rating a financial system – and critically, implementation of the codes and standards would be periodically incorporated as conditions for IMF and World Bank aid programmes.

Institutional changes would also reorient the relationships of both the BIS and IMF. Since its creation in the aftermath of the First World War, the BIS's position in the global monetary system had been questioned, and with the collapse of the gold standard its very existence threatened. By contrast, at the time of the IMF's birth, it was assumed to be the premier, and central, international organisation for global finance.

However, the Asian financial crisis, and the global responses to it, would redraw and reorient the place of the BIS in the international regulatory system. Its expert committees, and its role in helping shape and inform international standards, would give the institution a position in policymaking equivalent to – and in some ways even superior to – that of the Fund.[17] At the same time, the Fund (and to a certain extent the World Bank, too) would see its stature enhanced as surveillance activities expanded beyond monetary concerns to market microstructure and governance. In the end, the Bretton Woods institutions would not be elevated to sources of financial regulation per se. But they would be leveraged as a force multiplier for largely Basel-based soft law.[18]

3.6 The Reform of Modern Financial Soft Law

For all the changes wrought by the Asian financial crisis, the international regulatory system was still far from perfect. One of the biggest problems was that it was a largely voluntary model of governance. Many countries did not subject themselves to FSAPs. Instead, only countries receiving aid from the World Bank or IMF were required to undertake assessments and apply international best practices (Brummer 2014b: 163–4).[19]

Furthermore, information gained from the IMF and World Bank surveillance mechanisms could only be published or disseminated to other authorities at the consent of the assessed country. Having a choice enabled adverse-selection problems that would riddle efforts to promote transparency. In short, countries that performed the best were most inclined to discuss surveillance results, and those that did not could squash any disclosure as to strengths or weaknesses of their domestic financial systems.

Finally, the process was beset by problems of legitimacy. From its earliest days, the Basel Committee was an exclusive club. Smaller countries were purposely excluded, undermining the perceived fairness and robustness of the forum – a problem Tietmeyer at least tacitly acknowledged in his call for 'greater involvement' in standard-setting by emerging-market economies. Still, decision-makers including Tietmeyer advocated that decision-making be limited 'to a size that permits an effective exchange of views and the achievement of action-oriented results within a reasonable time frame'. In most instances, this meant the G10 members, and, where necessary, the IMF and World Bank. Eventually, some standard-setting bodies would establish regional liaison groups comprising emerging but still important regulatory voices like Brazil, China, India, Russia and South Africa (Alexander 2006: 42). Nevertheless, these countries had no seat on the Basel Committee and therefore exercised no direct influence on the standard-setting process, but some of these countries were eventually incorporated into the BCBS (Alexander 2006: 42).

The 2008 crisis would humble western policymakers and give new direction to the international surveillance system. Throughout the 2000s, speculation in the US real-estate market jumped to historic levels. Fuelling the lending spree were, among other things, varying forms of financial and regulatory arbitrage combined with complex financial instruments like derivatives subject to light or no regulation. With few checks in place, asset bubbles grew throughout the United States, attracting ever more loans and investments tied to the US housing market. Ultimately, the market crashed, unleashing chaos not only in the housing market, but also in US credit markets, threatening banks that had underwritten billions of dollars of loans. The turmoil would also have a distinctively cross-border character, as many European and emerging markets had helped fuel speculation as participants and investors.[20]

The crisis highlighted a series of gaps that pervaded not only national regulatory regimes, but also the greater corpus of international financial law. International regulatory forums like the Basel Committee and IOSCO had devoted very little time to thinking about financial products with hybrid features that either straddled or sat in between traditional sectors of the financial economy. The crisis also demonstrated that no one, not even the United States, was immune to the dangers of financial meltdowns. Every country, rich and poor, would have to consider the relevance of the rules for not only their domestic financial-market participants, but also their cross-border creditors, customers and investors.

Collectively, these observations would once again prompt considerable institutional change in the global regulatory system. In the most significant institutional step, the G20 was named the world's premier economic forum, essentially displacing what was at that point in time the G7/G10 and introducing a wider economic decision-making group including Brazil, Russia, China, India and South Africa (White House Office of the Press Secretary 2009). Additionally, the FSF was renamed the Financial Stability Board (FSB). The Board was elevated to a technocratic counterpart to the G20 to aid in coordinating standard-setting activities of different regulatory agencies and to ensure that complex, institutional topics did not fall through the cracks of different organisational mandates among standard-setters.

Together, the FSB and the G20 would more aggressively direct standard-setting processes and work streams, as well as coordinate between what had remained – despite Tietmeyer's initial aspirations in 1999 – rather disparate and disconnected standard-setting bodies. In effect, what was a somewhat disjointed system became vertically integrated under G20 and FSB leadership, the former of which would also include summits consisting of political heads of state (Brummer 2014b: 63).

Finally, to support the new integrated system of rule-making, surveillance was ramped up. The IMF and the FSB required FSAPs as part of their members' obligations, and would even require to varying degrees the publication of the results. Additionally, the FSB launched a series of thematic and country reviews to take stock of existing practices in particular policy areas, with a focus on progress made by individual FSB member jurisdictions in implementing FSAP regulatory and supervisory recommendations. Similarly, the Basel Committee, IOSCO, CPMI and other standard-setters introduced, refined and revamped their own in-house monitoring systems, including peer-review programmes, to better track and identify the implementation of international standards by members.[21]

These final reforms reflected, if anything, a broader political and regulatory awareness that soft law, whatever its informality, can – under certain circumstances – evidence not only moral suasion, but also coercion. International standards were increasingly deployed as best practices to guide not only regulatory supervision, but also best practices for market participants. To the extent that actors failed to comply with rules that ultimately would be considered market benchmarks – such as Tier 1 capital adequacy or proper disclosure accompanying the issuance of public securities – *market participants themselves could serve as discipliners for largely Basel-based regulatory products.*[22] But this, along with global buy-in, depended on more available transparency to markets about country-level compliance, and a sense that the rules were fair (or at least informed by a wide variety of market contexts) (Barr and Miller 2006: 15, 20–31, 41). At the same time, it highlighted just how far international policymaking and the BIS would move from the 'macroeconomic' compliance problems characterising reparation payments in the 1930s.

3.7 The End of the Beginning

Even in a time of political polarisation, the international regulatory system continues, at least operationally, to function along the path set immediately in the wake of the 2008 global financial crisis. In comparison with other institutions animating international economic law, it appears even as an odd lifeboat of continuity, with its flexible structures and regulatory products absorbing changes in political and regulatory priorities, as well as intermittent disagreements among economic powerhouses as to the implementation of regulatory commitments. The BIS in particular appears as a staple of consistency, even as it emerges from its institutional adolescence as a fully mature player in international regulatory affairs.

But make no mistake, the history of the BIS is one of changes. It is one that reflects as much the working theories and operations of international financial regulation and soft law as it does the vagaries and incidents of history.

In some regards, the development of the BIS has been a matter of circumstance. History, not infrequently, just 'happened' to the BIS. The Bank was from the start the product of the necessities of the first post-war period. But to serve even its initial purpose in facilitating reparations, it would have to deploy institutional structures to accommodate the cyclical nature of global economics (and politics). Informality was an intentional feature reflecting the ad hoc nature of monetary policymaking and the inherent need for flexibility in light of ever-changing economic circumstances; an emphasis on small committees a recognition of both its central-bank shareholder base and the technocratic nature of monetary rule-making.

The decay and ultimate abandonment of the gold standard would reconfigure international monetary relations, as well as introduce a new awareness of the importance of prudential and market oversight. Like monetary relations, financial regulation, too, is highly technocratic; and though guidelines can be written, the very objects of regulation – financial markets and products – are always evolving. The BIS, with its expertise in payments, the very infrastructure of banking and financial transactions – along with a ready-made infrastructure for informal norm-setting – would be quickly identified by central bankers and finance ministers as an ideal forum to formulate policies. And it would be at Basel-based committees that modern soft law would be born – and in the process, elevate the importance and relevance of the BIS. The story of the rise of the BIS is the story of soft law.

Since the Asian financial crisis, a critical aspect of that story has been institutional refinement. The turn to prudential policymaking would elevate the importance of the BIS, while at the same time leveraging the IMF's (and to a lesser extent, the World Bank's) legacy roles as surveillance operators. Their surveillance function would be changed dramatically to include the observance of compliance standards emanating largely from Basel-based committees, and coordinated by the Basel-based FSF. After the 2008 global financial crisis, surveillance would be upgraded, introducing more transparency into surveillance, as well as legitimacy into the membership of key standard-setting bodies, from the renamed Financial Stability Board to the Basel Committee itself. Both were ultimately designed to increase what was always intimated as a primary goal of coordination – the compliance pulls of multilateral standards that were, of necessity, informal.

Where the BIS goes from here is anyone's guess, but if its last ninety years are a guide, it will be the product of many forces: the next financial crisis, regulatory pragmatism, member preferences and its own expertise. And while such forces may shape other multilateral organs as well, the particular history suggests that the BIS's evolution as a practitioner of soft law promises that its path will be unique, not only as a bank, but as a member of the international regulatory community.

Notes

1. See *The Basel Process–Overview*, BIS: www.bis.org/about/basel_process.htm.
2. A number of other committees working at the BIS, such as the Committee on Payments and Market Infrastructures (CPMI), also provide standards, including for data. See www.bis.org/about/areport/areport2019/prom_int_coop.htm.
3. The Basel Committee also refined the framework to address risks other than credit risk, which was the focus of the 1988 Accord. In January 1996, following two consultative processes, the Committee issued the Amendment to the Capital Accord to incorporate market risks. *History of the Basel Committee*, BIS (Apr. 14, 2018), www.bis.org/bcbs/history.htm.
4. See Borio and Toniolo (2006: 24–5) for a discussion on how reparations, war debts and restoration of the international monetary system were linked.
5. This duality permeates the statutory arrangements of the BIS and had a lot to do with the Bank-specific institutional nature as a cooperative venture of central banks (Toniolo 2005: 49).
6. Modern networks are distinctly intergovernmental in nature, fostering affinities and professional collaboration among officials. See generally Slaughter 2004.
7. This practice achieved important results but also created deep resentment among the Fund's non-G10 members (Bossone 2008; see also James 1996).
8. On the broader impact of the end of the Bretton Woods par system on the international monetary and financial system, see Chapter 5 (Barry Eichengreen) of this volume.
9. 'The basic principles . . . that every banking establishment should be supervised and that the parental (home) supervisor should do so on the basis of consolidated account[s] were largely uncontroversial and incontrovertible.'
10. The Group of Experts on Payment Systems would follow up on this work in the late 1980s, inter alia by setting up a Committee on Interbank Netting Schemes. In 1990, the G10 Governors decided to give this group a firmer footing by creating the Committee on Payment and Settlement Systems (CPSS), as one of the permanent central-bank committees at the BIS reporting directly to the G10 Governors. The CPSS would be renamed Committee on Payments and Market Infrastructures (CPMI) in 2013. See www.bis.org/cpmi/history.htm.
11. The BIS had already begun to attempt to engage in limited standard-setting without the G10 members.
12. The Latin American sovereign-debt crisis of 1982–3 proved how badly exposed undercapitalised banks were, particularly in the United States and Japan. The US Congress then linked the provision of additional resources to the IMF, to deal with the outfall of the crisis, to a requirement for American banks to increase their capital buffer to prevent a repetition of the Latin American debacle. This naturally increased the incentive for US policymakers and banks to call for more stringent capital standards globally, in order to avoid a competitive disadvantage for US banks.
13. BISA 7.18(15) – *Papers Lamfalussy*, LAM25/F67, 1–2, 24 October 1979.
14. Mexico liberalised its trade sector in 1985 after nearly a decade of stagnant economic activity and high inflation. As part of its reforms, banks were privatised, lending and borrowing rates were freed, and reserve requirements, as well as rules regarding qualifications for bank officers, were eliminated. A credit bubble ensued, with

consumers taking advantage of the generous credit terms by reducing savings and increasing borrowing, just as banks ratcheted up their extension at a 25 per cent credit rate. Ultimately, the credit bubble popped and the government was forced to float the peso, and Mexico was faced with imminent default on short-term, dollar-indexed government bonds. With Mexico teetering on the brink, the IMF and the United States intervened to rescue the country, first by buying pieces in the open market and later by extending emergency loans of over $40 billion (Brummer 2014b: 13).

15. Increased lending brought lower credit standards as banks failed to undertake thorough evaluation and monitoring of borrowers. To encourage greater foreign investment, Thailand's domestic banking rules were liberalised and local banks were permitted to accept foreign deposits, thereby expanding their lending capacities. In Indonesia, the number of banks increased from 64 in 1987 to almost 239 in 1997, creating intense competition for investments. Korean policies allowed finance companies to engage in private-equity transactions, as well as lending and borrowing in foreign currencies, which were activities with which they had little experience (Brummer 2014b: 14).

16. IOSCO (International Organization of Securities Commission) had been created in 1983 as a forum for national securities regulators. Up to that point, standalone capital markets regulators were not an established feature in the regulatory landscape, especially in Commonwealth countries using British institutional models (Jordan 2014: 35).

17. On the BIS's role in helping shape and inform international standards before and after the Great Financial Crisis of 2007–9, see Chapter 4 (Andrew Baker) of this volume.

18. This process would be reinforced further after the Great Financial Crisis: 'At the height of the 2007–9 international financial crisis and following the Group of Twenty (G-20) summit in London in 2009, a new body – the Financial Stability Board (FSB) – was established as a successor to the Financial Stability Forum (FSF), with an expanded mandate to formulate and oversee the implementation of regulatory, supervisory and other financial sector policies' (Lombardi 2011).

19. 'The Financial Sector Assessment Program (FSAP) is a joint program of the International Monetary Fund and the World Bank. Launched in 1999 in the wake of the Asian financial crisis, the program brings together Bank and Fund expertise to help countries reduce the likelihood and severity of financial sector crises. The FSAP provides a comprehensive framework through which assessors and authorities in participating countries can identify financial system vulnerabilities and develop appropriate policy responses.' *Financial Sector Assessment Program (FSAP)*, THE WORLD BANK. See www.worldbank.org/en/programs/finan cial-sector-assessment-program.

20. See Wessel (2009) for a description of Federal Reserve assistance to the European Central Bank.

21. *Implementation of the Basel standards*, BIS. See www.bis.org/bcbs/implementation .htm. See in this context also Ingves (2014).

22. See Crockett (2002), who notes that 'for *users* [e.g. market participants], global standards hold out the promise of increasingly comparable information'. See also Arner and Taylor (2009: 11–12).

Tower of Contrarian Thinking

How the BIS Helped Reframe Understandings of Financial Stability

Andrew Baker

4.1 Introduction

Central banks' responsibility for financial stability was limited in the lead-up to the financial crisis of 2007–8. In developed countries it was largely believed that a dual approach, central-bank inflation targeting combined with robust risk management by market institutions, would be sufficient to guard against widescale financial instability and crisis (Borio 2011).[1] One of the most important developments since the crisis is that an intellectual framing and terminology, which staff of the Bank for International Settlements (BIS) played a prominent role in developing over several decades, now directly informs the design of national and international policy frameworks. The approach identifies long-run financial cycles and the build-up of systemic financial risks as a primary cause of financial crisis. It is widely known as the 'macroprudential' perspective and was endorsed by Group of Twenty (G20) summits in 2009. It has since involved the development of a range of prudential policy instruments that seek to constrain system-wide financial risks.

To some extent, the rise of macroprudential frameworks has ushered in a new departure and era in central banking. Central banks increasingly have financial stability mandates and powers reflecting macroprudential conceptual frameworks to varying degrees. This chapter examines the role the BIS played in a process in which macro-financial stability frameworks as a mode of conceptual understanding rose to prominence.[2] It also reflects on the financial stability regime-building that has resulted, including ways in which it remains incomplete, as well as current BIS thinking on these issues.

The chapter explains the emergence of this conceptual framing as an example of a primary contribution the BIS makes to contemporary global financial governance by practising a form of 'measured contrarianism'.

'Measured contrarianism' involves standing outside of and being prepared to challenge intellectual, policy and market consensus. It involves taking a sceptical and questioning approach to apparent market stability, acting as an early-warning mechanism for potential financial instability, through the presentation of careful and rigorous analysis of prevailing data patterns. In acting as a dogged and persistent voice developing and promoting a macroprudential conceptual framing, BIS staff effectively practised a form of measured contrarianism by encouraging central banks to think more systematically about macro-financial instability. At the same time, the macroprudential perspective's contemporary salience potentially puts the BIS's capacity to perform measured contrarianism on a firmer intellectual and institutional footing.

The first section of the chapter notes how relevant international organisations require niche specialisms (a form of comparative advantage) to remain relevant. The next section presents the macroprudential perspective as a significant conceptual shift, covering the origins of the term. The deepening of the BIS research programme between 2000 and 2008 is also described. In this period, significant elements of the macroprudential conceptual framework were not accepted in key technical regulatory committees, or by some national supervisors, especially in the United States. The third section examines how prior BIS work and related academic contributions found their way into the G20's programme of reform through G20 working groups. The perspective and prior BIS work subsequently informed the Basel III process in the Basel Committee on Banking Supervision (BCBS) and the agenda of the Financial Stability Board (FSB) as an umbrella body, following the crisis of 2007–8. The final section considers how the Basel III process has induced a programme of national regime-building, including why other institutions, most notably the International Monetary Fund (IMF), the FSB and the Committee on the Global Financial System (CGFS), have become sites of analysis and research on macroprudential policy. Finally, BIS positions relating to strengths, weaknesses as well as gaps in the evolving macro-financial stability framework requiring further analytical work are recounted.

4.2 Measured Contrarianism as a Niche Specialism

All international organisations (IOs) effectively compete in a marketplace to provide services, functions, tasks and skills to an international community of member states (Seabrooke and Henriksen 2017). Relevant, salient IOs pursue a comparative advantage by performing a specific function and offering skills and services not easily replicated or reproduced by others.

The BIS is no exception. There are tasks which it is well placed to perform, given its mandate, expertise, skills and intellectual culture; and also limitations or areas of activity that are beyond its capabilities.

The role BIS staff and their research programmes played in establishing a new macroprudential perspective on financial stability following the financial crisis reflected the particular niche strengths of the institution, as well as its limitations (Baker 2017). BIS work conducted prior to the crisis of 2007–8 developed the idea that there was a need for a new macro-financial stabilisation framework (Crockett 2000b; Borio, Furfine and Lowe 2001; Borio and Lowe 2002; Borio 2003; Borio and White 2004; White 2006; Borio and Shim 2007; Borio and Drehmann 2009). Following the crisis, a back catalogue of earlier work was drawn upon by key expert committees and institutional settings tasked by G20 leaders with diagnosing and responding to the crisis (Baker 2013).

Crucially, the case of the 'macroprudential shift' provides a good illustration of what the BIS is well equipped for. The BIS has a capacity to challenge orthodoxies and accepted practice by generating ideas, conceptual frames and data that help to redefine how policy challenges are understood. As a self-financing institution, with some degree of governance autonomy, it can develop its own independent research programmes, can access data from member central banks and has a staff profile with the expertise and the space to develop ideas and analyses. It also regularly interacts with both standard-setting committees and national authorities. BIS staff and management have access to the networks, expertise and data and the independence of thought to perform measured contrarianism.

The contrarian element of measured contrarianism is relatively straightforward. It refers to a willingness to lean against established intellectual and policy beliefs in the name of avoiding complacency, false confidence and excessive ambition; a preparedness to question market trends and prices as something necessarily rooted in deeper fundamentals; and a willingness to lean against collective societal and market expectations and sentiments by interrogating their foundations.

The measured component is less clear but has a double meaning. One relates to style, disposition and use of language. It is about avoiding alarmist, excitable or overly strong claims, but using a circumspect, cautious and qualified tone, which may gently escalate over time out of necessity (escalating candour). A second element is about ensuring positions and warnings are based on careful analysis of data and robustly tested measurement indicators.

Monitoring and thinking about financial vulnerabilities mean that the BIS is an organisation that worries. 'Reasoned worrying' is part of the DNA of the institution, as it is with many national central banks. For political economy reasons, however, domestic authorities are sometimes limited by mandates and constrained by prevailing public and political sentiment. The BIS's analyses and its independent voice can therefore lend force to and supplement the efforts of national central banks in taking action to temper financial booms.

In an area such as financial stability policy, which by its very nature involves monitoring the build-up of conditions that cause crises, it is important that the international community is served by an international institution that is prepared to challenge market and policymaking consensus. Excessive optimism and common collective thinking can quickly become a contributory driver of unsustainable financial booms (Brunnermeier and Oehmke 2012; Widmaier 2016).[3] In this context, considered and measured contrarianism becomes a much-needed and precious antidote.

Just as central banks can experience reputational damage if they follow 'time-inconsistent' monetary policies, adopting excessively contrarian positions in inappropriate circumstances can lead to the erosion of credibility and the attachment of pejorative labels such as 'Cassandra'. Contrarian thinking is an important commodity in the field of financial stability, but it has to be used sparingly.

More research is required on whether systematic criteria could inform and guide measured contrarianism, but the broad underpinning philosophy is similar to using 'constrained discretion' to build track record and credibility. It means operating with caution, and crucially neither overstating nor understating potential risks and threats to financial stability, while retaining a vigilant intellectual disposition.

Keeping abreast of financial risks that are by their nature dynamic and ever evolving also requires a framework, or way of thinking, that can explain and identify processes likely to cause financial disruptions and instability as part of longer-run cycles of risk-taking. A willingness to challenge assumptions of semi-permanent stability and equilibrium is essential in countering financial instability as a vital component of measured contrarianism.[4]

The BIS engages in measured contrarianism in different ways. One way is through collecting and analysing data that identify the build-up of system-level risks. Another way is through challenging complacent consensual thinking by developing accounts of how financial markets can be unstable, because of the evolving dynamic incentives, behaviours, practices and modes of thinking that characterise those markets. A further way is by creating tools and instruments to act as new technologies to constrain and offset some of these very processes. All three have been evident and at work in the macroprudential shift, but, without the conceptual shift, the contribution of the other two (indicators and instruments) would be much diminished.

In a favoured refinement of Milton Friedman's famous idiom, Claudio Borio, currently head of the BIS Monetary and Economic Department, wryly reflected that 'we're all macroprudentialists now' (Borio 2011b). While the BIS has certainly challenged and changed understandings of crisis and financial instability, the extent to which the BIS perspective is truly shared and present throughout the evolving international financial architecture is far from clear. Ultimately, the macroprudential case illustrates that while the BIS and its staff can author new ideas and set in train modes of thinking that can change how policymakers think about and approach financial stability, the organisation can also never control what happens to these ideas, as well as how they evolve and are interpreted once they leave the BIS tower.

4.3 The Macroprudential Perspective: Origins of an Intellectual Shift

The term 'macroprudential' refers to an approach in which prudential regulatory instruments and settings are adjusted (often in a time-varying fashion) to target system-wide financial risks and reduce potential harms to the wider macroeconomy. However, the macroprudential perspective goes beyond this simple literal description to encompass a conceptual framework for thinking about the functioning and processes that characterise financial markets and their capacity to hinder macroeconomic performance.

In the BIS conception, a macroprudential perspective involved two dimensions of systemic financial risk. A *time dimension of risk* refers to how perceptions of risk change over time. Financial market participants have difficulty in calculating the time dimension of risk, because short time horizons produce extrapolations of current conditions into the future, resulting in misperceptions of risk, which in turn could drive excessive risk-taking in boom periods. At some point, events cause a reassessment of the true nature of these risks. These behaviours and incentives produce cycles of risk-taking. Such cycles often move financial asset values and credit provision to extremes, lengthening and amplifying both upswing and downswing phases of such cycles in a phenomenon known as *pro-cyclicality* (Crockett 2000b; Borio, Furfine and Lowe 2001: 2). This so-called time-dimension aspect of risk, for example, later informed the development of countercyclical capital buffers.

A second *cross-sectional dimension* refers to how risk is distributed within the financial system. Financial stability problems can arise when many institutions have similar exposures and institutions are highly inter-connected, or when an outsized institution has a disproportionate impact on the system as whole. These factors can reduce systemic resilience and increase the vulnerability of individual institutions in ways that are not apparent when considered on a stand-alone basis. Regulators consequently need to pay attention to the systemic significance of institutions and their contribution to overall system-wide risk, with those of greater systemic significance being subjected to tighter standards (Crockett 2000b; Borio 2003). This cross-sectional framing later informed efforts to identify global systemically important financial institutions (G-SIFIs) and set prudential standards accordingly.

The first recorded usage of the term 'macroprudential' dates back to 1979 in a meeting of what is now the BCBS, 28–9 June 1979. The Chair of the Committee, Bank of England official Peter Cooke, referred to how microprudential problems could become macroprudential ones (systemic, with macroeconomic implications (Clement 2010)). A well-known favoured BIS definition is that a macroprudential objective involves limit-ing the costs to the economy from financial distress, by constraining 'systemic risk' (Crockett 2000b).

A macroprudential perspective sees systemic outcomes as being deter-mined by the collective behaviours of individual market institutions, or 'in economic jargon, as "endogenous" to the system'.[5] In this reading, first set out in a speech in 2000 by the then BIS General Manager Andrew Crockett, actions that seem desirable from an individual institution's perspective can result in 'unwelcome systemic outcomes'. Such 'fallacies of composition' occur when one wrongly 'infers that something is true for the whole, from the fact that it is true for each of the individual components of the whole' (Brunnermeier et al. 2009: 75). One example is when individual institu-tions may understandably tighten lending during a recession, with detri-mental effects for system-wide credit and stability if all banks do the same thing at more or less the same time. The resulting impact on economic activity can lead to a further deterioration in the credit quality of portfolios (Crockett 2000b). This is a key feature of the phenomenon of

Table 4.1 *The macro- and microprudential perspectives compared*

	Macroprudential	Microprudential
Proximate objective	Limit financial system-wide distress	Limit distress of individual institutions
Ultimate objective	Avoid output (GDP) cost	Consumer (investor/depositor) protection
Model of risk	Endogenous (in part)	Exogenous
Correlations and common exposures across institutions	Important	Irrelevant
Calibration of prudential controls	In terms of system-wide distress, top-down	In terms of risks of individual institutions, bottom-up

'procyclicality' in which financial cycles are amplified by such systemic forces and patterns.

Table 4.1, from Borio's 2003 paper, summarises the distinction between the macroprudential and microprudential perspectives as initially laid out in Crockett's 2000 speech. The table is a useful device for thinking about how the emergence of a macroprudential perspective represented an intellectual shift, or a shift in ideas, mindsets and conceptual framing. The emergence of a macroprudential perspective can be said to have some elements and characteristics of a shift in ideas (Baker 2013).

The shift in ideas represented by the macroprudential framing consists of three distinct elements. First, a macroprudential perspective provides a different causal account of the sources of financial crises, by elaborating on earlier endogenous accounts that had fallen out of fashion (Kindleberger 1978; Minsky 1995; Baker 2018). Prevailing conceptions during the 'Great Moderation' period tended to see primary risks to the financial system arising from exogenous shocks, through events or practices external to the financial system. An endogenous account of financial risk involves a qualitatively different causal claim about the origins, sources and mechanisms of financial crises. Here emphasis shifts to how practices and processes internal to financial markets propagate and amplify crises, through valuation techniques, risk models, investment decisions and the collective impact of individual decisions, as well as synchronised collective behaviours (Borio 2003; Shin 2010). On the upswing phase of a cycle such endogenous factors can combine to produce excessive risk-taking, leverage, credit provision and overextended balance sheets. On the downswing phase of a cycle risk aversion among market actors can shrink credit provision and macroeconomic activity. Crises in such a reading are primarily a function of these endogenous phenomena.

Second, a macroprudential perspective involves a shift in the primary unit of analysis from the micro or individual level to the systemic level. Analysis and focus move from the individual financial institution and the integrity of its risk models to the collective or system-wide consequences of the interactions between those models and institutions. As Andrew Crockett explained, focusing on individual institutions resulted in supervisors striving for too much (preventing individual failures), but delivering too little. Occasional individual failures, Crockett explained, are not a problem. Rather, what matters most is how the collective behaviours of institutions impact on (macro) economic outcomes (Crockett 2000b).

Third, a macroprudential perspective offers a different account of both individual and systemic behaviours, especially the combined, collective implications of those behaviours, with a broader range of unstable outcomes becoming possible. Even when agents behave rationally (sometimes they can behave myopically and herd), collective vulnerabilities can still result because of the collective impact of the interactions between those behaviours, reflecting the fallacy-of-composition problem noted earlier. More specifically, risks rose during expansions and later materialised in recessions.

In short, the emergence of a macroprudential frame has entailed: (1) a shift in a causal account of a given phenomenon; (2) a shift in the primary unit of analysis; and (3) a changed conception of agents' behaviours and their collective, systemic implications. These premises are a long way from an expectation that rational forward-looking agents will produce an efficient equilibrium most of the time. In the natural sciences, all of the above together might be said to resemble a Kuhnian-style paradigm shift. In the social sciences, however, and in the world of public policy, paradigm shifts require more than a shift in theoretical and conceptual framing. They also require a political driver, as part of a policy project, that presents a qualitatively different vision of state–society relations and of market systems (Ruggie 1982; Hall 2013; Baker 2018).

The macroprudential perspective has no such pretensions. It presents a different set of assumptions and account of the world of financial markets relative to assumptions of largely efficient financial markets (Fama 1991) or dynamic stochastic general equilibrium (DSGE) modelling (Smets and Wouters 2007; De Grauwe 2010). Both largely discount long-run financial cycles as a macroeconomic phenomenon. The perspective has, however, remained focused within the relatively technical domains of crisis diagnosis and financial regulation and supervision, rather than offering a prescriptive overarching vision of the 'good' financial system (Baker 2018).

The intellectual content and claims made within the macroprudential framing enable measured contrarianism in three ways: (1) conceptual; (2) practical instruments; and (3) data and indicators. The rest of the chapter provides an account of how the macroprudential perspective has proceeded and how it has enabled and represented measured contrarianism across these three levels.

4.4 A History of the Macroprudential Perspective

4.4.1 Usage of the Term, 1979–1999

After the first recorded mentions of the term 'macroprudential' in some of the documentation of the BCBS, further references came in October 1979, in a Bank of England background document. The document was submitted to a working group chaired by Alexandre Lamfalussy, BIS Economic Adviser and Chair of the Euro-currency Standing Committee (ECSC). It explained that a macroprudential approach considered problems that bore upon the *market as a whole* as distinct from an individual bank and that might not be obvious from a focus on individual institutions. The eventual Lamfalussy report mentioned the term 'macroprudential' seven times, although the term did not make it into the G10 Governors' public communiqué in April 1980.[6]

The Lamfalussy report made three main points of a macroprudential nature.[7] First, the growth of individual bank lending may look sustainable, while aggregate lending may not be. Second, perceptions of risk may focus narrowly on past performance, rather than broader future risk. Third, individual banks tend to underestimate the importance of liquidity risk, which requires a market-wide perspective. From the very outset a macroprudential perspective provided a framing that allowed for a mildly sceptical reading of the ways in which individual financial institutions assessed risks and the likely systemic financial vulnerabilities arising from this.

In 1986, some six years later, the term appeared in an official public document for the first time. A report by the ECSC considered how financial innovation (derivatives and securitisation) might raise risks for the financial system as a whole through regulatory arbitrage; the underpricing of risk on new instruments; overestimation of their liquidity; the opaqueness of risk resulting from interconnections in the financial system; the danger of risk concentrations; the overloading of payment and settlement systems due to a high volume of transactions; increased market volatility; and growth in overall debt.

After this 1986 report, the term 'macroprudential' largely disappeared from public documents but continued to be used in internal BIS paperwork and influenced the thinking of staff. The sixty-seventh BIS annual report in the mid-1990s (BIS AR 1997) raised concerns about a lack of transparency in derivatives markets and the concentration of market-making functions in a few institutions, which could undermine the robustness of market liquidity (Clement 2010).

In 1998, BIS staff conducted an in-house survey of financial stability arrangements among central banks. The document made brief reference to the need for more countercyclical provisioning in policy frameworks to counter procyclicality, with prudential standards and regulations being tightened or relaxed for this purpose, depending on the phase of the financial cycle.[8] Unfortunately, proposals under the Basel II process were moving in the opposite direction. They involved greater reliance on institutions' own risk models in the calculation of capital requirements that in turn were sensitive to and largely followed market prices.

BIS staff were beginning to raise the issue of financial cycles and highlight the need for countercyclical regulatory policy. Going public with such concerns, given the direction in which the Bank's dominant shareholder central banks were moving in the BCBS, was difficult. The 1998 document remained confidential and internal to the BIS, because it contained information on lender-of-last-resort and crisis-management practices that central banks were reluctant to make public.

The difficulty of engaging in public discussions of procyclicality was further illustrated a year later in 1999. BIS General Manager Andrew Crockett, acting as the first Chair of the new Financial Stability Forum (FSF), created by the G7 to consider cross-cutting financial stability issues in the aftermath of the Asian financial crisis of 1997–8, wrote a letter to the Chair of the BCBS, William McDonough of the Federal Reserve Bank of New York, dated 6 October 1999. The letter raised the issue of whether capital-adequacy standards could at times accentuate the financial cycle, by not constraining lending in the upswing phase of the cycle but restricting it in a downswing phase. Crockett asked whether a regime calibrated in the opposite direction by raising capital in the upswing phase of the cycle would be better placed to cushion losses in the downswing phase. The FSF asked for the opinion of the BCBS on these issues.

In March 2000, the BCBS published a ten-page response to the FSF and Crockett's letter. It addressed the question of whether capital regulations could potentially accentuate economic cycles (be 'pro-cyclical'). The BCBS expressed the view that supervisors should generally seek to reinforce rather than counteract signals coming from banks' own risk management models. Weak institutions should be encouraged to build up their capital, rather than expand risk-taking in a downswing phase of the cycle, because of the danger that this would create moral hazard incentives.[9] The BCBS did acknowledge that bank risk-taking could be procyclical but ultimately played down the extent to which its own work would fuel such a process. Rather, the softening of market discipline and the resulting moral hazard implied by a countercyclical framework was a far greater danger. At this point, the BCBS essentially opposed a countercyclical capital regime and instead focused on incentives facing individual institutions, rather than systemic patterns that might induce financial instability.

4.4.2 Deepening Conceptual Understanding in the 2000s

BIS management and staff reacted to the BCBS response by strengthening their research in the area and developing a more extensive conceptual framework to explain the occurrence of financial cycles and contagion across institutions. The path of least resistance in the circumstances would have been to remain quiet and simply accept the BCBS response, at least in public. Instead, displaying the traits of measured contrarianism, in which it is sometimes appropriate and desirable to push against dominant intellectual and market positions, the BIS went public with its framing. This body of work placed the need to counter procyclicality in financial markets centre stage, as a primary challenge for central banks in the new millennium.

The research effectively built on the earlier ideas noted above but deepened the conceptual framing for a macroprudential perspective. BIS staff and management's willingness to become more public in outlining some of their reservations about BCBS and Basel II positions was a new departure. Many within the BIS tower were clearly dissatisfied with the BCBS response to the concerns raised by the FSF.

In April and September 2000, having liaised with staff, General Manager Andrew Crockett gave two speeches setting out the need for a shift in the direction of a macroprudential perspective. The speeches were, in his own words, 'deliberately provocative' to 'sharpen the issues' and 'encourage a broader debate' (Crockett 2000a, 2000b). Much of the conceptual content of the speeches has been covered earlier in this chapter. The most marked feature, however, was a clear shift in tone. A polite request to consider questions was replaced with a stronger statement that financial risks *were* procyclical and endogenous.

The importance of the September speech was that it directly contradicted and contested the message contained in the earlier BCBS note. It was presented as an awareness-raising step in a longer journey to more fully developing a macroprudential perspective, as a process that was already under way. Not all BIS staff were comfortable with the organisation developing a public stance that seemed at odds with the prevailing view of the BCBS. While the BIS has a degree of intellectual autonomy, staff have to take care not to change or challenge the practices of standard-setting bodies that the organisation hosts, not least because they reflect the collective views of national authorities. Overt opposition to such collective views can risk undermining the legitimacy of the BIS and damaging the credibility of standard-setting bodies, as well as constituent central banks.

Nevertheless, the BIS research that followed revealed the determination of staff to keep the macroprudential perspective alive and to develop it further, at a time when the wider climate and environment were not especially favourable. For example, one leading figure from the Federal Reserve involved in Basel II expressed disapproval to senior figures at the BIS over the content and tone of Crockett's speeches. One observer recalled that Crockett's speeches were a courageous undertaking, in a generally unsympathetic context, and without it the macroprudential perspective might have withered.

A first major contribution to emerge following Crockett's speeches was a paper by Claudio Borio, Craig Furfine and Philip Lowe that explored the issue of procyclicality in the financial system in greater depth (Borio, Furfine and Lowe 2001). Prior to the paper, there was a sense in the central-banking community that procyclicality was a process much talked about but little understood, and the authors set out to rectify this.

Procyclicality was defined as the process through which the financial system 'unnecessarily' amplified swings in the real economy. A key driver of both procyclicality and financial instability was identified as the inappropriate response of financial market participants to changes in risk over time. Uncertainty created measurement difficulties, while 'market participants' incentives to react to changes in risk could often be socially suboptimal' in such a context (Borio, Furfine and Lowe 2001: 1). These measurement difficulties meant risks tended to be underestimated in booms, leading to rapid credit growth and inflated collateral values. In recessions, risk would be overestimated, leading to rapid retrenchment, downward spirals in asset values and plummeting collateral valuations. Measurement biases arose because market agents were better at assessing relative rather than absolute risk (Borio, Furfine and Lowe 2001: 2).

The paper had three purposes: (1) to extend empirical evidence on procyclicality; (2) to explore in more detail the underlying mechanisms causing procyclicality and the implications for monetary and prudential authorities; and (3) to position these ideas in relation to the extant academic literature. The paper called for supervisors to induce an increase in capital cushions during boom periods when they reached an assessment that risk was being mis-assessed by financial institutions, which could be linked to stress tests of particular institutions. Likewise, the possibility of minimum provisioning rates being varied and adjusted across time for the system as a whole was raised, as were loan-to-value (LTV) ratio adjustments, which would tighten the terms on which new mortgages were issued. This was seen as a potential means of moderating property price cycles.

Spanish provisioning rules, where banks took a charge on their profits, taking account of long-term loss experiences, were also cited. This charge was to be placed in a separate statistical fund. The aim here was to reduce fluctuations in year-to-year bank-recorded profits. Accumulated profits could then be drawn down from the statistical fund to compensate for bad years (Borio, Furfine and Lowe 2001: 44).

The kind of arguments being marshalled by the BIS were reinforced when a group of academics connected to the London School of Economics Financial Markets Group made a submission to the BCBS entitled 'An academic response to Basel II' (Danielsson et al. 2001). The submission argued that Basel II was failing to address many of the key deficiencies of the global financial regulatory system and even created the potential for new sources of instability. The submission drew on a body of academic work that explored asset price dynamics and the limits and mathematical inadequacies of private value-at-risk (VaR) models (Morris and Shin 1999; Embrachts et al. 2001; Danielson, Shin and Zigrand 2004).

Among the critiques advanced were that proposed regulations failed to consider risk was endogenous, so VaR could destabilise an economy and induce crashes where otherwise none would occur; statistical models forecasting risks were inconsistent and biased, underestimating downside possibilities; and financial regulation was inherently procyclical, with

Basel II significantly exacerbating that tendency and increasing rather than reducing the likelihood of systemic crisis.

Under the Basel II internal ratings approach, the analysis explained, banks would have less capital at the cusp of a cycle, when the danger of systemic crisis was greatest, and hold too much capital, or under-lend, during a downturn when macroeconomic stabilisation required an expansion of lending. Regulation of the sort proposed by Basel II therefore risked destabilising the economy as a whole (Danielsson et al. 2001: 15).

This was a powerful argument from some of the leading thinkers and financial risk modellers in academia. There was a clear resonance with the questions raised by Crockett in his letter and speeches, as well as the subsequent BIS work on procyclicality. While the academics noted difficulties in forecasting cycles and producing forward-looking capital adjustments, they also encouraged more thought being given to this question, because the procyclicality problem was so serious and revised capital regulations in Basel II potentially exacerbated it.

In short, support for the BIS research agenda was starting to emerge from leading academic authorities. An intellectual alliance sharing a similar diagnosis of issues around procyclicality and the flaws associated with placing too much weight on an internal ratings approach, together with the limits of private risk management strategies and models, was developing.

In 2003, Claudio Borio more fully sketched the macroprudential framework in a single-authored BIS working paper. Notably, Hyun Shin from the LSE academic group commented on drafts of the paper, indicating a growing interaction between the BIS's own research programme and academic work and modelling on endogenous risk. Borio explained that a macroprudential perspective could be regarded as a kind of looking glass, for putting old issues into new focus. The objective of a macroprudential approach was to limit the risks of financial distress in terms of the real output for the economy as a whole. A macroprudential approach would be top-down in that it would seek to set a threshold of acceptable tail losses across a portfolio as a whole.

Common exposures to macroeconomic risk, Borio argued, produced more severe financial crises and were the driver of the majority of major crises around the globe. Such processes and the mechanisms through which they occurred were little understood. Crises followed certain common patterns and phases, involving a build-up phase, booming economic conditions and benign risk assessments, access to credit, fewer external financing constraints and buoyant asset prices. Such conditions masked the accumulation of real financial imbalances as the system became over-stretched. At some point such a process went into reverse, with potential triggers, or shocks, located in both financial and real economies. When the system suffered from a lack of buffers and the contraction went far enough, financial crises were likely. In other words, crises were seen to be a function of a system-wide financial cycle (Borio 2003).

The macroprudential perspective had three primary differences relative to orthodox models of systemic risk. First, crises could only be understood in terms of how vulnerabilities build up over time, due to dynamic inter-actions between financial and real economies. Booms sow the seeds of bust, with the trigger the least interesting feature of the story. Second, crises result from common exposures to the same risks. Third, the real action is on the assets side of the balance sheet, rather than the liabilities side, because this is where exposures build up and where changes in value originate. Subsequent deterioration in asset quality and value drives the process of crisis.

In this vision, risks build up during a boom, but market participants operate as if they were falling, when in hindsight they were probably at their peak. In contrast, risks tend to be treated as highest during recessions. In reality, they rise in booms, then materialise in recessions when the boom unwinds. Losses and evaporations in wealth are then liable to being socialised or distributed broadly across society. The main concern of a macroprudential perspective was to limit the disruption to economic life and society as a whole as a consequence of generalised financial distress (Borio 2003: 8–9). The macroprudential perspective called for financial regulation to move away from narrowly conceived depositor protection, towards addressing these broader concerns.

The paper noted that while the price-sensitive calculations of minimal capital requirements proposed by Basel II might provide a better reading of *cross-sectional risk*, it also had troublesome implications for the *time dimension of risk*, or a potential procyclical impact. The paper was pep-pered with approving references to the work of Goodhart, Danielsson and Shin from the LSE financial markets group, referring to an LSE endogene-ity school of risk, who were making similar observations (Morris and Shin 1999; Danielsson et al. 2001; Goodhart and Danielsson 2001; Borio 2003: 8). A firmer set of intellectual foundations for a macroprudential perspective were gradually being laid.

A key moment in efforts to promote this mode of thinking outside of the BIS came at the Jackson Hole symposium, when Claudio Borio and William White were invited presenters (Borio and White 2004). Jackson

Hole is the annual flagship event for intellectual exchange in central-banking circles, hosted by the Federal Reserve Bank of Kansas City. This was an important litmus test of the reaction to the emerging BIS perspective on financial instability in the wider central-banking community, particularly in the United States as the world's leading financial power.

The Jackson Hole paper drew heavily on and synthesised some of the work conducted since 2000 (Borio, Furfine and Lowe 2001; Borio and Lowe 2002; White 2002). Its primary claim was that financial instability was beginning to replace inflation as the primary villain confronting the global economy. Simply focusing on price stability was therefore not an adequate guarantor of financial stability. Rather, the evidence pointed in the opposite direction. The conjunction of liberalised financial markets with credible price-stability-oriented policies was resulting in increasing instances of financial instability, often with double-digit GDP effects, significantly changing the dynamics of the economy (Borio and White 2004: 1).

Monetary policy focused on inflation, the paper argued, was likely to react too slowly to the build-up of financial imbalances, increasing the vulnerability of economies to boom-bust cycles. One of the consequences of lower and more stable inflation was also an increase in private risk-taking, with market actors assuming risks were lower and more benign. This was resulting in a greater prominence of asset and credit boom-and-bust cycles and a greater incidence of financial crises. At the same time, by the 1990s financial liberalisation had increased access to external forms of funding, and a much richer spectrum of tradable financial instruments, increasing the prospect for overextension during the up-phase of a financial cycle.

Expansions also potentially lasted longer, but also became increasingly costly when going into reverse. Financial factors were becoming more important drivers of business fluctuations, with this being fuelled by internal bank risk ratings and credit rating agencies (Borio and White 2004: 7). On the downswing side of the cycle, households and businesses struggle to restructure balance sheets, as falling profits, incomes and asset prices produce excessive indebtedness. Financial institutions react to this distress with a greater reluctance to extend finance, producing deep crises and recessions. Crises tend to have such common cyclical elements, with the credit-GDP ratio and inflation-adjusted equity prices deviating from long-term trends, being particularly good indicators of overextension and future crises (Borio and Lowe 2002).

To maximise the benefits of financial liberalisation, while minimising its costs, the paper argued, it was necessary to put in place mutually supportive safeguards, in both monetary and financial spheres, through monetary and prudential policies. In the BIS view monetary and prudential policies with a macroprudential orientation would be the key elements of a macro-financial stability framework. One element of this would be to require financial institutions to build up cushions during the upswing of a crisis, which could be run down in downswings. In monetary policy it was suggested authorities could tighten policy to reduce the build-up of financial imbalances, even when near-term inflationary pressures were not apparent (Borio and Lowe 2002). Such a move would also ensure authorities had more ammunition in the downswing phase of the cycle. This was a potentially controversial message because it involved moving central banks beyond narrow inflation-targeting mandates and building indicators such as credit-GDP gaps into existing monetary policy frameworks. While the macroprudential perspective was effectively a mindset, or way of understanding financial instability and its sources, macroprudential policies were only one element of the desired institutional response. The preferred BIS approach of creating broader macro-financial stability frameworks that went beyond prudential and regulatory policies, to encompass macroeconomic policy more generally (particularly monetary policy), was the logical outcome of adopting a macroprudential perspective or mindset (White 2006).

Audience reaction at Jackson Hole was mixed, but especially critical from US-based delegates. Mark Gertler of New York University acting as discussant argued that (1) the indicators the paper proposed were unlikely to be reliably predictive; (2) financial imbalances and instability were primarily due to regulatory inadequacies rather than cycles; and (3) there was no evidence that pre-emptive monetary policy responses to financial imbalances yielded significant benefits, but may actually do damage.

Frederic Mishkin, Ben Bernanke, Alan Greenspan as Federal Reserve Chairman and Allan Meltzer all rejected the idea that monetary policy could have a role in limiting bubbles and instances of financial instability, suggesting such moves would be counterproductive and induce recession (FRBKC 2003). Most notably, the central thesis of the paper that financial instability and crises have common features reflecting an inherent market procyclicality was not engaged with. The central term 'procyclicality' was referred to only once in post-paper discussion by Borio himself, illustrating that BIS attempts to inject this terminology and framing in international policy discussions were largely unsuccessful. The discussion did not even consider the proposition that cyclical market risk-taking caused financial instability, or that this was a characteristic of modern financial markets. Quite simply, the BIS lens on procyclicality was not being engaged with by many leading macro-economists and major figures in the world of central banking, particularly in the United States, revealing a discomfort and unfamiliarity with the terminology and the mode of thinking.

At national central banks the willingness to think in terms of non-equilibrium scenarios was increasing slowly. At the Bank of England, for example, an endogenous way of thinking about financial risk was beginning to develop. This was aided by the appointment of Hyun Shin (part of the LSE endogenous school of risk) as a consultant. Crucially, the Bank's financial stability team opted to keep this work private, based on a calculation that there was little appetite for it, either internally within the Bank or externally. Some parts of some central banks were becoming more receptive to thinking in terms of macro-financial stability, but narrow mandates, equilibrium modelling and a focus on inflation targeting did not make for an institutional environment that was especially conducive to progressing such thinking.

Signs that macroprudential thinking was beginning to permeate other settings and domains were also emerging in limited ways. Macroprudential monitoring was becoming more popular within the prudential supervision community, evident in macro stress testing and the development of indicators of financial distress. The IMF and World Bank's financial sector assessment programmes had encouraged such practices. There was also evidence of a macroprudential orientation filtering through into prudential instruments. Basel II, for example, produced some adjustments to its calibrations in response to concerns raised by the BIS and others about its potential to amplify procyclicality (Caruana 2004). Furthermore, the supervisory-review pillar could 'in principle' be adjusted in the light of a build-up of financial imbalances.

Some supervisory authorities had also developed through-the-cycle stabilising instruments. The most notable was the statistical provisioning scheme used by the Bank of Spain, which was calibrated according to average historical experience in loan losses to avoid excessive declines in provisioning in good times (De Lis et al. 2001). In some South East Asian economies, prudential standards were also tightened in good times, mainly loan-to-value ratios in Hong Kong, South Korea and Thailand, and tightened capital requirements against real estate lending in India, Norway and Portugal. Crucially, however, such measures were piecemeal and discretionary, rather than part of systematic macroprudential policy regimes, and were not present in the major financial jurisdictions.

The BIS perspective during this period was that the technologies and practices of countercyclical provisioning were still in their infancy. Macro-stress testing and indicators of distress still fell short of providing adequate financial stability safeguards, or a basis for discretionary policy interventions (Borio 2006: 19). Testing, experimenting with and refining macroprudential instruments remained difficult. Institutional factors also potentially inhibited such instruments. Supervisory authorities focused on depositor and investor protection would have difficulty using instruments for systemic stabilisation. International accounting standards also potentially clashed with the kind of statistical provisioning being used in Spain. BIS staff raised these issues in exchanges with the International Accounting Standards Board (IASB) but made little progress on an agreed way forward.

More significantly, the expertise and mindset of supervisory authorities were not always conducive to a macroprudential perspective. The legal and accounting backgrounds present in the supervisory community were often not compatible with the perspective's macroeconomic logic (Borio 2006: 20). The idea that standards and capital requirements would be varied through the cycle based on evolving conditions and judgements was not easy to represent in either legal codes of practice or on spreadsheets, and would inevitably be constrained by political economy considerations (White 2006).

Overall, BIS staff spent the 2000s gently promoting an intellectual shift that would allow measured contrarianism to flourish. However, staff also noted that this alone would be insufficient. A more far-reaching shift would require the creation of specific institutional mandates, indicators and instruments that would institutionally hardwire such a perspective (Borio 2006; White 2006).

By 2008, evidence from the financial disruptions of 2007 was being analysed and lessons were being drawn at the BIS. Reflecting earlier work, the emerging crisis was interpreted as a long-run financial cycle resulting from an overextension of risk-taking and balance sheets in good times (Borio 2008: 12). This reflected a broader 'paradox of financial instability', according to which financial system risk is greatest at precisely the point when it appears lowest and most benign to a majority of actors (Borio 2008). It is at this moment that aggressive and eventually destabilising risks are undertaken. Analytical devices like the 'paradox of financial instability' provided an intellectual framework for thinking and acting on a contrarian basis, issuing warnings or advocating a countercyclical tightening of policy. In the lead-up to 2008, the BIS issued several warnings that excessive risks were building up (BIS AR 2005, 2006, 2007; Knight 2007).

The evolving crisis was seen as a further rationale and justification for strengthening the macroprudential orientation of policy frameworks. In reality, concrete proposals for policy instruments had not progressed much since 2002, when Borio and Lowe's paper developed early-warning indicators. Two primary proxies had been advanced: an asset price gap, measured by the deviation of inflation-adjusted (real) equity prices from their long-term trend, and a credit gap, measured by deviations of the ratio of private-sector credit to GDP from its trend. The best warning signal had been found to be where the credit gap exceeded 4 percentage points and the equity price gap was greater than 40 per cent (Borio and Lowe 2002). BIS work during 2008 and 2009 updated this. Property prices were included in the indicator.[10] Revised results found the best predictors to be where the credit gap exceeded 6 per cent and at the same time either the equity gap exceeded 60 per cent or the property gap exceeded a threshold from 15 to 25 per cent (Borio and Drehmann 2009: 34).

As the crisis of 2008 materialised, a sense of urgency was imparted to this BIS research agenda on warning indicators and policy guides – not least because one of the primary lessons emerging from the episode was that the policy armoury for containing procyclicality remained hugely underdeveloped. In July 2009, BIS staff produced a research report jointly with Bank of Spain officials formulating proposals on counter-cyclical capital buffers.

The research developed a proposal for a countercyclical capital buffer scheme around the following principles or features: a time-varying target would be based on either the ratio of credit to GDP or credit growth, deviating from the long-term trend (credit-GDP gap); the target would be suspended in bad times for a pre-announced period based on aggregate losses and credit conditions, with banks allowed to use the additional regulatory capital built up in good times; and there would be a blanket restriction on dividend payments for the period of the suspension of the target. The credit-GDP gap was found to be the best indicator for guiding policy in the build-up phase, while some measure of aggregate losses, possibly combined with indicators of credit conditions, seemed best for signalling the beginning of the release phase. A prompt and sizeable release of the buffer was seen as desirable, as a gradual release could reduce the buffer's effectiveness. The research concluded that some degree of judgement, both for the build-up and the release phase, would be inevitable (Drehmann et al. 2009; later Drehmann et al. 2010).

4.5 Tackling Procyclicality as a Post-crisis Priority, 2008–2009

In April 2008, the FSF produced a report on the unfolding crisis for G7 finance ministers and central-bank Governors, entitled 'Enhancing market and institutional resilience'. The report contained no mention of strengthening the macroprudential orientation of policy frameworks. Its central message was the reiteration of a trinity of greater transparency, greater disclosure and better risk management by financial firms (Eatwell 2009). The report did, however, call for further study of the forces driving procyclicality in the financial system, pledging to further investigate options for mitigating it on behalf of the finance ministers and central-bank Governors (FSF 2008: 2). With the FSF looking to catalyse further work on procyclicality, the earlier research of the BIS was an obvious first port of call.

In this respect, the BIS enjoyed a 'first-mover advantage', having already conducted much of the analytical and conceptual legwork around the issue of procyclicality (Lall 2012; Baker 2013). Other institutions needed to draw on the BIS work, precisely because it already existed, and was the primary work in the field. On some occasions, various committees and bodies even deferred to the BIS's expertise, asked its advice or directly used previous work. In the changed climate after the crisis, this earlier BIS foundational work became a means of making sense of unfolding events and market fragility, while also pointing towards a programme of reform (Blyth 2002). For politicians and officials charged with establishing reform trajectories and conveying a sense that action was being taken to prevent future crises, the macroprudential perspective became important for the symbolic purpose of demonstrating that something concrete was being done (Lombardi and Moschella 2017).

One of the last acts of the George W. Bush administration in the United States was to convene a new G20 leaders' summit to discuss and develop responses to the crisis. As part of this ongoing process a working group of finance-ministry and central-bank officials was established to consider regulatory overhaul in more detail. Ahead of a second G20 leaders' summit in London in April 2009, the working group published a sixty-two-page report setting out a regulatory reform agenda in February of that year.

Recommendation three in the report called for authorities to be equipped with suitable macroprudential tools to address systemic vulnerabilities. More explicitly it noted that such tools should be developed by the BCBS, the International Organization of Securities Commissions (IOSCO), the International Association of Insurance Supervisors (IAIS) and the newly expanded FSF (soon to become the Financial Stability Board (FSB)). A number of potential instruments were listed, including simple measures to contain the build-up of leverage with enhanced sensitivity to off-balance-sheet exposures, capital requirements that adjust over the cycle, forward-looking loan loss provision standards, longer historical samples for assessing risk and margin requirements, and a greater focus on LTV ratios for mortgages (G20 2009: 9). This was the first time the development of a macroprudential policy toolkit had been formally recommended in an international policy document by major central banks and ministries of finance. Crucially, earlier BIS conceptual points were also taken up, such as the importance of the collective behaviour of economic agents being taken explicitly into account, and not simply reduced to the sum of individual component parts (G20 2009: 16).

This G20 working group was chaired by Tiff Macklem of the Canadian Ministry of Finance (and formerly of the Bank of Canada) and Rakesh Mohan of the Reserve Bank of India. In this sense, the report reflected that a number of officials in the central-banking community had quietly begun to accept the need for a macroprudential perspective. The ideas had gained currency at the Bank of England, the Bank of Canada and in a number of Asian countries, including India and South Korea. In the United Kingdom, Charles Goodhart, together with John Eatwell of Cambridge and Avinash Persaud, explained the macroprudential perspective to the new head of the UK prudential regulator, the Financial Services Authority (FSA), Adair Turner, who became a speedy convert to the perspective (FSA 2009). In Canada, Paul Jenkins and David Longworth of the Bank of Canada were advocates of creating an extensive macroprudential regime. Important national delegations – those of Canada as Chair of the working group and the United Kingdom as Chair of the G20 – were therefore beginning to advocate a macroprudential perspective.

The process of greater acceptance at key central banks was given additional momentum by the publication of the Geneva Report in July 2009, which brought together some of the primary academic authors from the endogenous school of risk with Andrew Crockett. One prominent Bank of England official, in conversation with the author, recalled that this report made the biggest difference in terms of acceptance by the central-banking community, because the standing of the academic voices involved markedly increased the credibility of the ideas. The report claimed strongly that countercyclical capital charges were the way forward and that capital-adequacy requirements should be adjusted over the cycle by two multiples: the first related to above-average growth of credit expansion and leverage;

the second related to the mismatch in the maturity of assets and liabilities (Danielsson, Shin and Zigrand 2004; Adrian and Brunnermeier 2010; Segoviano and Goodhart 2009; Adrian and Shin 2010).

On procyclicality, the G20 working group noted that FSF working groups would be tasked with developing recommendations for mitigating procyclicality with respect to bank capital, provisioning practices, and valuation and leverage. The working group also noted that the FSF and its member committees should be given a mandate to mitigate procyclicality in the financial system and for developing approaches to this end (G20 2009: 11). As part of this effort, staff at the BIS were tasked with writing a foundational paper for the FSF on procyclicality. The BIS contribution took the form of a conceptual note drawing on the previous research described elsewhere in this chapter (BIS AR 2009). Gradually, the BIS prior research and many of the ideas and concepts on which it was based were being diffused into key settings in the global financial architecture.

The FSF report on addressing procyclicality was published in April 2009 and was produced through three working groups: one on bank capital jointly with the BCBS; one on provisioning involving securities regulators and IOSCO; and one on leverage and valuation in conjunction with the CGFS. The reports produced by these working groups together with the BIS conceptual note on procyclicality were drawn together in a series of strong FSF recommendations to strengthen the macroprudential orientation of existing regulatory frameworks. The BCBS in particular was the target of a number of specific FSF recommendations, given the reluctance to do much to directly counter procyclicality earlier in the decade.

The first recommendation was that the BCBS should develop a countercyclical capital buffer. The second was that the BCBS should revise the market risk framework of Basel II to reduce the reliance on cyclical VaR-based capital estimates. A third recommendation included a non-risk-based measure to help contain the build-up of leverage in the banking system and put a floor under the Basel II framework. Other recommendations directed at the BCBS included enhanced stress testing to validate minimum capital buffer requirements as well as making appropriate adjustments to dampen excessive cyclicality of the minimum capital requirements (FSF 2009: 2–3). Further recommendations on provisioning asked the International Accounting Standards Board (IASB) to take action to reduce procyclicality by considering an incurred-loss model.

Notably, eleven of the seventeen recommendations made by the FSF report were directly targeted at the BCBS. This reflected a sense at G20 leader and ministerial levels that the BCBS had underperformed and needed to be subjected to greater accountability and oversight. To secure this, the FSF was converted into the FSB and given a much stronger mandate to direct and monitor BCBS activities, given that the FSB involved finance-ministry and supervisory-authority representatives. This FSF report was a strong statement of its new role as an intermediary between the G20 and more technical standard-setting bodies, in which these bodies would still be central in establishing new regulatory practice and frameworks but would be subject to a greater degree of direction and scrutiny than before.

For the BIS, the contents and tone of the report represented recognition of the work the institution had been undertaking a decade earlier. That the wider international community eventually came to accept and push these positions also illustrated the value of having an institution prepared to stand outside of and challenge accepted and established thinking, by adopting more contrarian alternative positions in a public fashion. In an area like financial stability, cyclical processes inevitably necessitate the periodic deconstruction and overhaul of policy regimes. BIS analytical and conceptual work has helped to guide and critically inform this process since the financial crisis.

The FSF report on procyclicality set a trajectory for regulatory reform, in particular the agenda to be pursued in reforming Basel II. Crucially, the report called on the BCBS and the CGFS to conduct a research programme to define robust measures of funding and liquidity risk. Stress tests could then gauge the likelihood and magnitude of a future liquidity crisis in different market environments. The FSF also called for information to be collected on leverage and maturity mismatches, on a coordinated international basis, including from off-balance-sheet vehicles and money-market funds by both the IMF and the BIS, to be made available to authorities (FSF 2009: 6).

Another notable aspect of the FSF document was that the section describing the conceptual framework drew almost entirely on the BIS note. It defined procyclicality as 'dynamic interactions (including positive feedback mechanisms) between the financial and the real sectors of the economy. These mutually reinforcing interactions tend to amplify business cycle fluctuations and cause or exacerbate financial instability' (BIS AR 2009: 1; FSF 2009: 8). The sources and drivers of procyclicality were also taken directly from BIS work. These were identified as limitations in risk management, particularly difficulties around the time dimension and distortions in incentives, evident in a direct link between asset valuations and funding that exacerbates procyclicality (BIS AR 2009: 2; FSF 2009: 9). The conceptual framing that the FSF used to draw up and set an agenda for Basel III therefore drew heavily on prior BIS work.

4.6 Basel III and the Macroprudential Framework

The revision of Basel II in the Basel III process through the BCBS, chaired by Dutch central-bank Governor Nout Wellink, began in the summer of 2009, following on from the activity of the G20 and the revamped FSF.[11] This was a substantially more inclusive process than that for Basel II. G20 Treasury officials were raising questions about the extent of BCBS involvement and centrality in preparing a new Basel accord. In this context, the new FSB was able to shield the BCBS from a diminished role in the process, but was also able to initiate a widening of the preparation process to a broader range of voices, reflecting a sense that Basel II had been too insular and narrow and that there was a need to broaden thinking. Accordingly, BIS staff were granted a much more active participatory role in Basel III than in Basel II.

The financial regulatory reform agenda since the crisis has been a broad one. It has increased the quality and level of capital requirements at banks, introduced and legitimated leverage ratios, set a framework for systemically important financial institutions and developed policies on institutional resolution and reform of over-the-counter derivatives and shadow banking. The arguments for the necessity of such systemic-resilience-enhancing measures were given extra force by the conceptual and data work developed by the BIS over the previous decade. In practical concrete terms, the biggest BIS influence has been on the discretionary time-varying policies addressing procyclicality, which have been a relatively small part of the overall reform agenda, but were most clearly driven by earlier BIS research and conceptual work. BIS staff were also involved in the discussions and conducted work relating to the methodology for developing the G-SIFI agenda and the capital surcharge for systemically important banks (SIBs) (BCBS 2011a). Here, however, national delegations, particularly that of the United States, had much more developed positions they wished to pursue in negotiations, aimed at least in part at countering the size of some European banks.

The countercyclical elements for Basel III, together with work on the capital conservation buffer, were handled by a group of officials, chaired by a representative from the New York Federal Reserve. Despite the new directions emerging from the FSF, there was still a limited receptiveness towards and understanding of the macroprudential perspective in this group. BIS officials directly involved in the work of the group recall that many other members of the group, particularly those from the micropru-dential supervision community, had difficulty thinking in terms of coun-tercyclical policy and had little sense of what it would involve. There was a particular difficulty in grasping how time-varying policies would be adjusted on the basis of discretionary interpretations of prevailing condi-tions, rather than being based on the precise implementation of a specific regulatory code and sets of rules. Some of the earlier opposition from the BCBS in 2000 was repeated in these discussions.

In the first round of debates and exchanges, BIS officials found their voice went largely unheard. Drafts of a first text were sent to the most senior BCBS Committee. The Committee responded by asking where the countercyclical element in this first text was. They instructed a second group to revisit the issues. Bank of England Governor Mervyn King was believed to be prominent in highlighting the need for a stronger counter-cyclical element. As noted earlier, the Bank of England itself had under-gone a partial conversion to a macroprudential perspective, through regular interactions with the LSE endogenous risk group, many of whom were former colleagues of King. The Bank was also in the process of being handed a new financial stability mandate.

The second group also had a new chair from the Bank of Canada, who invited BIS staff to present their ongoing work with the Bank of Spain on the design and operation of countercyclical capital buffers. In this second round of discussions, in the absence of other concrete proposals, the BIS idea of using a credit-GDP gap indicator to build up the capital buffer went unopposed. Data from computational thresholds were presented to sup-port this choice. The regular publication and communication of this indicator became part of the recommendations emerging from Basel III. Monitoring and publicising of credit-GDP gaps have since become an activity for both the BCBS and the BIS.

Basel III went on to call for countries to deploy a countercyclical capital buffer (CCyB) when aggregate credit growth was deemed to be excessive, with jurisdictions probably only deploying the buffer on an infrequent basis. The buffer for internationally active banks was to be a weighted average of the buffers deployed across all the jurisdictions to which they had credit exposures. The requirement would in turn be released when system-wide risk crystallised or dissipated. The relevant passage in Basel III reads: 'If the relevant national authority judges a period of excess credit growth to be leading to the build-up of system-wide risk, they will consider, together with any other macroprudential tools at their disposal, putting in place a countercyclical buffer requirement. This will vary between zero and 2.5 per cent of risk weighted assets, depending on their judgement as to the extent of the build-up of system-wide risk' (BCBS 2011b: 58).

Many staff within the BIS recognise that the 2.5 per cent buffer itself will do relatively little to push against the cycle and might only make a small contribution to enhancing financial system resilience. The CCyB has greater power as a soft communication and signalling device that can dampen market expectations by encouraging market actors to modify their investment patterns in anticipation of its deployment, increasing resilience through this indirect route. In this respect, building the CCyB requirement into Basel III was also important in signalling an international expectation that national authorities and internationally active banks would now develop such buffers. At US insistence, however, the CCyB did not become compulsory.

Since June 2016, the BIS has published time series data on the credit-GDP gap for more than forty countries since 1961 (Drehmann et al. 2016). The credit-GDP gap captures the difference between the credit-GDP ratio and its long-run trend. BIS quantitative work has shown it to be a reliable early-warning indicator of impending financial crises (Drehmann and Juselius 2014). Compared with other early-warning indicators of crisis it has the best overall statistical performance among single indicators across a large panel of countries over the past several decades (Drehmann and Tsatsaronis 2014: 59). It also performs well on timing, providing pre-emptive warnings and allowing policy measures time to take effect at least two years prior to crisis.

Importantly, while the use of these total credit series as input data facilitates comparability across countries, the credit-GDP gaps published by the BIS differ from those considered by many national authorities as part of their CCyB decisions, because they may use different data series. The gap indicator was adopted as a common reference point under Basel III to guide the build-up of countercyclical capital buffers. Authorities naturally have to apply judgement in setting buffers in their jurisdiction, rather than mechanistically applying a credit-GDP guide. Nevertheless, the BIS data work in this area can act as a central independent reference point that national authorities, the BCBS and the IMF can all draw upon. As such, its role is to inform, rather than dictate, supervisors' judgemental decisions regarding the appropriate level of the CCyB. Questions remain, of course, regarding the traction of the data and the fashion and extent of their usage by others.

Basel III, together with the FSB's mandate to encourage and monitor macroprudential policies, has to some extent triggered and supported the building of national macroprudential policy regimes. Many major central banks, from the Bank of England to the Federal Reserve (somewhat belatedly) and the European Systemic Risk Board at the European Central Bank, have been given varying macroprudential mandates, and many national central banks have been equipped with a wider range of instruments. Post-crisis reform proposals and their formalisation through Basel III have given some degree of energy and momentum to this process of national regime-building.

For the BIS, however, national regime-building has also meant that the institution has become less the go-to authority on macroprudential matters. Nevertheless, the macroprudential story illustrates the BIS's capacity to develop intellectual agendas that challenge accepted wisdom both in markets and academia, and among national central banks and regulatory bodies. Having an organisation that is prepared to stand outside of and sometimes challenge accepted wisdom has proven to be valuable. The persistence and intellectual independence of BIS staff, together with the cultivation and identification of important high-level academic allies, enabled the creation and diffusion of the macroprudential perspective as an intellectual framing for understanding systemic financial crisis. Such intellectual creativity is an undoubted strength of the organisation.

Once national regime-building commenced, with all its country specificities and peculiarities relating to market structures, institutional and cultural traditions, as well as coalitions and growth models, the BIS's lack of country expertise has made it less well equipped to advise on, input into or monitor this process. For these reasons, much of this work of assessing and monitoring national regimes has gravitated to institutions with stronger country expertise, such as the IMF, or bodies with greater national representation, such as the CGFS. Nevertheless, BIS positions on the process and direction of regime-building still matter because, as primary creator of the frame, the BIS remains well positioned to identify shortcomings in existing frameworks and to identify future challenges.

4.7 Current Macroprudential Policy Frameworks and the BIS

The general approach of the BIS to national macroprudential frameworks, and the contribution it is best suited to make in this domain, is consistent with the overarching disposition of measured contrarianism. Macroprudential and financial stability regime-building is not a one-stop fix. Reflecting the nature of markets and financial risk, it is an evolving and dynamic challenge, requiring forward-looking anticipatory adjustments and responses. Viewed through this lens, building adequate regulatory and policy regimes is never settled but an ongoing responsive process of evolution and development. In this sense, an important current role of the BIS is to identify new frontiers for financial stability frameworks and gaps that need to be filled, rather than advising on the fine-grained details of national arrangements or devising best-practice toolkits.

One example of the kind of concern that the BIS may be well placed to push is the extension of macroprudential instruments to shadow banking and other forms of asset management. For instance, recent BIS research has shown asset managers' cash hoarding to protect themselves from redemptions is an increasingly common practice that can amplify fire sales and procyclical dynamics (Morris, Shim and Shin 2017). Again, analysis identifying new evolving threats to financial stability within the conceptual frames developed by the BIS is an example of measured contrarianism in practice.

The FSB has since tried to take the issue of how macroprudential policies might be extended to asset management forward, through several reports, but has encountered institutional and intellectual barriers (FSB 2013a, 2013b, 2015). For example, margin-setting in central counterparties (CCPs) would fall under the remit of securities regulators, requiring both institutional consent and mandate amendment. It would also require an understanding of the purpose and benefits of such instruments among securities regulators.

A growing concern relates to whether there are enough revenue profits to meet long-term debt obligations for certain investment funds. Pension investments, for example, seek long-term returns, but also have large daily bond redemptions. Potential problems occur if such funds have to sell assets to meet redemptions, producing procyclical downward price spirals, which in turn creates a risk of sharp increases in bond funding (Morris, Shim and Shin 2017). Further analytical work on such discontinuities as a cause of systemic financial disruption, including an investigation of how arrangements for suspending redemptions among asset managers might be implemented, together with including cash hoarding in stress-testing, would undoubtedly be useful (Morris, Shim and Shin 2017: 20).

Mandates and mindsets remain a major issue in relation to extending macroprudential policy into asset management. Securities regulators who would have responsibility for overseeing such measures adopt a buyer-beware attitude and see their role as ensuring adequate transparency standards for informing individual transactions, rather than introducing measures to prevent systemic discontinuities. The issue illustrates how the perimeter of macroprudential thinking and concepts has struggled to extend beyond credit and banking markets.

Since the financial crisis there has been a clear increase in the use of macroprudential instruments by national authorities. BIS research shows that instrument usage in emerging markets doubled between 2006 and 2012, and in advanced economies it trebled between 2007 and 2018. The primary responsibility for monitoring macroprudential instrument usage within the international community now rests with the IMF, together with the FSB. LTV ratios and debt service-to-income ratios have a much higher statistical-significance impact than countercyclical capital buffers in restraining growth in credit and asset prices. There is also a recognition of a need to develop and extend tools targeted at the non-bank sector such as asset managers and other capital markets (due to risks of regulatory arbitrage) and to consider a variety of reciprocity measures that reduce the likelihood of cross-border leakages (Borio 2018: 5).

On desirable national institutional arrangements, there is no clear BIS position on optimum arrangements. Generally, the BIS view is that central banks need to be actively involved because of their macroeconomic expertise. The need for macroprudential bodies to have independence from government, so as to resist the political economy pressures that arise with financial booms, is believed to have been underestimated. BIS member central banks report that the common arrangement of having a committee made up of multiple agencies such as the Financial Stability Oversight Council (FSOC) come with significant collective action and coordination problems (Borio 2018: 7).

Most of all, the BIS continues to illuminate and identify areas on which too little is known, including which are the best intermediate targets; how different macroprudential tools interact with one another and with monetary policy; the appropriate balance between rules and discretion in macroprudential policies; how macroprudential policies should be calibrated in a bust; and potential distortionary side effects, including political risks (Claessens 2019).

Perhaps the boldest claim, and one in keeping with the broad philosophy of measured contrarianism, is the need to make vigilance against financial instability a broader macroeconomic priority. This position effectively revisits themes explored in the Borio–White contribution from Jackson Hole in 2003. It is a view that macroprudential policy itself is only one element of a broader macro-financial stability framework (Borio and

White 2004). In such a conception, financial stability concerns and responsibilities need to inform both monetary and fiscal policies (as well as structural policies) to avoid the risk of overburdening macroprudential policy (Borio 2018). The logic here is for more pronounced countercyclical regimes in both monetary and fiscal policies, as part of a holistic macro-financial stability framework (Claessens 2019).

Under such arrangements, monetary policy would be tightened, sometimes in the absence of inflationary pressures, to contain asset price and credit growth, but also to provide more ammunition in the downswing phase of a cycle. Foreign exchange market intervention could also be used to build up exchange reserve buffers that could be used in a downswing phase. A significant part of the current BIS research agenda is considering how financial stability considerations might be extended into monetary policy frameworks. In fiscal policy, taxation can be used to influence asset prices and credit, such as by reducing the tax bias favouring debt over equity. Having fiscal space to respond to the burdens of crisis and downturns can help also in reducing the macroeconomic effects of financial instability (Borio 2018: 8).

There are relatively few signs, however, of progress towards this kind of broader macro-financial stability framework. It is even possible that the emergence of macroprudential policies enables monetary and fiscal policies to remain insulated from financial stability considerations (Baker 2014, 2015). In this sense, and in keeping with the spirit of measured contrarianism, the construction of macro-financial stability frameworks from a BIS perspective remains a partial and incomplete project.

4.8 Conclusions

This chapter has provided an assessment of BIS contributions to the conceptual reframing of understandings of financial stability that followed the financial crisis. After 2008, a macroprudential perspective gained a higher profile and new policy frameworks were built. A recent citation analysis showed that academic modelling providing measures of systemic risk since the crisis still remains wedded to formal modelling that excludes many of the observable phenomena and amplification mechanisms characterising longer-run financial cycles that are identified by the BIS (Thiemann, Aldegwy and Ibrocevic 2017: 21). This could be interpreted as raising serious questions as to whether the macroprudential perspective truly has travelled outside of the BIS, especially into academic research. As a methodology, however, citation analysis has limits. There is today clearly a greater understanding of and sensitivity to processes such as procycli-cality among policy authorities around the world, even if efforts to build macro-financial stability frameworks remain incomplete, in the BIS view.

The obvious counterfactual question to pose is whether the macropru-dential perspective and macroprudential policy regimes could have come into existence without the BIS. Some academic work certainly dovetailed with the BIS research and developed a similar, if not identical, set of concerns and premises. But without the BIS's persistence in making submissions and developing arguments for policymakers in the FSF/FSB, BCBS, G20 and other forums, it is difficult to see how the perspective would have either had the prior analytical and institutional presence or gained the momentum required to produce the macroprudential policy frameworks that have emerged since the crisis (Baker 2013). That is not to say that the BIS achieved this on its own. In emerging markets, macroprudential-style policies were being experimented with prior to the crisis, though without being labelled as such. Both the Bank of Canada and the Bank of England were becoming more sympathetic due to their own in-house analytical work, and both played an important role in producing crucial political support for the perspective in the G20 in 2009, while the Bank of Spain's experience with dynamic provisioning was a crucial reference point throughout.

In persistently and doggedly pursuing these themes at a time when the receptive outside audience was limited, especially in the United States, the BIS effectively practised a form of measured contrarianism. As a function and service the BIS provides to its member central banks, but also wider society, the organisation's capability to perform measured contrarianism has somewhat deeper institutional foundations than it did prior to the crisis as a consequence of these efforts.

These deeper institutional foundations have been pushed forward in three ways. Firstly, in relation to instruments, the BIS itself effectively designed and created a blueprint for using countercyclical capital buffers that was imported into the provisions of Basel III. BIS work has also heralded a range of other more direct through-the-cycle, non-discretionary instruments such as LTV and loan-to-income (LTI) ratios. Analytical arguments relating to procyclicality have also helped to strengthen the case for the use of leverage ratios, for more robust capital requirements and for extending macropru-dential policies into shadow banking through margins and haircuts, even if the latter has not made much progress to date. Experimentation with a much broader range of macroprudential policy instruments and indicators is ongoing in many jurisdictions around the world, and BIS work has legit-imised and given energy to these efforts. The BIS itself can now advocate a more targeted set of interventions to contain emerging financial risks in its own public communications, though it seldom does so in terms of national specifics, preferring to talk more broadly about global systemic risks.

Secondly, the BIS itself now has a more focused set of data-collection activities around the credit-GDP gap, as its own favoured and most reliable early-warning indicator. Becoming more systematic in the collection and public communication of data adds substance and rigour to performing its function of measured contrarianism, while enabling the organisation to be more public and transparent in doing so. Analytical data-driven work at the BIS also continues to help identify new potential frontiers for macro-prudential policy and new potential sources of financial instability, such as cash hoarding by asset managers (Morris, Shim and Shin 2017).

Thirdly, and most significantly of all, the BIS created a new conceptual framing in a language that was intelligible to many interested and informed observers. Thinking in terms of financial cycles and recognising their endogenous sources have become more commonplace not only in central banks but also in the financial press (Borio 2018: 4, Graph 4). Expert public discourse more readily accepts such terms and understandings. Notions such as the 'paradox of financial instability', explaining that risks are sown and are highest in booms precisely when they appear lowest but materialise in recessions, have helped to foster the kind of vigilant mindset and intellectual disposition required to practise measured contrarianism.

Nevertheless, the shift to macro-financial stability frameworks remains incomplete and many gaps in knowledge remain. For example, we are still a substantial way from the more holistic macro-stability frameworks envisaged by the BIS. Indeed, it is possible that the emergence of a separate macropru-dential policy field may be slowing down the introduction of financial stability considerations into other areas of economic policy, most notably monetary policy. The latter remains a particular priority and target for the BIS as the next frontier for macro-financial stability frameworks. One possible irony is that, contrary to BIS views, monetary policy may become more insulated from financial stability concerns by the new emerging macroprudential policy pillar, which in part, as this chapter has documented, owes its existence to a prior body of BIS intellectual work that stretched over several decades.

Notes

1. In BIS conceptual work, financial instability and crises were distinguished from simple financial distress. The former took more systemic forms affecting entire markets, evident in system fragility, while the latter related to idiosyncratic diffi-culties encountered by individual institutions (Borio and Drehmann 2009: 2).

2. This chapter draws on a number of confidential interviews with BIS staff, macro-economists conducting policy work and national central bankers. It also draws on confidential archive material to which access was facilitated by the BIS for the purpose. This material is not individually referenced in the chapter, but at many points the material is drawn directly from interviews or archive material.

3. In economics this relates to the Minskyan notion that excessive optimism about the future might generate leverage cycles (Brunnermeier and Oehmke 2012; Bhattacharya et al. 2015; Caballero and Simsek 2017), but also to how herding behaviours amplify financial volatility (Devenow and Welch 1996; Nofsinger and Sias 1999; Welch 2000; Persaud 2000). Political scientists have also considered how ideational stability and consensus can induce complacency, policy fine-tuning or narrowing, as a cause of economic and financial instability, ultimately producing ideational instability, redundancy and renewal due to the anomalies that develop in established approaches accumulated over time (Hall 1993; Widmaier 2016).

4. While institutions such as the IMF have highly skilled personnel and much macroeconomic expertise, the financing operations and pool of capital the organi-sation presides over involve the direct monitoring of member countries' financing positions. This, together with the formalism associated with Article IV surveillance, conditionality agreements and greater board-level vetting of intellectual content and agendas, has traditionally made it more difficult for the IMF to play a role of challenging conventional accepted wisdom and optimism, because of greater political sensitivities and contention surrounding its role, the analysis it develops and what the analysis is used for. In contrast, the BIS has traditionally had a greater degree of intellectual autonomy, though this fluctuates across time and is contin-gent upon circumstances.

5. Earlier accounts of endogenous forces in the financial system are evident in Kindleberger 1978 and Minsky 1995.

6. 'Report of the Working Party on possible approaches to constraining the growth of banks' international lending', 29 February 1980, in BIS Archive 1.3a(3)J – *Working Party on constraining growth of international bank lending*, vol. 2 (Clement 2010).

7. On the macroeconomic background to the emergence of macroprudential con-cerns at the BIS, see Chapter 5 (Barry Eichengreen) of this volume.

8. This document is one of the confidential sources to which the author had access, as referred to in note 2.

9. BCBS, 'Discussion Note: Financial Stability and the Basel Capital Accord', BS/00/14, 9 March 2000, In BISA 10.4.1 – *BCBS Numbered Documents 2000*.

10. An absence of reliable data had prevented this in 2002. The 2002 paper had also considered the use of built in stabilisers, in addition to discretionary measures, through conservative loan-to-value ratios based on through-the-cycle valuations.

11. On the role of the BIS and BCBS in developing soft law in the wake of the Great Financial Crisis under the guidance of the G20 and FSB, see Chapter 3 (Christopher Brummer) of this volume.

Exchange Rates, Capital Flows and the Financial Cycle

On the Origins of the BIS View

Barry Eichengreen

5.1 Introduction

One way of tracing the development of the Bank for International Settlements (BIS) is through the analyses in its annual reports, which provide a distillation of staff and management thinking.[1] In what follows, I focus on the post–Bretton Woods period that saw the emergence of the modern BIS that is relevant to today, and hence on annual reports published in 1971 and after. But it is important to put those reports and the themes and issues they emphasise in their broader historical context. Because the Bank originated as fiscal agent for the Dawes and Young Plan loans and subsequently acted as trustee for the Marshall Plan and European Coal and Steel Community, Dawes-, Young-, Marshall- and Community-related matters figure prominently in its early reports.[2] Starting in the 1960s, the focus was then on money, credit and capital markets and their relationship to exchange rates and the balance of payments. That the challenge of maintaining exchange rate stability and managing payments imbalances should have featured prominently in the Bank's analysis of credit and capital markets reflected the fact that the Bretton Woods system of pegged but adjustable exchange rates was the institutional basis for such markets in the third quarter of the twentieth century. Insofar as the BIS was now charged, or took it upon itself, to monitor the operation of credit and capital markets, it was centrally concerned with the operation of the Bretton Woods system and the stability of its exchange rates in particular.

But no sooner did the BIS adopt this perspective than the Bretton Woods system went by the board. The collapse of Bretton Woods was both a consequence and cause of the recovery of international capital mobility from the restrictions of the Great Depression, the Second World War and the agreement reached at the Mt Washington Hotel in 1944.[3] The growth of capital flows reflected the recovery of domestic and international financial markets from the damage wrought by the 1930s and the war, and also the general trend towards financial deregulation, as the prevailing mood of suspicion towards such markets faded in policy and political circles. As regulation lightened and financial markets recovered, the scope for financial volatility expanded as well. Increasingly, the focus of the BIS, as reflected in its annual reports, became financial-stability-related issues and, specifically, how international monetary and financial arrangements could best be adapted to this new environment.

There is of course no official BIS view of feasible and desirable exchange rate and international monetary and financial arrangements. Referring to a single BIS view is at best a useful figment. Whether at the level of management, staff or members, the Bank is not a monolithic institution. That said, my own experience with international organisations is that such institutions do, in fact, develop a culture and set of analytical emphases as a result of their histories and the intellectual influence of individual members of management and staff.[4]

Thus, it is possible to discern, at various points in time, the outlines of an unofficial, unstated, unconscious institutional consensus. Allen, Bean and DeGregorio (2016), focusing on the recent period, refer to a 'house view' whose most prominent element is the proposition that lax credit conditions create incentives for risk-taking that threaten systemic stability. To this I would add the proposition that, in contrast to the standard Keynesian presumption that international capital flows can be important for sustaining demand in economies where spending is otherwise constrained by weak external accounts, it is important to monitor gross as opposed to net debt flows and to gather data on their development so that their implications for financial stability can be assessed. A further element of the house view is that the nature of the instruments and institutions that convey capital flows across borders (whether flows are mediated by the interbank market or the bond market, as well as the currency denomina tion and tenor of the instruments traded) is important for understanding financial-stability risks. Related to this is scepticism about the insulating properties of flexible exchange rates in the face of 'powerful waves' of financial capital.[5] A final element is that there is a role for macroprudential policy in restraining the excesses giving rise to these risks.

These views grew organically out of the Bank's earlier history. The BIS's early intellectual leaders, such as Alexandre Lamfalussy, came of age in the

1970s, when the institution began exercising oversight of international financial markets.[6] The 1970s was a period of lax monetary policy that culminated in a Third World and global debt crisis.[7] From April 1971, when the central-bank governors of the Group of Ten (G10) countries created the Euro-currency Standing Committee, the BIS was involved in monitoring the sources and uses of loans and securities denominated in currencies other than that of the political jurisdiction in which they were issued. The Basel Committee on Banking Supervision was established following the failure of Herstatt Bank, with its cross-border repercussions, in 1974. As early as 1982, when Lamfalussy produced a note for G10 central-bank governors on 'The Current Position and Policies of the G10 Countries' Commercial Banks: Some Macro-Economic and "Macro-prudential" Issues', the BIS was identified with the view that macroeconomic and microprudential policies should be supplemented by macroprudential measures.[8] Thus, a specific view of capital flows and the financial cycle, emphasising loose money, risk-taking, macroprudential regulation and the structure of the interbank markets, germinated in Basel already half a century ago in response to the circumstances the BIS faced.

A house view of exchange rates is harder to identify. Following the collapse of the Bretton Woods system, the BIS was slow to acknowledge the challenges of putting back in place a system of pegged but adjustable exchange rates. In part this reluctance reflected the dominance of European central banks, with their historical preference for stable rates, in its membership and the prominence of European economists amongst its staff. The Bank in its annual reports was critical of floating rates for their volatility and limited insulating properties. It regularly warned that currency depreciation intended to restore competitive advantage could be beggar-thy-neighbour. It characterised floating rates as drifting away from equilibrium and taking on a life of their own. Once it reluctantly acknowledged that fixed rates had become a thing of the past, it became a pragmatic proponent of foreign exchange market intervention – intervention guided not by rigid rules but by intuition and discretion – as a means of driving misbehaving currencies back towards sustainable levels.

In addition, the Bank was sensitive to the defects of the dollar-based international monetary and financial system, especially when US policy was unstable or formulated with little regard to the rest of the world. But it also expressed scepticism about the prospects for devising less dollar-centric arrangements.

The BIS tended to be cautious in advancing proposals for monetary and financial reform. It did not exactly point the way forward to the development of a more desirable set of international monetary arrangements or specifically identify urgent reforms. This caution reflected the fact that the Bank is an organ of its members, and those members did not always share a consensus view of feasible and desirable reforms. As in earlier crises, lack of a shared conceptual framework, where different conceptual frameworks reflected different historical experiences, was an obstacle to agreement on the way forward.[9] Some members subscribed to Keynesian logic emphasising the implications for aggregate demand of international capital flows, for example, while others were more sensitive to the consequences for financial stability. Some members convinced by the need for an international lender of last resort supported BIS involvement in emergency rescue measures for countries experiencing capital flow reversals, while others preoccupied by the risk of moral hazard advocated a more restrained approach. Members with powerful voices resisted proposals that might disadvantage their constituencies: US resistance to measures that might have clamped down on the operation of the international interbank market in the run-up to the Latin American debt crisis are a case in point.

To be sure, the Board of Directors, representing member central banks, which is responsible for 'determining the strategic and policy direction of the Bank', did not give staff and management explicit marching orders or caution them against specific warnings and recommendations.[10] Still, BIS documents convey a sense that staff and management were generally reluctant to get out too far ahead of the consensus in the committees hosted by the Bank.

But one can also discern occasions when BIS staff and management pushed back against national positions and challenged national members of its committees. These occasions were exceptional: generally, they occurred after crises and when BIS staff and management felt frustration over lack of progress on the part of the Bank's committees and members in addressing structural and policy problems.[11] They also reflected personalities: the willingness of a general manager to stick out his neck, and the existence of a level of trust between that general manager and his national counterparts, such that he could be confident that his head would not be chopped off when extended above the parapet.

5.2 After Bretton Woods

The focus in this chapter on the post–Bretton Woods period makes the Bank's 1971 report a logical starting point. That 1971 report opened in now traditional fashion with discussions of gold reserves and gold production, the fixed dollar price of gold being a central pivot of Bretton Woods and gold reserves being a traditional determinant of international liquidity. From there it moved to a country-by-country accounting of reserve gains and losses, followed by a review of foreign exchange market conditions. Among new developments it highlighted the growth of Eurodollar transactions and negotiation of a European Monetary Agreement to foster cooperation among the continent's monetary authorities and prepare for the eventual move to a single European currency. These developments, by implication, pointed towards a future in which the international monetary system would be less US- and dollar-centric. That said, the Bank did not obviously have an inkling of what was to follow, namely the imminent collapse of the Bretton Woods adjustable peg.

The first substantive chapter of the 1972 report focused predictably on the events of the second half of 1971: the US decision to close the gold window in August and the negotiations leading up to the Smithsonian Agreement in December. The chapter was entitled 'The Crisis of the Dollar and the Monetary System', indicating the shock with which these events were received. The Bank blamed the crisis on a combination of factors: excessive demand pressure and inflation in the United States; the reluctance of other countries to revalue against the dollar (the *n*-1 country problem); and the Triffin Dilemma, which suggested that US deficits were a consequence, at least in part, of the appetite of other countries for liquid dollar reserves.[12]

The Bank was studiously agnostic about the form that the post–Bretton Woods system might take, indicative presumably of the absence of a consensus among its members.[13] Reflecting this institutional caution, the 1973 report again adhered to the earlier tripartite focus on the level of gold and foreign exchange reserves, developments in the Eurodollar market and the evolution of the European Monetary Agreement. The format was again the same in 1974. Judged from its reports, the Bank had no firm convictions at this point about the form of feasible and desirable reforms of the international monetary system.

Efforts to design that new system were spearheaded in practice not by the BIS but by the International Monetary Fund (IMF), which established and coordinated the Committee of Twenty.[14] The BIS obtained observer status in the C20, to which it contributed a detailed memo on the Eurocurrency market, a phenomenon that had been on the Bank's radar screen for years.[15] This memo was an early recognition of the rapidity of the growth of international capital flows, increasingly from commodity- and oil-exporting economies to London and other European financial centres, which in turn recycled them to developing countries in Latin America and elsewhere. It highlighted the challenge posed by those flows for the maintenance of a stable international monetary and financial system and the need for international cooperation in their management and regulation. In its words, such flows had been 'an element in the various problems, both for national monetary authorities and for the operation of the monetary system'.

The memo then went on to highlight as concrete problems (i) complications for the conduct of monetary policy, (ii) intensification of inflationary pressure and (iii) scope for capital flight and speculative attacks on exchange rates.[16] This list sounds positively modern in light of subsequent experience with short-term capital flows.[17]

These concerns were then amplified in subsequent reports. The 1973 instalment warned, in somewhat antiseptic terms, of the unprecedented growth of the foreign-currency liabilities of European banks.[18] It noted that the Euro-currency market was primarily an interbank market and hinted at risks that might arise from extensive bank lending and borrowing on the wholesale market. In 1974 the BIS pointed to the striking growth of Euro-currency lending to developing countries and to the increasing prevalence of syndicated loans, which 'served to remove virtually all limitations on the size of loans which could be handled by the market'.[19]

In March 1973, six of the nine members of the European Community jointly floated their currencies against the US dollar, signalling the final demise of the Smithsonian Agreement and the inability of governments, under conditions of heightened capital mobility, to maintain pegged exchange rates.[20] In its report three months later, the Bank commented on these developments. The realignment of currencies and policies in December 1971 and after, it argued, had been too little, too late. The 7.9 per cent devaluation of the dollar negotiated at the Smithsonian was too small to materially strengthen the US balance of payments. Nor was it adequately reinforced by US monetary and fiscal consolidation (BIS AR 1973. 21). In 1972, the UK government had then responded to high unemployment and weak growth with fiscal and monetary stimulus, causing sterling to weaken relative to its new Smithsonian level and doubts to spill over to the dollar.[21] The US authorities, reluctant to tighten monetary and fiscal policies, chose instead to devalue the dollar a second time in February 1973. Having been burned twice, currency traders moved their funds into European currencies, forcing the joint float in March.

One conclusion that might have been drawn from these observations was that governments were increasingly reluctant to subordinate monetary and fiscal policies to the imperatives of exchange rate stability and that this rendered the maintenance of pegged exchange rates unrealistic in the prevailing environment of rising capital mobility. For the moment, however, the Bank was unprepared to take this intellectual leap, reflecting its reservations about the alternative of more flexible rates. It highlighted three such reservations in its 1974 report. First, 'a feature of recent experience is that floating rates did not provide as much domestic monetary autonomy as had often been expected'. Second, national authorities, displaying what we would now call 'fear of floating', 'found it appropriate to intervene in the markets in order to prevent excessive swings in their exchange rates'. Third, the depressing impact of exchange rate variability on international trade was more limited than anticipated (BIS AR 1974: 32).

All three observations were amply confirmed by subsequent experience. But at this point there was no effort to elaborate what they implied for feasible and desirable exchange rate arrangements or for the future of the international monetary system.

In 1976, the BIS published its first comprehensive assessment of the post–Bretton Woods 'nonsystem'.[22] The transition to floating rates, it concluded with evident reluctance, was irreversible.[23] This reality reflected divergent national policy preferences and the explosive growth of international capital flows. Whether and to what extent the exchange rate changes in fact facilitated external adjustment remained to be seen, however. For the United States and Japan, the Bank's assessment was positive: dollar and yen movements had visibly contributed to the narrowing of the external imbalances of the two countries.[24] In the United Kingdom and Italy, on the other hand, weaker currencies had not translated into commensurate strengthening of external accounts. In these cases, the Bank observed, expenditure switching was frustrated by the absence of significant expenditure reduction.

Nor had exchange rate adjustment proceeded smoothly. The Bank was evidently aware of academic analyses (e.g. Dornbusch 1976) suggesting that exchange rates tended to overshoot. As the 1976 report put it, appreciations and depreciations not infrequently 'overshot the mark' (BIS AR 1976: 103). More generally, increased attention to the connections between exchange rates and interest rates, as opposed to the earlier focus on exchange rates and relative output prices, indicated an awareness that exchange rate movements were driven increasingly by capital flows and the capital account of the balance of payments, not by trade and current-account balances.

The Bank's next several reports focused on other issues, such as the business cycle and its determinants, although the 1977 instalment included additional discussion of floating rates. It highlighted differences of opinion between the authorities in large, relatively closed economies such as the United States, who favoured relatively free floating, and those of smaller, more open economies, such as in Europe, who preferred heavily managed rates. It reiterated the overshooting view, augmented now by the observation that large exchange rate movements could create expectations of further movements and become self-perpetuating. One implication, documented in academic studies such as Frenkel (1978), was that floating did not obviously reduce the need for international reserves, since the authorities, in order to limit self-fulfilling dynamics, might still have to intervene extensively.

The dollar weakened sharply in 1978, with destabilising spillovers to other countries. For the BIS, writing in its 1979 report, this was another 'dollar crisis' – the most serious threat to the stability of the international monetary system since the breakdown of Bretton Woods (BIS AR 1979: 3). The Bank took the opportunity to restate its scepticism about floating rates: it pointed to a fact that deserved

careful consideration in the analysis of this crisis ... that it happened while all the major currencies were floating – not freely, admittedly, but floating nevertheless. It thus contrasted sharply with the crises of both early 1971 and early 1973, which had taken place under a regime of pegged rates. At that time many economists – and even some central bankers – had come to believe that floating rates, whatever their short-comings, had at least one virtue, namely that they did not allow exchange crises to occur. Experience with floating rates since 1973 has brought about a progressive revision of these views. (BIS AR 1979: 3)

Cogent observations all, but to what conclusions they led was unclear.

Finally, 1978 was notable for the decision to create the European Monetary System (EMS), which the Bank understood as another effort by European governments to insulate themselves from the effects of dollar weakness.[25] The BIS saw some justification for these efforts; it was duly critical of the failure of the American monetary and fiscal authorities to commit to sound and stable policies and positive about the stabilising potential of the EMS (BIS AR 1979: 5).

5.3 The Birth of Macroprudential Policy

The dollar's sharp decline in 1978 prompted a more ambitious review of international financial markets. The ongoing deliberations of the Euro-currency Standing Committee (ECSC) chaired by Lamfalussy provided an obvious context for discussions. The committee noted the alarmingly rapid growth of borrowing and lending on Euro-currency markets. It suggested that this had eased the diversification of foreign reserves out of dollars, accentuating the weakness of the greenback. It worried that by facilitating the movement of funds between currencies, growth of the Euro-currency market amplified exchange rate fluctuations generally (anticipating the modern critique of multiple reserve-currency systems). It warned that ease of borrowing on Euro-currency markets was enabling 'a number of countries to postpone taking prompt adjustment measures'.[26] And it flagged commercial banks' exposure to concentrated country risk.

These concerns about the growth of cross-border lending and financial-stability risks extended beyond the confines of the Euro-currency market, however. To address them, G10 central-bank governors established under Lamfalussy's direction a Working Party on Possible Approaches to Constraining the Growth of International Bank Lending (known for ease of reference as the Lamfalussy Group). Its charge was to investigate whether international bank lending had 'contributed to an excessive growth of international liquidity' and to consider 'prudential concerns arising out of the international banking developments of the past four years'. The chairman's first progress report described general support for the motherhood-and-apple-pie recommendation of more and better data, but noted also limited enthusiasm for regulatory measures to constrain the growth of international lending, other than the view that capital require-ments should not be biased *in favour* of international business.[27]

Lamfalussy's report on the Group's second meeting included what appears to be the first official invocation in a BIS document of the term 'macro-prudential'.[28] In a section entitled 'General Considerations on the Use of Prudential Measures for Macro-Economic Purposes', Lamfalussy referred to 'concerns of a macro-prudential nature, which may not readily be perceived at the level of the individual bank, to which the supervisor should have regard'.[29] Beyond acknowledging the validity of macropru-dential 'concerns', however, there was again no agreement on steps to be taken. Members discussed the possibility of applying higher capital requirements to banks' foreign assets but rejected the possibility for its 'undesirable arbitrariness' and specifically on the grounds that different international loans carried different degrees of risk.[30]

The Group's final report elaborated those same macroprudential con-cerns. It observed that 'not only the prudential risks to which individual banks are subject but also the macro-prudential risks, i.e. those affecting the international banking system taken as a whole, will be greater in the future than they were in the past'.[31] The report listed four sets of measures that might be taken in response.[32] The first two, measures regulating banks' foreign exchange and country exposures, were primarily microprudential in nature but might have some useful macroprudential effects. The other two, attempts to regulate maturity mismatches and to apply capital surcharges to risky international lending, faced what it described as technical problems of implementation.

At this stage, in sum, an awareness had developed of macroprudential concerns. But there was no agreement on measures to be taken in response.

5.4 The Materialisation of All Risks

Capital flows and the challenge they posed to economic and financial stability took centre stage in 1982 with the eruption of the Latin American debt crisis.[33] This episode was, in effect, the materialisation of many of the fears and worries about the operation of the interbank Euro-currency market voiced in earlier BIS reports. Already in 1978, Lamfalussy had warned of the danger of a sudden stop.[34] The Bank then reiterated this warning in the annual report in June 1982 (BIS AR 1982: 188), a few months before Mexico closed its foreign exchange market.[35]

In late 1980, discussions in the ECSC had shifted from how to prevent the further build-up of international debt to how to deal with the fallout of a crisis that seemed increasingly likely.[36] In its meeting on 9 November 1980, the Committee discussed a Bank of England paper on 'Possible consequences of a debt service failure by a major borrowing country'.[37] In April 1981, it administered a questionnaire to G10 central banks on means for providing liquidity support to banks in crisis. The results, reported to members of the Committee in June 1982, a little over a month before the eruption of the Mexican crisis, were not encouraging.[38] As the report noted, it was impossible to anticipate the scale of losses incurred by banks in the event of a sovereign default, since syndicated bank lending to sovereigns was a new and novel development.[39] Central banks thus had no way of knowing whether they were lending into a liquidity or solvency crisis.

In response, the Bank undertook several initiatives to improve statistical coverage of commercial bank lending to emerging markets.[40] This, in effect, was the genesis of the BIS banking statistics collected by the ECSC (from 1999 named the Committee on the Global Financial System).[41] There was also more discussion of the possible use of capital requirements and related measures to regulate and restrain the growth of international

bank lending. Again, however, there was no consensus, much less mean-
ingful action.

The BIS, in the person of Lamfalussy, also expressed worries about the
official response to the crisis, as led by the IMF and the US government.[42]
Lamfalussy questioned whether a strategy of concerted lending – of leaning
on members of bank syndicates to lend distressed governments enough
new money to permit the authorities to stay current on their interest
payments – was in fact viable. As he put it, 'If bank managements want
to reduce their global exposure to LDCs [less-developed countries], they
will display remarkable skill in taking back with the left hand what they
have given with the right.'[43] Lamfalussy also warned that requiring crisis
countries to compress spending sharply in order to eliminate their external
deficits 'exposes them to the dangers of a domestic financial crisis'.[44] Sharp
fiscal consolidation, he observed, might only consign the crisis countries to
deeper recessions and additional debt problems. Indeed, even adjustment
programmes that were viable when taken in isolation might lose that
viability when considered collectively – 'the wider use of tightly conditional
IMF medicine is not exactly conducive to world growth'.[45]

Ultimately, the developing-country debt crisis threatened not just developing economies but the stability of the global banking system.[46] The
experience led the BIS to adopt a still more sceptical perspective on
international bank lending. The 1983 annual report described how competition for international business had 'squeezed the banks' margins to
levels that left little room for building up reserves and led, in some
instances, to lending that took little account of the borrowing countries'
situations and policies.[47] Moreover, the fact that these funds were readily
available at very low, or sometimes negative, real interest rates . . . tempted
a number of LDCs to overborrow' (BIS AR 1983: 120–1). And the short-
term, variable-interest-rate debt to which the commercial banks had
turned in the effort to maintain their margins in the face of volatile interest
rates only passed on the associated interest-rate and rollover risk to the
debtor countries.[48]

As the 1983 report noted, the BIS played an important role in organising
central banks to put together a facility for Mexico. In addition, it provided
a bridging facility for Brazil in advance of disbursements from that country's IMF programme and then helped to establish a similar facility for
other Latin American countries in December 1982. The Mexican crisis, like
those that followed, is typically portrayed as having been managed by the
US government (which first provided resources to Mexico in August 1982)
and by the IMF (which approved its programme with the Mexican

government in December). In the intervening period, however, the BIS organised an additional credit, guaranteed by member central banks, which was matched by the US Treasury and the Federal Reserve.

The BIS had the advantage of an exclusive membership, an expansive mandate and the ability to move quickly. According to Bederman (1988), negotiating the bridge loan for Mexico required only forty-eight hours.[49] Events unfolded in the same sequence in Argentina, Brazil and elsewhere.

But this new departure was controversial. German officials criticised these bridging loans on moral-hazard grounds. As the debt crisis deepened, the duration of BIS loans lengthened, troublingly for an institution whose resources derived from its ability to manage the liquid foreign reserves of member central banks. The Bank had no power to impose conditions on the borrowers, and in any case lacked the staff needed to enforce them. Reflecting these problems, the BIS turned its emphasis instead to augmenting the resources of the IMF, collaborating with G10 central banks on the expansion of the General Arrangements to Borrow.[50]

Finally, reflecting ongoing concerns about capital flows, the operation of the interbank market and the risks to which they gave rise, the ECSC established a study group to examine the workings of the interbank market. Its report warned that some banks whose balance sheets had expanded as a result of their access to the market had engaged in inappropriate lending heavily concentrated in high-risk countries and that the market's lack of transparency led the banking system as a whole to lend more than otherwise to those high-risk borrowers.[51] The group's own conclusion was that these problems were not, in fact, attributable to the existence of the interbank market per se. Rather, they arose from the failure of national regulators to apply capital, concentration and liquidity requirements rigorously and consistently and from the failure of banks to observe them, not from how they raised their funds.

In introducing the study group's report to G10 governors in February 1983, the ECSC chairman (Lamfalussy) noted the dissenting views of a significant minority of study group members.[52] Non-bank depositors, they suggested, were willing to lend more to risky sovereign borrowers when their funds were intermediated by a major international bank, perhaps reflecting the existence of an implicit government guarantee of the bank in question or perhaps responding to signals from the authorities that they regarded interbank lending as low-risk.[53] The large number of participants in this market, they suggested further, led to excessive competition and overlending to non-bank borrowers.

Still, the majority and minority agreed that interbank lending was inadequately discriminating: there was too little attention to the country and other risk of the borrowing bank counterparty. There was inadequate management of liquidity risk and too little awareness that interbank liabilities were less liquid than claims on governments. Interbank liabilities were not backed by adequate capital, reflecting in part the fact that some supervisors required less capital against interbank transactions. The report emphasised the need to renounce implicit guarantees with the goal of strengthening market discipline. It recommended gathering more comprehensive statistics on lending to individual countries – not just to the government but also its banks – so that lending institutions could accurately gauge their aggregate exposure. National supervisors should encourage banks to upgrade their risk-management systems. They might contemplate upward revisions in capital requirements, reflecting new awareness of the riskiness of interbank lending.

But the emphasis at this stage was on self-regulation. 'There is, in the view of the Study Group, substantial advantage in emphasising that banks themselves clearly bear the risk of lending in the interbank market and are responsible for maintaining their own creditworthiness. This approach, which could be termed "self-regulation", would in all probability be greater than has hitherto been evident.'[54] The motivation for this official review was concern about the stability of individual banks and the international banking system as a whole, but the measures recommended in response were mainly of a microprudential, not a macroprudential, nature.

5.5 Back to Floating

In 1983 the Bank offered an assessment of ten years of floating. '[I]t is hard to avoid the conclusion,' it judiciously observed, that real and nominal exchange rates were volatile. Where policy credibility was incomplete – that is to say, in most circumstances – sharp exchange rate movements could alter expectations in self-reinforcing ways. Where volatility led to overvaluation, it could fuel protectionist pressures, such as those in the United States. Again, the implication was that flexible rates enhanced monetary autonomy to only a limited extent; instead of enhancing autonomy, floating rates 'in practice sometimes had the opposite effects' (BIS AR 1983: 150). That said, efforts to stabilise exchange rates would only succeed if backed by credible and consistent monetary and fiscal policies. In issuing this caution, the Bank was pushing back against contemporaneous calls for exchange rate target zones to rein in dollar appreciation (inter alia Roosa 1983).

The BIS was less than forthcoming about what alternative it had in mind. A hint can be found in a BIS paper by Mayer (1982), which served as input into the annual report. The author first acknowledged that fixed rates were feasible in a 'stable and predictable political and economic environment'. He then went on to observe that freely floating rates would also function smoothly in this hypothetical stable and predictable environment. In the real world, however, the imagined levels of political and economic stability were unlikely to prevail. Thus, the preconditions were lacking for either extreme regime to produce satisfactory results. This pointed to the need for periodic interventions guided by discretion and intuition rather than simple rules. A companion paper (Mayer and Taguchi 1983) concluded that intervention in the sterling-dollar, deutschemark-dollar and yen-dollar markets between 1974 and 1982, guided by just such official intuition and discretion, had exercised a modestly stabilising influence on exchange rates.

Over the subsequent two years, the sharp ongoing rise in the dollar became a major preoccupation. In pondering its causes and consequences, the BIS applied the analysis developed earlier to explain petro-dollar recycling and international bank lending to LDCs, but now to the availability of finance for the US current-account deficit. Analysts disagreed, the authors of the 1985 report observed, about whether the large capital inflows supporting the dollar resulted from the attractiveness of the investment climate in the United States or instead from large budget deficits that drove up interest rates. Either way, however, it was international banks, and not foreign direct investors or purchasers of bonds or equity, that were the principal conduit for capital flows to the United States. It followed that interest-rate-sensitive flows into dollar-denominated assets, intermediated by international banks, were the main factors driving exchange rates between the dollar and other currencies.

This state of affairs was desirable to the extent that bank-intermediated flows responded to supply-side reforms that improved the economic climate and created investment opportunities. It was undesirable insofar as it produced exchange rate movements that could become 'self-perpetuating' and to the extent that financial conditions and asset prices might unwind in disorderly fashion (BIS AR 1985: 8–9). What previously was perceived as a mechanism enabling imbalances in developing countries was now seen as facilitating global imbalances, including those of the country at the centre of the system, the United States. In this sense there was a straight line from the Bank's concern about the operation of the interbank Euro-currency market in the 1970s to its analysis of the developing-country debt crisis in the 1980s and now to its interpretation of global imbalances. This emphasis on cross-border bank flows and their connection with global imbalances would become an enduring focus.

The 1986 report was another step forward in analytical quality and presentation.[55] The authors first supplemented their new focus on bank-intermediated flows with their second consistent theme: underappreciated risks in the global banking system.[56] Their question was 'whether the [financial] institutions involved are themselves fully aware of the risks they are incurring and are taking them properly into account'. Prompted in part by the recommendations of the Lamfalussy Group, regulators had been hardening capital requirements with the goal of giving the banks, especially money-centre banks weakened by the developing-country debt crisis, a more generous cushion against risks. At the same time, however, the banks were inventive in circumventing regulation. As a result, 'the above-mentioned strengthening of the banks' capital base may be more apparent than real' (BIS AR 1986: 5).

A plausible trigger for financial distress, the authors reiterated, was the disorderly correction of global imbalances ('large current-account imbalances' was the term used at the time). The Plaza Accord negotiated in 1985, the Bank argued, had effectively and appropriately stemmed the rise of the dollar, which had 'taken on a life of [its] own' (BIS AR 1986: 184), becoming dangerously overvalued.[57] But since current accounts were slow to respond to exchange rate changes, imbalances remained, as did the risk of their disorderly correction if financing suddenly dried up. The implication was that large imbalances were best avoided, although, as the report acknowledged, that this was easier said than done.

Moreover, the BIS failed to single out policies that might have been pursued in earlier years to avoid the problem. It pointed to the desirability of better coordinating monetary and fiscal policies across countries, but it was not specific about the content of that coordination. It did not describe what would have constituted appropriate international adjustments in prior years, evidently reflecting disagreements between the Bank's US and European stakeholders about the role of budget deficits and anti-inflationary monetary policies in the emergence of global imbalances. Lamfalussy, now General Manager of the BIS, drew the obvious conclusion: 'We are much better at crisis handling than at crisis prevention.'[58]

A related issue was whether such attempts to coordinate domestic policies ex ante and foreign exchange intervention ex post should be regularised through an agreement to hold currencies within exchange rate target zones. The BIS cited the stability of exchange rates within the EMS as evidence that variability could be limited if governments and central banks committed to the objective. But it reiterated its scepticism about pegged exchange rates, now in the context of target zones. It questioned whether monetary policy could be credibly subordinated, in practice, to exchange rate policy, disregarding other domestic objectives.[59] Where this was not possible, it warned, international policy coordination could be counter-productive (echoing contemporaneous academic work such as Rogoff 1985). Had an agreement to cooperate been in place in 1983–5, the authors observed, the US authorities might have been compelled to counter dollar appreciation with monetary expansion, fuelling global inflation with un-desirable consequences all around.

Moreover, an agreement to hold currencies within target zones that collapsed in short order owing to the reluctance of governments to subordinate to it the other objectives of policy would cause reputational damage. As the report put it, 'premature implementation of even a watered-down version of target zones, at a time of major payments imbalances between the countries concerned, is also fraught with danger, since failure on the part of the authorities to live up to their explicit or implicit commitments could have an equally destabilising effect' (BIS AR 1986: 186). The conclusion was sound, but what to do instead was unclear.

The 1987 report, published in the aftermath of the Louvre Agreement, again fretted over the US current-account deficit but also expressed scepti-cism about the feasibility of more extensive international policy coordina-tion to correct it (BIS AR 1987: 7). Its successor cautioned further against 'excessive reliance on monetary policy' when attempting to stabilise cur-rencies. It pointed to the need for supportive action by the fiscal authorities to ensure that stabilisation initiatives were sustainable (BIS AR 1988: 164), reflecting disappointment that more fiscal action had not been taken and that interventions at the Plaza and Louvre had not delivered a smooth realignment of currencies. The deeper question, of course, was whether governments, and specifically a US government that could finance its deficit by issuing debt denominated in its own currency, were prepared to adjust fiscal policies in order to stabilise exchange rates at desired levels.

The 1988 report offered additional reflections on the role of capital flows. Notwithstanding its concerns with the operation of the international interbank market, the BIS view of international capital mobility remained cautiously positive. Capital flows, it observed, were important for the smooth operation of the floating-rate system, since they provided financing for current-account balances, which fluctuated significantly over the seasons and year to year. At the same time, it cautioned, 'short-term capital flows, including transactions in long-term assets for short-term speculative purposes, may at times have a strong destabilising impact on the exchange market. Moreover, it is certainly true that, as a result of the increasing global integration of national markets, these destabilising capital flows can assume vast proportions.'[60] The solution, the Bank insisted, was not restrictions on capital mobility but rather more stable and better aligned national policies (BIS AR 1988: 177–8). Given the Bank's historical embrace of macroprudential policies, one might think that there would have been some sympathy for the idea of capital controls as macroprudential measures. However, this was not the case.

In 1988 there were heightened strains within the EMS, as the decline in the dollar led the Deutsche Mark to strengthen against the currencies of its EMS partners in the phenomenon known as 'dollar-Deutsche Mark polarisation' (McCauley 1997). The Bank noted that nominal convergence within the EMS remained incomplete. But with the relaxation of capital controls as part of the single market, realignments had become problematic, since expectations of devaluation and revaluation might now precipitate enormous anticipatory capital flows. The Bank recommended that countries allow their currencies to move more freely within their existing ±2.5 per cent fluctuation bands as a way to 'increase the cost of speculation and minimise its effect on interest rates', while remaining agnostic about whether this would be enough to sustain the system (BIS AR 1988: 160).

If rising capital mobility could not be reconciled with exchange rate stability, the Bank suggested, then in Europe there was a case for moving to monetary union.[61] This conclusion anticipated remarks regarding the fragile stability of rates in the exchange rate mechanism (ERM) made by Lamfalussy in his capacity as a member of the Delors Committee in January 1989. 'I am extremely preoccupied by what might happen to the EMS, not in three years' time', the General Manager observed, 'but in one year and that is very much along the line of the argument because we have now gone very far in liberalising capital movements … This liberalisation is happening in a world environment where expectations may run in all possible directions, where the speed of transmission of interest rate movements is extremely speedy, and because also I do see basic imbalances in terms of current accounts within the EMS … It is for this reason that I would be in favour of a first stage which could be implemented as quickly as possible and not in a two or three-year distant future, but starting this autumn or at least at the end of the year.'[62]

Lamfalussy's comments about the fragility of the EMS and the urgency of planning for monetary union were made in private so as not to excite the markets. In its 1988 annual report, the BIS was predictably more cautious. The argument for monetary union was generously hedged by a discussion of the challenges. The authors flagged the importance of arrangements to ensure that price stability would be the central objective of a new European central bank. They observed monetary union would not be secured by currency arrangements alone; although oblique, this was a reference to the need for some pooling of fiscal authority.[63] 'Clearly, many far-reaching political issues are involved,' was the Bank's understated gloss on the point (BIS AR 1988: 161). '[T]he essence of the problem,' it observed, 'is the need for hard political decisions involving sacrifices of national sovereignty. It is by no means clear that governments and electorates are prepared to make these.'

5.6 Crisis to Crisis

The EMS crisis came as a shock to the BIS as it did to Europe. Real-time crisis-management discussions took place in the European Community Committee of Governors, which met at the BIS but was (of course) distinct from it.[64] In addition, the BIS convened a special meeting in December 1992 of high-level representatives of all countries participating in its reporting system for international banking statistics to investigate the role of banks in the crisis.[65] Attendees concluded that commercial banks had not been active position-takers; rather, it was hedge funds and other non-bank investors that had actively shorted the embattled currencies.[66] Banks, however, were the source of the credit that speculators used to finance their positions, and they had profited from the surge in volumes. To be sure, some banks acting as market-makers in foreign exchange-related options and derivatives had suffered losses because volatility exceeded the levels predicted by their models. But with the dollar-Deutsche Mark and dollar-yen rates remaining stable, the resulting losses did not undermine the solvency of major financial institutions. Still, delegates to this meeting acknowledged that there was no guarantee that these major rates would exhibit similar stability in the future. The episode thus pointed up the need to address the derivatives exposures of banks as well as market-makers.[67]

The BIS addressed the broader implications in its 1993 report. The ERM crisis was described as one of 'the most significant events in the international monetary system since the breakdown of the Bretton Woods arrangements twenty years ago' (BIS AR 1993: 182), echoing a phrase the Bank had used in 1978. Turning to causes, the report highlighted the 'insidious fact' of inadequate nominal convergence, which made for weak current accounts in the United Kingdom, Spain, Italy and Sweden.[68] It pointed to doubts about the depth of the official commitment to the arrangement, doubts that rose further in the wake of the Danish referendum on 2 June in which that nation's voters rejected the Maastricht Treaty. It highlighted the role of tight monetary and loose fiscal policies in Germany following reunification, which drove up interest rates and drew capital from other countries.[69] Foreign exchange market intervention, it warned, would stabilise exchange rates only if backed by sustained changes in interest rates. But the Bank warned of limited political tolerance of high interest rates, given 17 per cent unemployment in Ireland and indexed mortgages in the United Kingdom. It observed the growing virulence of contagion and the danger that one devaluation would fuel expectations of others.

This crisis, like other crises, did not have a single cause; rather, it reflected a confluence of factors. The BIS emphasised above all high international capital mobility and 'the scale of the pressures which can now be brought to bear' on currency pegs, not solely in Europe but especially there, given the removal of capital controls in conjunction with completion of the single market (BIS AR 1993: 196). It reiterated that orderly realignments were no longer possible, since even quiet negotiations could now unleash a tidal wave of capital flows. The implication was that European countries would have to accept greater exchange rate flexibility, 'including the floating of two major currencies' (meaning sterling and the lira). The Bank appended the standard caution that floating was no panacea and that exchange rates could range far 'out of line with the requirements of domestic and external equilibrium' (BIS AR 1993: 224). But the implication was clear.

In principle, European countries might instead choose to 'reinforce [their] . . . exchange rate commitments, and speed up their move towards monetary union' (BIS AR 1993: 223). But as the report sagely judged the prospects for monetary union, 'Some might find such a prospect acceptable, others not.' One is reminded of the Bank's early response to the collapse of the Bretton Woods system, when it acknowledged the growing difficulty of maintaining exchange rate pegs but also expressed reservations about more flexible rates, providing little guidance on the way forward.

The Bank's 1994 report elaborated the challenges posed by high and rising capital mobility. The explosive increase in flows reflected financial deregulation and capital-account liberalisation, on the one hand, and advances in data processing and communications, on the other. As a result, gross flows now outstripped even those of the period before the Second World War. International capital markets also differed from those of that earlier historical era by the range of financial assets available and by virtue of the more active role of institutional investors, notably mutual funds and pension funds, whose actions complicated capital-flow management. The Bank supplemented these observations with an extensive analysis of cross-border banking and of transactions in various new and novel derivative securities. The expansion of capital flows, it observed, now extended not only to new instruments but also to new countries, given the negotiation of Brady deals by a growing range of emerging markets.

Much as the 1971 report commending the operation of the Bretton Woods system appeared just before the final crisis of that regime, the 1994 report appeared just months prior to the Mexican crisis. In fairness, the Bank anticipated the tendency for capital flows to emerging markets to fuel excessive consumption and produce real exchange rate overvaluation. Asia, it observed, was better positioned than Latin America because a larger share of capital inflows took the form of foreign direct investment and because inflows into Asia tended to finance investment rather than consumption. The report again cautioned that the growth of capital flows called into question the ability of central banks and governments to hold currencies within predetermined fluctuation bands, given the absence of an overarching exchange rate commitment like that of the gold-standard era.

The timeliness of this observation was quickly pointed up by the Tequila crisis. The BIS was actively involved in preparing for that crisis, which suggests that the silence of its 1994 report was intended to avoid exciting investors. Already in November 1993, with encouragement from the Federal Reserve, the BIS approached G10 central banks about assembling a $6 billion support package for the Bank of Mexico as a cushion against turbulence surrounding US Congressional votes on the North American Free Trade Agreement (NAFTA). The Mexican central bank quickly declined this facility as unnecessary. The following July the Fed again approached the BIS with a request to reactivate the facility in response to investor unrest over the Zapatista uprising in Chiapas.[70] This time the initiative, although meeting with resistance from other members of the G10, went ahead. The Bank of Mexico accepted the terms and conditions of the credit but declined to activate it on the grounds that conditions in Mexican financial markets made it unnecessary. When in January 1995 it then became urgent to assemble a $15 billion package, the BIS agreed to organise $5 billion from other G10 central banks to supplement the $9 billion stumped up by the United States and the Can$1.5 billion contributed by Canada.[71] By February, this $5 billion had become $10 billion.[72]

The Bank's assessment of Mexico's experience in its 1995 report in many ways anticipated the Asian crisis two years later. In contrast to earlier crises, the BIS observed, Mexico's crisis did not reflect large budget deficits financed by capital inflows; the Mexican government had run primary surpluses averaging 5.3 per cent of GDP between 1983 and 1992. The government had undertaken structural reforms enhancing the economy's flexibility and responsiveness to market signals and was about to enter into a free-trade agreement with the United States. Economic fundamentals were 'healthy by many standards' (BIS AR 1995: 160–1).[73]

Instead, the Mexican crisis was a capital-account-centred crisis fuelled by financial inflows subject to abrupt reversal. If there was a lesson, it was that capital flows had been unnecessarily encouraged by a pegged exchange rate adopted as an expedient for bringing down inflation. The peg had led investors to underestimate currency risk. That the Mexican authorities had failed to adopt 'macroprudential' policies limiting the expansion of domestic credit accentuated the resulting imbalances and heightened financial risks. They relied on volatile portfolio investment, much of it directed towards the country by US mutual funds, over more stable foreign direct investment. They responded to the reluctance of investors to hold long-term peso-denominated securities by issuing short-term, dollar-linked securities, known as *tesobonos*, heightening the fragility of the capital account.[74]

The bottom line, once again, was that international capital flows were a mixed blessing. In its report the BIS acknowledged the all-but-universal tendency for countries to move towards more open capital accounts in the course of economic and financial development. But now it also conceded a role for temporary capital controls on what would today be called 'macroprudential grounds' (BIS AR 1995: 152).[75] This concession was a significant shift from as recently as 1988, when the Bank had opposed resorting to capital controls in response to problems created by international capital flows (see above). The ongoing increase in the volume of flows was presumably one factor prompting the rethink. In addition, in 1988 the problems created by capital flows had centred on the advanced economies. Now, in contrast, emerging markets were centrally implicated. Supervision and regulation were weaker in emerging markets, creating a case for using controls to pre-empt those problems by stopping capital flows at the border.

The BIS also emphasised the growing size, complexity and connectedness of the global banking system. It pointed to the role of weak banks in Mexico and Argentina and warned of bank fragility as a factor in a prospective Brazilian crisis. Loan portfolios, it observed, were weighted too heavily towards government-directed credits. Loan concentrations were excessive, and the connections between banks and commercial firms were too close. The risks were greatest in countries experiencing credit booms, and especially in those where liquidity flowed disproportionately into the housing market. While microprudential supervision was too timid to rein in these risks, 'macroprudential' policies were prominent by their absence.

In the advanced countries, by implication, these problems of internal governance and external supervision were less severe. But risks were by no means absent, given how cross-border and non-bank competition was squeezing profits, giving banks an incentive to gamble in order to survive. The salience of these observations would be underscored, soon enough, by events in East Asia and then by the global financial crisis in the United States and Europe.

5.7 From Exchange Rate Stability to Financial Stability

As a result of these events, the Bank's focus shifted decisively from exchange rate stability to banking and financial stability. While the shift was a function of the recent crises in Europe, Mexico and Argentina, it may have also reflected the appointment of William White as BIS Economic Adviser, White bringing to the BIS a laser-like focus on financial-stability issues.[76]

The 1997 annual report, which went to press in May, warned of financial weaknesses in Indonesia, Malaysia, the Philippines and Thailand, all countries that had experienced rapid credit growth and whose banking systems were exposed to the property market. As causes of these problems, the report pointed to lack of experience on the part of loan officers in evaluating credit risk, inadequate prudential oversight and expectations of official support. But it now cited, in addition, the tendency for banks in countries with liberalised capital accounts to incur dangerous currency mismatches and the role of pegged exchange rates in encouraging foreign investors to lend in ignorance of these risks. It pointed to what became known as the financial cycle, namely the tendency for banks to expand their lending with increases in the market valuation of the assets held as collateral, and the strongly procyclical implications of that behaviour. It emphasised the importance of tightening prudential guidelines and cited favourably the practice in some countries of placing higher reserve requirements on foreign short-term bank deposits than on other credits. It recommended reducing loan-to-value ratios when real estate markets were booming but could mention only Hong Kong as an economy that had successfully utilised such measures. It encouraged governments to move towards more flexible exchange rates as a way of creating the perception of two-way risk and deterring excessive capital inflows.

Tighter capital controls were notably absent from the menu of policy responses recommended in its 1997 report. This may have reflected political sensitivities, 1997 being when the IMF was making the case for further capital account liberalisation.[77] Behind the scenes, however, another attitude was evident. In late 1996 and early 1997 the Basel Committee on Banking Supervision drafted what became the Core Principles for Effective Banking Supervision in an effort to establish benchmarks for sound banking supervision.[78] The Core Principles were intended to apply not just to G10 countries but also to emerging markets. Their development was accompanied by other initiatives to bring emerging markets into policy discussions previously dominated by the G10.[79] These included the admission of nine emerging markets as shareholding members of the BIS in 1996-7, and by the establishment of a working party on financial stability, including representatives of both the G10 countries and emerging markets.

The result was a more nuanced view of the relationship of capital controls to financial stability. As Mario Draghi, chairman of the G10 deputies, described the working party's conclusions to his colleagues in April 1997, capital-account liberalisation remained desirable, but as part of an integrated strategy in which prudential arrangements were strengthened and the macroeconomic environment was stable and robust.[80] Thus, the retention of controls was justifiable if the macroeconomic and structural preconditions necessary in order for the benefits of capital-account liberalisation to exceed the costs were not yet present. In addition, there was support in some circles for the reintroduction of controls for a limited period under exceptional circumstances (not specified).

It is clear from the tone of the working party's report that there was disagreement within the central-banking community about how rapidly countries should proceed to capital-account convertibility and the circumstances under which exceptions might be permitted. This may have been why none of this thoughtful discussion made it into the Bank's 1997 report.

5.8 The Emergence of the BIS View

The Asian crisis was the next obvious turning point. BIS staff prepared a note for G10 governors analysing both country-specific and systemic aspects, and much of this analysis made its way into the 1998 annual report.[81] The following year's annual report, emphasising the pervasiveness of problems in banking and financial systems, contained the Bank's most strongly worded endorsement yet of selective controls:

> While current problems in the financial systems of emerging market countries were primarily domestically generated, international capital flows clearly exacerbated them. The underlying reality is that even flows that are modest from the perspective of international capital markets can have highly disruptive effects on small economies. This suggests that such countries should dismantle controls on short-term inflows only very cautiously, particularly if there are doubts (and there normally will be) about the inherent stability of the domestic financial system. (BIS AR 1999: 147)

The 1999 report then went on to advocate wider use of market-based prudential instruments, such as differential reserve requirements to discourage short-term foreign-currency-denominated borrowing. It again endorsed greater exchange rate flexibility to discourage carry trades, in what effectively constituted a repudiation of the earlier IMF-led status quo.

This crisis, together with the failure of the Greenwich, Connecticut-based hedge fund Long-Term Capital Management, led the BIS to adopt a still more critical view of international capital markets. Banks in the advanced countries, it observed, had been encouraged to engage in 'imprudent lending' by the existence of a safety net and shrinking profit margins. Moreover, investors and institutions that lent to emerging economies through securities markets might be inclined to cut and run, to a greater extent than international banks that had built relationships with the borrowing governments and/or enterprises.

In a passage whose full implications would become evident only in 2007, the 1999 report highlighted the importance of market liquidity and the limitations of banks' internal risk models in the face of 'non-linear payoffs' (BIS AR 1999: 149). It questioned whether it was wise to shift responsibility for banking supervision to self-standing agencies while still making the central bank responsible for overall financial stability and the provision of emergency liquidity to financial markets.[82] It alluded, in this, the first year of the euro, to the dangers of monetary union without banking union: as it antiseptically put it, to 'the additional complications posed by having a supranational central bank interacting with diverse national supervisors' (BIS AR 1999: 149).

Finally, the last BIS annual report of the twentieth century contained what may have been the first full-throated statement of the BIS view of low interest rates. Economic instability and imbalances have many causes, the authors observed, but prominent among them is an extended period of low interest rates that can heighten vulnerabilities in advanced economies as well as emerging markets. Interest rates had been 'unusually low' in the United States in the first half of the 1990s. These accommodating monetary conditions were transmitted to Asian emerging markets that pegged their currencies to the dollar. Similarly, the 'very low levels' to which Japanese policy rates had been pushed contributed materially to the difficulties of Japanese banks and spilled over to neighbouring countries.[83]

The consequences included an overly rapid expansion of credit, falling lending standards and increases in risk-taking (BIS AR 1999: 6). The prices of financial assets had been pushed up unsustainably. The capital now flooding into emerging Asia owing to these low US and Japanese interest rates could equally well flood out again. Better, the implication followed, would have been for the United States and Japan to normalise the level of interest rates and to rely less on monetary policy for supporting their economies. Also better would be to somehow reform the international monetary and financial system to avoid this excessive elasticity of credit conditions.

In 2000 Andrew Crockett, in his role as BIS General Manager, gave a high-profile speech widely interpreted, both internally and externally, as giving the green light to additional analytical work on the relationship between monetary stability and financial stability.[84] The 2001 annual report correspondingly highlighted the dangers of the financial cycle and related these to the conduct of monetary policy. While financial factors had long played a role in business cycle fluctuations, the report argued, that role had grown more prominent with the liberalisation of capital markets. In the good old days, an accommodating monetary stance adopted in response to weak growth could be accompanied by tighter controls on bank lending, which limited increases in debt and leverage and the associated financial excesses and imbalances. But in the deregulated financial system of the early twenty-first century, this was no longer the case. Now asset prices, in general, and property prices, in particular, responded disproportionately to changes in money- and credit-market conditions (BIS AR 2001: 123–4). The report pointed to a series of amplification mechanisms that worked to accentuate the financial cycle. These included behavioural quirks such as 'disaster myopia' and 'poorly anchored' extrapolative expectations; approaches to risk management that mechanically projected current conditions into the future; the slow reaction of credit-rating agencies and procyclical impact of their rating adjustments; and distorted accounting and regulatory rules. The authors recommended changes in regulatory practice to address these concerns, such as counter-cyclical adjustments in capital ratios and dynamic provisioning *à la* the Bank of Spain. They also raised the possibility that monetary policy should be used to lean against the financial cycle and not just to target inflation.[85]

And with this, the modern BIS view of exchange rates, capital flows and the financial cycle was effectively complete.

5.9 Coda

The balance of the 2000s was dominated by the build-up of the financial vulnerabilities that set the stage for the global crisis and then by the crisis itself. These developments deserve a treatment of their own and are analysed in other contributions to this volume. Relevant here are how the BIS view shaped the institution's interpretation of the crisis, and how the crisis in turn influenced the BIS view of international monetary and financial reform.

The BIS was initially sanguine about the performance of the international monetary system in the crisis. Its 2008 annual report provided a generally upbeat assessment of the role of the exchange rate system, noting that the foreign exchange market had been relatively stable and resilient in the face of financial stress, a happy outcome that reflected the diversity of participants in the market and the improved risk-management practices of investors and dealers. Insofar as the roots of the crisis lay elsewhere – in the originate-and-distribute model of securitisation, inadequate bank capitalisation, flawed risk management and the procyclical responses of the rating agencies, for example – the international monetary system was not the problem, nor was international monetary reform the solution.

There was, to be sure, the view that global imbalances were central to the crisis, an argument repeated in the Bank's 2009 report. The authors pointed to global imbalances as a source of fragility and a leading indicator that things could go badly wrong (BIS AR 2009: 5). The ease with which they financed their external imbalances allowed advanced countries such as the United States to crawl out further on an unstable financial limb, increasing their leverage and indebtedness. And there were two sides to the global-imbalances coin, as noted in the Bank's 2010 report. In particular, emerging markets, by absorbing US treasury and agency securities in the course of accumulating international reserves, had 'contributed to the mispricing of assets and to the global spread of the crisis' (BIS AR 2010: 12).

The structure of the international monetary and financial system contributed to these imbalances, given the observed reluctance of governments to allow real exchange rates to adjust.[86] Surplus countries could intervene, accumulating additional reserves as a way of preventing their real exchange rates from appreciating. In turn, this placed the burden of adjustment entirely on deficit countries.[87] But real exchange rate changes having costs as well as benefits, imposing all the costs on the deficit countries rendered them similarly reluctant to adjust. This impasse created an argument for international coordination of the monetary and fiscal policies responsible for different values of the real exchange rate, the advantages of coordination being a long-standing theme, and indeed a rationale for the very existence, of the BIS. But the authors noted also another long-standing BIS theme, namely that coordination is easier in theory than practice.[88]

Importantly, the 2009 report had highlighted the role of low interest rates in fuelling credit booms not just in the United States, and not just in the advanced countries, but globally (BIS AR 2009: 6). It emphasised that low rates encouraged financial firms to take on risk in the hope of generating the returns needed to stay profitable. Low rates boosted spending on interest-rate-sensitive sectors and activities such as construction. They encouraged households to take on not just mortgage debt but also revolving credit. The Bank's 2010 report expanded this critique into a stand-alone chapter, whose title posed the question: 'Low interest rates: do the risks outweigh the rewards?' While no answer was given, the implication was clear.

As explained in that chapter, low interest rates in the advanced economies, and specifically the United States, were then transmitted to other countries, for two reasons. First, international contracts were denominated in dollars and therefore subject to arbitrage. Second, many emerging markets, in their wisdom, pegged their currencies to the dollar. These observations both pointed to directions for international monetary reform, although the point was not pursued.

Over time, one could detect in BIS research and in the interventions of staff at international meetings a growing scepticism that global imbalances were at the root of the crisis. Borio and Disyatat (2011), for example, challenged the presumption of a link between current-account imbalances and the crisis. They observed that the bulk of financial inflows into the United States, the principal current-account deficit country, came from advanced economies (the United Kingdom and the euro area) whose current accounts were roughly balanced, rather than from emerging-market countries running current-account surpluses. Hence, there was little trace in the data of a global savings glut placing downward pressure on interest rates, causing institutional investors to stretch for yield, and leading to a build-up of risk. Insofar as credit aggregates had expanded and liquidity had flowed into riskier assets, these developments reflected not excessive savings but the procyclicality of the global financial system, owing to the positive feedbacks intrinsic to the financial cycle.[89]

The 2009 and 2010 annual reports did not include separate chapters on or even much discussion of exchange rates and international monetary reform. But in 2011 the report featured a chapter on the role of the international monetary system in the crisis. It again questioned the traditional emphasis on global imbalances and sought to shift the focus from net to gross capital flows. The chapter emphasised that large financial inflows matched by outflows can occur even in the absence of current-account imbalances. When they did, they could pose risks to the balance sheets of financial institutions and national economies, insofar as those flows gave rise to currency and maturity mismatches, and because the resulting assets were held by different agents (viz. pension funds versus others) whose claims were not interchangeable. At the same time, the report pointed out the difficulties in measuring such systemic risks accurately (BIS AR 2011: 95 – building on i.a. Cecchetti, Fender and McGuire 2010).

In the self-conscious culmination of this intellectual evolution, the Bank's 2015 report advanced a 'different perspective', departing from the 'common diagnosis' that the fundamental problem was the chronic nature of global imbalances and the asymmetry between surplus and deficit countries. The central problem instead was the tendency for the international system to 'heighten the risk of financial imbalances' and produce 'unsustainable credit and asset price booms that overstretch balance sheets and can lead to financial crises and serious macroeconomic damage. These imbalances occur simultaneously across countries,' the report observed, 'deriving strength from global monetary ease and cross-border financing' (BIS AR 2015: 83). This, then, was a definitive statement of the BIS view that the intrinsic flaw in the international monetary and financial system was not its asymmetry but rather its 'excessive elasticity'.

The mechanisms underlying this excessive elasticity were several. '[P]owerful waves' of freely mobile financial capital had a tendency to 'wash across currencies and borders, carrying financial conditions across the globe' (BIS AR 2015: 83). The monetary and financial influence of the key international currencies, notably the US dollar, extended beyond their issuers' national borders. The Fed's reluctance to take these repercussions into account therefore constituted a problem for the operation of the system. Moreover, the extent of these cross-border spillovers pointed to the limited insulation properties of flexible exchange rates and the destabilising effects of large exchange rate changes, facts that rendered other central banks reluctant to countenance large interest-rate differentials vis-à-vis the issuers of the main international currencies. This reluctance further heightened the transmission of financial conditions across borders.

This powerful summary statement was somewhat less forthcoming, predictably, about what to do in response. Given the emphasis in preceding annual reports on the role of pegged exchange rates as a transmission belt for credit booms, one might have expected a stronger call for exchange rate flexibility. Given the less than efficacious role of dollar-denominated debts, one might have anticipated recommendations for proactive measures to speed the move to a less dollar-centric international system. Given the tendency for capital flows to 'wash across ... borders', one might have expected a more explicitly sympathetic endorsement of capital controls.

Instead, the authors emphasised the need to 'adjust domestic policy frameworks', meaning that policy should be tailored to avoid or at least limit credit booms and busts, and not merely target inflation and seek to moderate the business cycle (BIS AR 2015: 94–6). Returning to a long-standing BIS theme, they reiterated the desirability of strengthening international cooperation so as to take better account of cross-border spillovers, feedbacks and exposures.

All of which was easier said than done. As the report noted, in understated fashion, 'It may be difficult to go beyond enlightened self-interest and to revisit rules of the game more broadly.' Although the dollar and a handful of other key currencies play disproportionately important international roles, the central banks issuing them have domestic mandates, making policy adjustments on behalf of other countries politically fraught. By implication, not only adjusting the goals and execution of policy but also seeking to coordinate policies internationally might be problematic. Still, the authors ended on an optimistic note, observing how '[t]his interpretation of domestic mandates contrasts sharply with successful international cooperation in the realm of financial regulation and supervision. There, national mandates have not precluded extensive international cooperation and the development of global rules. A better understanding of the shortcomings of the current IMFS [international monetary and financial system] would already be a big step forward' (BIS AR 2015: 99).

Understanding the shortcomings of the current system and the nature and extent of interdependencies is well and good. But whether it would be enough to facilitate international cooperation, much less systematic reform, remains an open question.

5.10 Conclusion

The BIS, even more than other international financial institutions, has focused throughout its history on the connections between monetary and financial stability. This focus is ingrained in its DNA. The creation of the BIS was a response to tension in the 1920s between the monetary constraints of the gold standard, on the one hand, and the financial challenges of transferring German reparations across the exchanges, on the other. The Bank's activities in the era following the collapse of Bretton Woods, the period considered here, reflected a similar focus. They were concerned with reconciling a system of stable exchange rates with financial stability, and then with reconciling a stable system of exchange rates with financial stability, to paraphrase the Second Amendment of the IMF's Articles of Agreement.[90]

Addressing these connections required conceptualising three aspects of the international monetary and financial system. First, it was important to understand the operating properties, both strengths and weaknesses, of the international monetary system. Second, BIS researchers had to characterise the salient features of the international financial system, notably the international interbank market, which meant gathering heretofore unavailable data before proceeding to analysis. Third, they had to understand the interaction of the monetary and financial systems.

The BIS's views of these issues evolved over time. BIS researchers, like other researchers, responded to events. Indeed, the idea that there was such a thing as the BIS view, even at a point in time, is a useful abstraction. Economists do not always agree, not even economists in small and cohesive international financial organisations. The BIS is a creature of its shareholders, which may lead staff and management to temper, if not their analysis, then at least their rhetoric. Much of the business of the Bank goes on in its committees, where its staff is one voice among many and in which it has limited agenda-setting power.

That said, the history recounted here suggests that BIS staff and management, when they dissent, can make a difference. But dissent has costs, so it occurs only occasionally, generally in response to extreme circumstances – that is to say, crises.

Over time, the BIS view of the international monetary system, such as it is, evolved from highlighting asymmetries in the adjustment mechanism to emphasising the excessive elasticity of its liquidity provision and the threat posed by this excessive elasticity to financial stability.[91] It evolved from channelling the textbook view of countercyclical monetary and fiscal policies to highlighting the risks to financial stability created by an extended period of low interest rates. Throughout, the BIS was an advocate of macroprudential measures, ideally coordinated internationally, as a means of reconciling monetary and fiscal activism with financial stability.

But in contrast to efforts at fostering cooperation in the development of macroprudential policies, where the BIS and its committees made headway, progress in coordinating monetary policies and addressing the 'excessive-elasticity problem', whether on an ad hoc basis or through fundamental reform of the international monetary system, has been notably less. The narrow central-bank mandates that are the political quid pro quo for delegating monetary-policy authority are invoked as a binding constraint. Lack of agreement on the nature of feasible and desirable reforms is a perennial obstacle. What to do about this conundrum is an enduring problem.

Notes

1. While I supplement my discussion with material from archives and secondary sources, it is the annual reports that are my organising framework. An advantage of this focus is that the Bank's annual reports, uniquely perhaps among the publications of other international financial organisations, are not vetted by the Board or members prior to their presentation and publication. Thus, the views of staff and management, as expressed in the annual reports, are not necessarily the same as those of the central banks that are members of the BIS or the committees through which those central banks deliberate and, on occasion, issue their own reports. Except where noted otherwise, I do not also attribute the views described below to the member banks. For the moment, I ignore the question of whether an organisation or institution like the BIS can 'have a view', as opposed to its employees espousing a variety of different views. For more on this, see below.
2. Where early, in this context, means the first thirty years or so (1930–1960).
3. This is the central argument of Eichengreen (1998), Chapter 4.
4. For perspectives on this process from political theory, philosophy and business, see Haas (1992), Vahamaa (2013) and Kantor (2011).
5. The quote is from the Bank's 2015 annual report, discussed further in Section 5.9.
6. Before that, as Bederman (1988: 103) puts it, 'the Bank's activities remained limited. Indeed, at this time there was no need to expand its functions.'
7. Lamfalussy was Economic Adviser to the BIS from 1976 to 1981 and Assistant General Manager from 1981 to 1985, before ascending to the post of General Manager. For more on his role and influence, see below.

8. Lamfalussy, A., Note to the G10 Governors, 'The current position and policies of the G10 countries' commercial banks: some macro-economic and "macro-prudential" issues', In BISA 7.18(15) – *Papers Lamfalussy*, LAM 35, 89. Before that, in 1980, there was mention of 'macro-prudential concerns' in the deliberations of the Lamfalussy-chaired Working Party on Possible Approaches to Constraining the Growth of International Bank Lending (see below).

9. The focus here on the lack of common conceptual frameworks and domestic political constraints as obstacles to international cooperation, and on the role of history in shaping conceptual outlooks, draws on Eichengreen and Uzan (1992).

10. The quote is from the page of the Bank's website where the Board of Directors is described.

11. See on this issue also Chapter 4 (Andrew Baker) of this volume.

12. And of the absence of adequate alternatives. Special Drawing Rights were created in 1969, and a first allocation was distributed to IMF members starting in 1970. But disbursement of that allocation was spread over three years, and it was too small to dent countries' dependence on dollar reserves. See Bird (1998).

13. Other documents pointed to a recognition within the institution of the need for at least a modicum of greater exchange rate flexibility. For example, Milton Gilbert, Economic Adviser to the Bank from 1960 to 1975, consistently advocated increasing the price of gold, which would have entailed devaluing the dollar against gold if not necessarily against the currencies of other countries – see Gilbert (1968).

14. The Committee of Twenty, formally the Committee on Reform of the International Monetary System and Related Issues, was established in July 1972 on the basis of a resolution adopted by the Board of Governors of the IMF, and made up of representatives of the IMF's 20 executive directors. The committee issued its recommendations for the orderly evolution of the international monetary system two years later, without much substantive effect, official attention having been diverted towards the oil crisis, development challenges and the deficits of less-developed countries. See McCauley and Schenk (2014).

15. 'The Euro-Currency Market', confidential report to the Committee of Twenty by René Larre, 3 March 1973, BISA, 7:18(23), Milton Gilbert Papers, box GILB1. See also Toniolo and Clement (2005: 468). In early 1971 BIS governors called a series of meetings of their deputies to discuss possible joint supervision of the Eurodollar market, which was seen as creating growing problems for monetary control. Later that year the Standing Committee on the Euro-currency Market was established under the umbrella of the BIS; creation of this committee had been recommended in a subsequent memo also attributed to Larre: 'Report of the President's ad hoc group on the Euro-currency market', 18 April 1971, BISA, 7.18(23), Milton Gilbert Papers, box GILB1. This group evolved into today's Committee on the Global Financial System. These efforts to arrange cooperative management of the Euro-currency market were unavailing. Continental European governments favoured stricter regulation, while the UK government and the Bank of England opposed international measures that might stifle the growth of Euro-currency business, London being the main centre in which it took place.

16. Op cit, p. 1.

17. See e.g. Eichengreen and Gupta (2018).

18. Three-quarters of those liabilities being in dollars, while an even larger share of the increase in liabilities in the course of the previous year took that form (BIS AR 1973: 154, 161).
19. BIS AR 1973: 159. There was no mention (yet) of the threat that large loans to developing countries might pose to the stability of money-centre banks or the difficulties that syndicated lending might create for debt restructuring.
20. The joint float reflected the intense desire of European governments, mindful of their earlier monetary history, to maintain pegged rates or at least narrow bands within Europe. Experience with subsequent arrangements (the Snake, the Snake in the Tunnel) was not entirely happy (Eichengreen 1998).
21. Much as they had in 1931.
22. The term in quotes is evidently from Williamson (1977), who was involved, as an adviser to the IMF, in the deliberations of the C20.
23. Alexandre Lamfalussy for one had concluded years earlier, even before the collapse of the Bretton Woods system, that greater exchange-rate flexibility was both inevitable and desirable (Maes 2011b). Lamfalussy joined the BIS in January 1976, and the 1976 annual report, issued in June, bore his imprint. More generally, Lamfalussy was more concerned with financial-stability issues than Milton Gilbert, his predecessor as Economic Adviser, who focused more on the real economy and country analysis.
24. In the US case, it observed, adjustment was helped along by strong recovery from the oil-shock-induced recession.
25. On this, see also Chapter 1 (Harold James) of this volume.
26. Euro-currency Standing Committee, 'Chairman's report on policy problems related to the growth of the Euro-currency market and international lending since the oil price increase', copy dated 4 July 1978, In BISA 7.18(15) – *Papers Lamfalussy*, LAM 20, p. 4.
27. 'Chairman's progress report on the activities of the Working Party on Possible Approaches to Constraining the Growth of International Bank Lending', 28 November 1979, In BISA, 7.18(15) – *Papers Lamfalussy*, LAM 25, 67. Even when more timely data were available, however, it remained for market partici-pants to take notice and act on them. In this context, note might be made of Lamfalussy's open letter of 11 January 1983 to the *Financial Times* refuting the criticism that bankers had had no way of knowing how much of Mexico's debt was short-term: 'By December 1980 anyone who cared to look at our figures could see that an increasing proportion of Mexico's external borrowing was short-term ... Actual and potential creditors did have early warnings ... well before the eruption of the Mexican crisis.' For more on the Mexican crisis, see Section 5.4.
28. Google's Ngram Viewer flags 1982 as the first year when the word 'macro-prudential' or 'macroprudential' appeared in the books in its database.
29. Committee on Banking Regulations and Supervisory Practices, 'Report on the use of certain prudential measures to constrain the growth of banks' interna-tional lending', February 1980, In BISA, 7.18(15) – *Papers Lamfalussy*, LAM 25, 67, p. 2.
30. Ibid., p. 6. There was both opposition from the Basel Committee to macropruden-tial measures and resistance from the United States in the Euro-currency Standing

Committee. Edwin Truman at the Federal Reserve Board, C. Fred Bergsten at Treasury and Richard Cooper at the US State Department, adopting standard Keynesian logic, all viewed the recycling of capital flows by banks to less-developed countries as a positive process that supported global demand. BIS staff, in contrast, were concerned with the unsustainable growth of stocks of debt, their maturity and their allocation of interest-rate risk (through floating-rate syndicated loans). Again, we can see here early inklings of what came to be the BIS view.

31. 'Final Report of the Working Party on possible approaches to constraining the growth of banks' international lending', 29 February 1980, In BISA 7.18(15) – *Papers Lamfalussy*, LAM 25, 68, p. 3.

32. A fifth set of measures concerned possible compulsory balance-sheet provisioning in respect to involuntarily rescheduled international loans, a topic not pursued here.

33. The first instance of BIS assistance, in March 1982, was actually to the National Bank of Hungary, a country that saw large-scale withdrawals of external funding when neighbouring Poland experienced political and financial turmoil in late 1981 and which was not yet an IMF member.

34. Clement and Maes (2013: 5) quote him as follows: '[T]he only way private banks can set into motion domestic adjustment policies is when they stop lending. This has happened in some cases; and when it happened, it did so abruptly.'

35. I owe this reference to Clement and Maes (2013).

36. Maes and Clement (2012: 20).

37. Bank of England (1980). This paper was submitted by the Bank of England for discussion by the ECSC. It should not therefore be considered as the official position of the Bank of England on the matter.

38. ECSC, 'Report to the Governors on possibilities for central bank co-operation in handling liquidity crisis situations affecting banks' foreign establishments', 29 June 1982, In BISA 7.18(15) – *Papers Lamfalussy*, LAM 22, p. 60.

39. 'Since there are virtually no recent precedents . . . ' Ibid., p. 4.

40. This can be seen as an outgrowth of the recommendations of the Lamfalussy Group, lent further impetus by the de facto default of Mexico, Poland and a growing list of other debtors, and the absence of 'internationally comparable and properly consolidated banking data'. Quoting from Lamfalussy, A., Note to the G10 Governors, 'The current position and policies of the G10 countries' commercial banks: some macro-economic and "macro-prudential" issues', 22 September 1982, in BISA 7.18(15) – *Papers Lamfalussy*, LAM 35, 89, vol. 1.

41. The Mexican crisis in 1982, by revealing the incompleteness of publicly available statistics on Mexican borrowing, finally provided effective impetus for improving reporting systems.

42. See Lamfalussy, A., Note to the G10 Governors, 'The international debt situation: prospects for 1983 and policy options', 1 February 1983, In BISA 7.18(15) – *Papers Lamfalussy*, LAM 35, 89, vol. 1.

43. Ibid., p. 2. Evidence on the incomplete effectiveness of concerted lending is in Caskey (1989).

44. Lamfalussy, A., 'Speaking notes for an introductory statement to the G10 Governors' exchange of views on the international debt situation', 7 September 1983, In BISA 7.18(15) – *Papers Lamfalussy*, LAM 35, 89, p. 4.

45. Lamfalussy, A., Note to the G10 Governors, 'The international debt situation: prospects for 1983 and policy options', In BISA 7.18(15) – *Papers Lamfalussy*, LAM 35, 89, p. 5.

46. A contemporary discussion of the connections is Cline (1982–3).

47. At the same time, the relevant section concluded somewhat anomalously with a defence of the banks. 'Looking at developments since 1974 from the standpoint of the banks, the fact that so many countries have had to have recourse to rescheduling operations and/or official assistance has given rise in some quarters to the view that in the past nearly all bank lending to certain groups of countries was misdirected and irresponsible. This view is, to say the least, far too sweeping. It appears almost entirely to overlook the extent to which the functioning of the world economy and the international financial system has since 1974, and in particular following the successive oil shocks, depended on the role of intermediary played by international banks' (BIS AR 1983: 130).

48. Analysis of these issues was developed more fully in Monetary and Economic Department (1983), which presumably served as input into the annual report.

49. Clement and Maes (2013) show that the entire process from assembly of information on exposures to Mexico to agreement on the final loan took longer, on the order of twelve days – still very fast by IMF standards.

50. This goal was achieved in 1984.

51. 'Report of the Study Group on the International Interbank Market', BISA, 7.18(15) – *Papers Lamfalussy*, LAM 22, 61. A sanitised and toned-down version of the report was published as Bank for International Settlements (1983).

52. The ECSC Chairman's speaking note introducing the Interbank Market Study Group report to the G10 Governors, 21 February 1983, BISA, 7.18(15) – *Papers Lamfalussy*, LAM 22, 61.

53. As the final report (reference note 52) put it, 'Many banks assume that the authorities would be extremely reluctant to allow any major bank to fail. Some banks have referred to the G10 Governors' Communique of 1974 as support for their view that banks which are unable to honour their obligations because of temporary liquidity difficulties may well be supported by the authorities. Banks may be basing their judgements on the experience of the past decade or so, when a number of banks in difficulty have benefitted from officially-sponsored rescue efforts' (p. 28).

54. 'Report of the Study Group on the International Interbank Market', p. 30 (references see note 52).

55. 'The topics discussed in this Report have been arranged in a somewhat different order from that of previous Reports,' as the Bank put it (BIS AR 1986: 5).

56. In turning its intellectual attention in this direction, the authors were building on the conclusions of the Cross Report (Committee on the Global Financial System (1986)), published in April.

57. This positive assessment of the agreement was not one that subsequent scholarly studies necessarily shared – for discussion, see Frankel (2015).

58. Lamfalussy (1989a: 99).

59. One hears here echoes of Mayer (1983), now as applied to target zones.

60. Shades of what would transpire in 1992–3.

61. The year 1988 also saw the establishment of the Delors Committee, charged with sketching the roadmap to European Monetary Union, on which Lamfalussy, still head of the BIS, served as a member. See also Chapter 1 (Harold James) of this volume.

62. Quoted in James (2012: 329).

63. Lamfalussy had concurrently observed that some form of central oversight and coordination of national fiscal policies was 'a vital component of a European EMU'. Lamfalussy (1989b: 83).

64. On the deliberations of the Committee of Governors, see James (2012).

65. ECSC Invitation to 6 December 1992 meeting, BISA 7.18(15), LAM37.92.

66. ECSC Summary of 6 December 1992 meeting, BISA 7.18(18), BOC 17.1.

67. In addition, certain US-based money-market and bond funds had taken long unhedged positions in ERM currencies, having been attracted by their relatively high yields and convinced that, with the need to comply with the 'convergence criteria' for euro adoption, those yields were poised to come down. These US money managers, in their wisdom, were confident that European central banks would do whatever it took to defend their ERM parities, and when this conviction proved false, they incurred significant losses. In turn, this pointed to the need to address how those funds were managed and regulated (whether bond funds should be subject to concentration limits or hedging requirements, whether money market funds should be permitted to offer their shareholders redemption at par under all circumstances).

68. Sweden was not formally a member of the EMS but pegged the krona to it.

69. In this connection, it attributed a subsidiary role to dollar weakness and the associated tendency for the Deutsche Mark to strengthen against other EMS currencies as investors moved funds out of dollars in favour of the strongest European currency.

70. This time the total package was to be $12 billion, half from the United States and the other half from other G10 central banks plus the Bank of Spain.

71. Half of that $5 billion was to prefinance the IMF package then still under negotiation, and the other half to be disbursed only with the unanimous consent of G10 central banks guaranteeing the loan. 'Extracts from Minutes of the 571st Meeting of the Board of Directors held in Basel on 9th January 1995', BISA 2.403, Banco de Mexico vol. 10.

72. 'February 1995 BIS Credit Facility in Favour of Banco de Mexico', 13 February 1995, BISA 7.18(31), Papers of Andrew Crockett, ADC 23,1. The BIS credit was formally extended to the Banco de Mexico on 2 March 1995 but never drawn.

73. This assessment of structural reform efforts and accomplishments was more sanguine than those of certain other observers, such as Dornbusch and Werner (1994).

74. The Bank's confidential assessment for the meeting of Governors some four months earlier, in February, anticipated this analysis. 'The Causes and Lessons of Financial Turbulence in the Emerging Markets', 13 February 1995, BISA 7.18(42), Papers of Philip Turner.

75. Anticipating what became known two decades later as the IMF's 'new institutional view' – see Ostry et al. (2012).

76. The Economic Adviser held the pen for the annual report (or at least its concluding chapter).

77. See the speech of First Deputy Managing Director Stanley Fischer at the September 1997 IMF–World Bank meetings in Hong Kong (Fischer 1997). See also Fischer (1998) along with the other essays included in the volume in which it appears. On the political context, see Abdelal (2006).

78. Basel Committee on Banking Supervision (1997). BIS General Manager Andrew Crockett alluded to the Bank's role in the development of the Core Principles in his report to G10 finance ministers and central-bank governors at the Spring 1997 IMF–World Bank meetings. 'Recent Work Under the Auspices of the G10 Governors to Promote Finance Market Stability', BISA 7.18 (31), ADC 33,1 (28 April).

79. On this, see also Chapter 2 (Catherine Schenk) of this volume.

80. 'Meeting of the Ministers and Governors of the Group of Ten', BISA7.18 (31), ADC 33,1, Washington, DC (28 April). Draghi's report to his colleagues summarised a longer document entitled 'Financial Stability in Emerging Markets. Report of the Working Party on Financial Stability in Emerging Market Economies' (April 1997), BISA 7.18(31), ADC 33,1.

81. 'International Responses to External Financing Crises', Note for a Meeting of Governors at 6 p.m. on 9th December 1997, BISA 7.18(31), ADC 12,2.

82. This, recall, was when the supervisory responsibilities of the Bank of England were shifted to the newly created Financial Services Authority. The statement in the BIS annual report was based on the outcomes of a survey among central banks the BIS had conducted in 1998. The resulting report 'Central bank involvement in safe-guarding financial stability', authored by Claudio Borio, Thorvald Moe, Masao Okawa and João Santos, had been discussed at a central-bank meeting in Basel on 9–10 February 1999.

83. Recall that this was the period when other observers, such as Krugman (1998), criticised the Bank of Japan for doing too little to fend off deflation, not for doing too much.

84. See Crockett (2000a). There was also a companion speech some five months later elaborating the same themes (Crockett 2000b). See also Chapter 4 (Andrew Baker) of this volume.

85. In contrast, the authors of the report did not say what should be done about the rating agencies or how the banks' own risk-management practices might be reformed. These issues would be the subject of considerable discussion and debate, of course, following the global financial crisis.

86. This argument appeared most clearly in the 2011 report (BIS AR 2011: 37).

87. Here the real exchange rate should be understood as the relative price of traded and non-traded goods. Otherwise (were it understood as the relative price of domestic and foreign goods) the statement would make no sense.

88. Jaime Caruana, having taken over as General Manager, emphasised the value of, but also the obstacles to, international coordination of financial and, especially, macroeconomic policies in Caruana (2012) – more so in a period when the imperatives of the crisis had caused monetary and fiscal policies to diverge sharply across countries.

89. See Section 5.8.

90. The Second Amendment to the Articles, adopted in the 1970s, modified the traditional wording in the Fund's 'constitution' to refer to a stable system of

exchange rates rather than a system of stable rates, acknowledging that the central parities and fluctuation bands of the Bretton Woods system had become things of the past. See IMF (1978).

91. One is reminded of Fritz Machlup's characterisation of the three salient aspects of the international monetary system: adjustment, liquidity and confidence. The BIS focus on liquidity was further highlighted in the 2011 CGFS report 'Global liquidity – concept, measurement and policy implications' (Landau Report), as well as by the publication of 'global liquidity indicators' on the BIS website. It can be argued that confidence has also figured importantly in the BIS view: see inter alia Section 5.9.

6

The Bank for International Settlements

If It Didn't Exist, It Would Have to Be Invented
(An Insider's View)

William C. Dudley

In July 1944, the country delegations gathered at the Bretton Woods Conference created the International Monetary Fund (IMF) and the International Bank for Reconstruction and Development (World Bank). One of the other decisions made at Bretton Woods was to close down and liquidate the Bank for International Settlements (BIS), which had been set up in 1930 in Basel, Switzerland, but was now thought to be irrelevant. Fortuitously, this decision was never implemented. Not only did the BIS escape the fate of being closed and liquidated, it has instead come to play an essential role in the global financial system. In a global economy that does not respect national borders, it is critical that central bankers, supervisors and regulators from around the world understand what each is seeing and doing and that their actions are well communicated and coordinated. In that sense, the BIS plays an important complementary role to that performed by the two institutions established by the Bretton Woods Conference: the IMF and the World Bank.

Initially, as head of the Markets Group of the Federal Reserve Bank of New York, and later as President of the Federal Reserve Bank of New York, I had the opportunity to participate actively in the BIS's work. This included as a member of the Markets Committee (2007–8), which focuses on global financial market developments and the execution of monetary policy; as Chair of the Committee on Payment and Settlement Systems (2009–12), now the Committee on Payments and Market Infrastructures (CPMI), which focuses on payments and financial market infrastructure issues; as Chair of the Committee on the Global Financial System (2012–18), which has a financial stability orientation through its focus on developments within the global financial system; as a member of the Economic Consultative Committee (2009–18), which acts as the Steering Committee for policy work and discussions at the BIS; as a member of the BIS Board of

Directors (2009–18), which is responsible for oversight of the BIS management and business strategy; and as a member of the Steering Committee of the Financial Stability Board (2009–18), which the BIS hosts and supports and is responsible for monitoring and making recommendations about the global financial system.[1] My experiences, which I relate in this chapter, underscore the important role that the BIS plays in relation to the IMF and the World Bank.

By way of background, the BIS was established in 1930 to administer Germany's First World War reparation payments. But, as part of its mission, it was also given the statutory authority to provide banking services to central banks and other international authorities and to serve as a place where central bankers could exchange views and coordinate their activities. When German reparation payments were suspended in 1931 and then abolished in 1932 as part of the Lausanne Agreement, the BIS did not fold up its shop but continued to provide banking services and act as a forum for central bankers.

Over time, as the process of globalisation has continued, the role of providing a forum for central-banker discussions has, in my judgement, become the most significant activity of the BIS. Today, we operate in a global financial system, with large systemically important financial institutions that do business in many different countries but within a regime in which monetary policy and bank supervision are still conducted on a national basis. Thus, there is a need for a place where central bankers can exchange information about recent and prospective monetary policy developments and where best practices can be established to help ensure greater consistency in how banks are regulated and supervised on a cross-border basis.

This role of providing a forum for central bankers provides value in several ways. Importantly, it results in improved understanding of why policy is evolving in the way it is in particular countries and regions; it provides insights into important lessons that can lead to better policy-making in the future; it helps coordinate and improve bank regulatory and supervisory standards; and it facilitates the development of personal relationships and trust, which become particularly valuable during times of crisis.

In my experience, US policymakers have used visits to the BIS to explain new innovations in US monetary policy that potentially have implications for global capital flows, financial asset prices and policy elsewhere. For example, in 2017 and 2018, the balance-sheet normalisation process that the Federal Reserve had commenced received considerable attention.

Similarly, US policymakers have learned from the experience of other
countries that have implemented negative interest rate policies about the
advantages and disadvantages of such policies.

The lessons from these past experiences that have been discussed at the
BIS have also helped guide policy. Thus, the experience of Japan following
the bursting of the country's real estate bubble informed US policymakers
that they needed to aggressively ease monetary policy following the bursting of the US housing bubble. In the same vein, I have no doubt that
ongoing discussions about the US experience with balance-sheet normalisation will inform the choices made by policymakers in other countries
when they start the process.

The bimonthly discussions about monetary policy and the economic
outlook in Basel and the work of the various BIS Committees also perform
another very valuable role. They help build important professional relationships across the central-banking community. These relationships are
important because they establish the trust and common understanding
that help to facilitate international policy coordination when such actions
are needed.

In my eleven and half years at the New York Federal Reserve, I made the
trip to Basel more than fifty times, each time meeting with colleagues
tasked with similar responsibilities in other central-banking
organisations.[2] This provided me with the personal contacts and relationships that proved critical in responding to some of the important international dimensions of the financial crisis. In particular, during the autumn
of 2008, these personal relationships helped facilitate the rapid deployment
of a system of coordinated dollar auctions by the European Central Bank,
the Bank of England, the Bank of Japan and the Swiss National Bank in
a few short weeks.[3] It took only a few conference calls to enable us to agree
on all the details, ending up with auctions conducted with similar terms
and conditions around the world. These auctions of dollar funding were
backstopped by foreign exchange swap agreements that each central bank
had executed with the Federal Reserve System. These auctions were an
important complement to the Term Auction Facility in the United States in
providing dollar liquidity to foreign commercial banks whose access to
traditional dollar funding markets was impaired. At its peak, the amount of
dollars extended through these foreign dollar auctions totalled more than
$500 billion. By facilitating the flow of dollar liquidity to the global banking
system, these auctions helped to stabilise bank funding following the failure of Lehman Brothers. The relationships established at the BIS helped
make this go smoothly.

The BIS also plays an important role in the realm of financial stability. Because we operate in a global financial system with a high degree of interconnectivity, no central bank can ensure financial stability just through its own actions. Thus, there is a need for a multinational entity to play an important role in this area.

The BIS does this in a number of ways. First, it provides a forum and the infrastructure (including permanent staff) that work on issues that are relevant to financial stability. This includes the work of the Basel Committee on Banking Supervision (BCBS) in developing liquidity and capital standards for systemically important banking organisations. Although the work of the BCBS is well known, the other Basel Committees also play important roles.

For example, when I chaired the Committee on Payment and Settlement Systems (CPSS) in 2009–12, the main focus of our work was to strengthen the standards that should be applied to important financial market infrastructures with respect to issues such as oversight, governance, liquidity and risk management. We did this working jointly with the International Organization of Securities Commissions (IOSCO). This work was particularly important in two respects. First, the prior standards were out of date, were not comprehensive, and lacked teeth – being more in the form of recommendations than standards. Second, the agreement among the G20 countries to mandate the central clearing of over-the-counter derivative transactions increased the importance of global financial market infrastructures. A consistent, global approach was necessary.

The CPSS–IOSCO work resulted in the Principles for Financial Market Infrastructures (PFMI). Not only do the PFMI provide a guide for the conditions that financial market infrastructures need to meet in order to operate effectively and safely, they have become the global basis for the implementation of regulatory standards on a country-by-country basis.

Similarly, the successor committee to the CPSS, which I chaired, the Committee on Payments and Market Infrastructures, has played a pivotal role in a number of important payments issues – some of which are relevant to the issue of financial stability. For example, the CPMI, after evaluating the Bangladesh cybersecurity theft (2016), took a number of actions to make the international payments system safer. In particular, the CPMI – with my wholehearted encouragement and support – worked to clarify the responsibilities of those involved in global payment chains – the party initiating the payment, the payment infrastructure provider and the party clearing and settling the payment. The CPMI also worked to ensure that there would be an effective assurance regime in place so that participants in global payments could be confident that each participant in the global payments chain would meet a minimum set of global standards.

On the financial stability front, the BIS also plays an important role in a number of other ways. It hosts the Financial Stability Board, which has played a leading role in terms of assessing the emerging risks in the global financial system and in coordinating international work on numerous topics, such as the resolution and recovery of systemically important banks and financial market infrastructures. Moreover, the BIS Monetary and Economic Department (MED) has conducted pioneering research into financial stability issues for several decades. For example, before the onset of the financial crisis, the then head of the MED, Bill White, was quite prescient in his analysis of emerging financial stability risks.

As part of this work, the BIS has played an important role in highlighting the potential use of macroprudential tools to address financial stability risks. The Committee on the Global Financial System, for example, has produced a number of papers that document what has been achieved to date and some of the issues that make the use of macroprudential tools difficult. While this subject is still in its infancy, over time I expect that macroprudential tools will prove to be an important complement to microprudential tools such as bank regulation and supervision in helping to foster financial stability.

The BIS also plays an important role in developing and compiling international banking data. It systematically keeps track of cross-border banking capital flows and global derivatives activity. The BIS also maintains a secure database of supervisory information on systemically important banking organisations. Both of these databases are important tools for use in assessing the risks to the global financial system and in determining appropriate prudential standards such as capital and liquidity requirements.

Finally, the BIS provides financial services and assistance to central banks and other international authorities. As a provider of banking services, the BIS has a reputation for high-quality service, safety (due to its low-risk balance sheet and high level of capitalisation), confidentiality and security. Especially when times are uncertain, the strength of the BIS balance sheet and its operational capabilities help support international financial activity and enhance financial stability.

I think it should be apparent from the foregoing that I am a big fan of the BIS. Nevertheless, there are some areas for improvement that could make the BIS even more effective.

First, the BIS should strive towards greater transparency about its role and responsibilities. This is particularly important at a time that many established institutions are viewed with suspicion and hostility. For example, some observers in the United States believe that the BIS imposes international capital standards on US banking institutions. Nothing could be further from the truth. The Basel capital standards are voluntary and developed via consensus. US central bankers and bank regulators view the Basel standards positively because they help establish a floor for capital requirements around the world, which helps prevent a 'race to the bottom'. This benefits the United States, where national bank capital standards are generally higher.

Providing more insight into how these types of international standards are developed and the other activities of the BIS would presumably increase the perceived legitimacy of these efforts. At a minimum, it would help quash conspiracy stories about what the BIS central banker cabal is up to! Transparency might also be enhanced by greater outreach and by publishing more detailed agendas and minutes of the activities of the various BIS Committees.

Obviously, there is a limit to how far transparency should go. Too much transparency might prove counterproductive by inhibiting candour and the willingness to exchange sensitive information on a confidential basis. But I don't think the BIS is close to that limit. In my opinion, the perception that it is a secretive organisation outside the control of elected governments serves to undercut its mission.

The second area for improvement is for the BIS to continue to broaden its membership and to provide a greater role for emerging-market economies. When the BIS was established it had a predominantly European focus because administering the German First World War reparations was its primary purpose. While, over time, the European role has lessened and important emerging-market economies such as China and India have played greater roles, European countries still have outsized representation, such as on the key BIS Committees and on the BIS Board of Directors, relative to their weight in the global economy.

While there is more to do here, the BIS is moving in the right direction. Thus, in 2019, the composition of the BIS Board of Directors has changed in a fundamental way – several European countries have lost their second Board of Director seats, and the proportion of non-European Directors has increased even as the number of Board members shrunk to eighteen from twenty-one. Similarly, it is gratifying to see officials with an emerging-market country background taking on key roles in BIS management – Agustín Carstens, the former head of the Bank of Mexico, is the first BIS General Manager from an emerging-market country.

The third area for improvement is to increase diversity and inclusion at the level of BIS management. Currently, for example, women are very underrepresented, with most of the major management positions of the Bank held by men. While one can argue that the underrepresentation of women and minorities is also true for central banking more generally, the BIS could do better and show greater leadership in this area. Put simply, for the BIS to be viewed as fully credible, the composition of its leadership needs to be more diverse.

A final area for focus – and this goes back to the earlier issue of transparency and communication – is to clarify how the work of the BIS fits in relative to the activities of the IMF and the World Bank. In my own experience, the three cooperate well. Representatives from the two Bretton Woods institutions are often included in BIS working groups, and the IMF participates, on a regular basis, in the Global Economy Meeting at the BIS, which focuses on international economic developments. Also, the Standing Committee on Assessment of Vulnerabilities (SCAV) of the Financial Stability Board includes representatives of the IMF and the World Bank and works closely with the IMF in the ongoing assessment of emerging financial system risks and vulnerabilities. But, it is not always clear where the boundaries are or where they should be, and at times this can lead to tensions between the institutions and redundancy in terms of work efforts. Obviously, because it takes two to tango, this is not an issue that the BIS can address on its own. It also requires a commitment from the IMF and the World Bank.

In conclusion, I believe that the globalisation of the economy and financial system has generated huge benefits for people around the world, literally lifting hundreds of millions of people out of poverty over the past few decades. In such a world, there is an important role for international organisations like the Bank for International Settlements – to provide a forum for central banks to discuss and debate, to provide a coordination mechanism to establish coherent global international banking standards and to provide an independent voice in analysing those issues that may impinge on the ability of the global financial system to function efficiently in allocating risk and intermediating the flow of funds between savers and borrowers. These are very important functions that complement the roles played by the IMF and the World Bank.

Notes

My thanks go to Sandra Lee of the Federal Reserve Bank of New York for her helpful comments in the preparation of this chapter.

1. I also served as a member of the Group of Governors and Heads of Supervision (GHOS), which is responsible for approving the work of the Basel Committee on Banking Supervision, and on the BIS Audit and Risk Committees.
2. Typically, once a year – usually in March – the BIS meetings are held elsewhere.
3. Although the Federal Reserve also established swap lines with a number of other countries, the coordinated auctions of dollar liquidity were undertaken just with these four central banks.

Annex 1

BIS Chronology

This chronology chronicles some of the main events in the BIS's institutional history.

1929–1939

3 October–13 November 1929	A committee to elaborate the structure and statutes of the Bank for International Settlements meets in Baden-Baden, Germany.
20 January 1930	The Final Act of the Second Hague Conference is adopted by heads of state and government representatives. This includes the agreement between the central banks of Belgium, France, Germany, Italy, Japan and the United Kingdom and a financial institution representing the United States to set up the Bank for International Settlements.
26–27 February 1930	Governors of the founding central banks meet in Rome to officially create the BIS, nominating its President and the members of its Board of Directors.
17 May 1930	The BIS opens its doors for business in the former Savoy Hôtel Univers in Basel, Switzerland.
30 July 1936	The Brussels Protocol, signed by government representatives, gives effect to Article X of the Hague Agreement protecting the BIS's property, assets and deposits.
September 1939	Following the outbreak of the Second World War, all meetings of the BIS Board of Directors are suspended. The BIS adopts a code of neutral conduct for the duration of the war.

1940–1949

20 May–7 October 1940	The BIS seat is temporarily moved from Basel to Château-d'Oex, following the German invasion of France and the Benelux countries.

(continued)

(continued)

1 July 1944	The United Nations Conference in Bretton Woods agrees to the creation of the International Monetary Fund (IMF) and the World Bank; it also adopts Resolution V calling for the liquidation of the BIS at 'the earliest possible moment'.
9 December 1946	First post-war meeting of the BIS Board of Directors.
13 May 1948	Washington Agreement: the BIS reimburses to the Allied Tripartite Commission gold it had received from the German Reichsbank during the war that after the war turned out to have been looted. The Bretton Woods resolution calling for the liquidation of the BIS is put aside.
1950–1959	
19 September 1950	The agreement establishing the European Payments Union (EPU) is signed by eighteen European governments. The BIS is appointed to act as agent for the EPU.
31 December 1958	Full current-account convertibility is restored for most European currencies. The EPU is wound up and replaced by the European Monetary Agreement (EMA).
1960–1969	
13 April 1964	Formal establishment of the Committee of Governors of the Central Banks of the member states of the European Economic Community. The Committee decides to have its secretariat and meetings at the BIS in Basel.
1 September 1964	The ten main central banks represented at the BIS (G10) inaugurate regular meetings of gold and foreign exchange experts in Basel. The Gold and Foreign Exchange Committee is renamed the Markets Committee in May 2002.
9 June 1969	A BIS Extraordinary General Meeting amends the Statutes to delete all references to the 1930 Young Plan (reparations settlement).

(continued)

(continued)

1970–1979	
18 April 1971	The G10 Governors establish the Euro-currency Standing Committee (ECSC) to monitor developments in the eurocurrency markets. The Committee is renamed the Committee on the Global Financial System (CGFS) in February 1999.
1 June 1973	The European Monetary Co-operation Fund (EMCF), a joint support mechanism between European central banks, becomes operational. The BIS assumes functions of the Fund's agent.
1 December 1974	In response to international bank failures, the G10 Governors establish the Committee on Banking Regulations and Supervisory Practices (renamed the Basel Committee on Banking Supervision in September 1989). The BCBS holds its first meeting in Basel in February 1975.
1 December 1975	The Basel Concordat calls on host- and home-country authorities to share supervisory responsibility for banks' foreign activities.
1 May 1977	The BIS completes its move from the former Savoy Hôtel Univers to its new premises in the Tower building.
1 January 1978	The BIS Data Bank of monetary, financial and economic statistical time series becomes operational.
1980–1989	
1 April 1980	Governors entrust the ECSC with regular and systematic monitoring of international banking developments.
1 October 1981	First meeting at the BIS of the Group of Payment System Experts. The Group is formally established as the Committee on Payment and Settlement Systems (CPSS) in November 1990 and renamed the Committee on Payment and Market Infrastructures (CPMI) in 2014.
1 April 1983	Creation of the International Organization of Securities Commissions (IOSCO).
21 March 1986	Signature of an agreement between the BIS and the ECU Banking Association (EBA) assigning the function of agent of the private European currency unit (ecu) clearing and settlement system to the BIS.

(continued)

(continued)

10 February 1987	Conclusion of the BIS Headquarters Agreement with the Swiss Federal Council; creation of the BIS Administrative Tribunal.
28 June 1988	Creation by the European Council of the Committee for the Study of Economic and Monetary Union (the Delors Committee), which is to meet at the BIS in Basel and presents its report on economic and monetary union to the European Council on 12 April 1989.
1 July 1988	Central bank Governors endorse the BCBS document *International convergence of capital measurement and capital standards*. Known as the Basel Capital Accord or Basel I, it is to be implemented by the end of 1992.
1990–1999	
1 September 1992	Creation of the Joint Vienna Institute (JVI) by the IMF, European Bank for Reconstruction and Development, International Bank for Reconstruction and Development, Organisation for Economic Co-operation and Development and BIS. The JVI provides technical training mainly to officials from the formerly planned economies in central and Eastern Europe, the former Soviet Union and a number of Asian countries.
31 December 1993	The European Community (EC) Committee of Governors, created in 1964, is wound up and replaced by the European Monetary Institute (EMI). In November 1994, the EMI leaves the BIS in Basel and moves to Frankfurt am Main in Germany (it is replaced by the ECB in June 1998).
15 May 1995	Termination of the BIS agency functions for the EMI.
1 January 1996	Establishment of the Joint Forum, under the aegis of the BCBS, IOSCO and the International Association of Insurance Supervisors (IAIS), grouping senior bank, insurance and securities supervisors representing their supervisory constituencies.
23 October 1996	The IAIS decides to locate its secretariat at the BIS in Basel.

(continued)

(continued)

8 June 1997	First meeting of the Central Bank Governance Steering Group at the BIS.
1 July 1998	Opening of the BIS Representative Office for Asia and the Pacific in Hong Kong SAR. Host Country Agreement signed with the People's Republic of China.
1 July 1998	The BIS and BCBS create the Financial Stability Institute (FSI) to provide practical training to financial-sector supervisors worldwide.
1 February 1999	The G7 Finance Ministers and Central Bank Governors create the Financial Stability Forum (FSF). The FSF secretariat is based at the BIS in Basel.
8 February 1999	First meeting of the BIS Global Economy Meeting (GEM), which comprises the Governors of BIS member central banks in major advanced and emerging-market economies.
1 October 1999	Establishment of the Central Bank Governance Network at the BIS.
2000–2009	
October 2000	Regional Treasury dealing room commences operations at the BIS Representative Office for Asia and the Pacific in Hong Kong SAR.
8 January 2001	An Extraordinary General Meeting of the BIS limits the right to hold BIS shares exclusively to central banks and approves a mandatory repurchase of privately held shares.
1 March 2001	Establishment of the BIS Asian Consultative Council (ACC) as a forum between Asian central banks and the BIS Board of Directors and Management.
1 May 2002	The International Association of Deposit Insurers (IADI) decides to locate its secretariat at the BIS in Basel.
1 November 2002	Opening of the BIS Representative Office for the Americas in Mexico City. Host Country Agreement signed with Mexico.
1 April 2003	The BIS changes its unit of account from the gold franc (in force since 1930) to the SDR (IMF Special Drawing Rights).

(continued)

(continued)

26 June 2004	The central bank Governors and Heads of Banking Supervision endorse the release of *International convergence of capital measurement and capital standards: a revised framework*, better known as Basel II.
1 January 2006	The BIS agrees to host the Irving Fisher Committee on Central Bank Statistics (IFC) and its secretariat. The IFC was created in 1995 and is an affiliated member of the International Statistical Institute (ISI).
1 May 2008	Establishment of the BIS Consultative Council for the Americas (CCA) as an advisory committee to the BIS Board of Directors.
2 April 2009	The Group of Twenty (G20) creates the Financial Stability Board (FSB), replacing the FSF, with a new macroprudential supervision mandate. The FSB secretariat is based at the BIS in Basel.
2010–2020	
1 January 2010	Creation of the BIS Economic Consultative Committee (ECC), which comprises eighteen (subsequently nineteen) central-bank Governors and supports the work of the GEM (see entry for 8 February 1999).
12 November 2010	The G20 Leaders endorse the FSB policy framework for addressing systemically important financial institutions (SIFIs).
1 June 2011	The BCBS releases *Basel III: a global regulatory framework for more resilient banks and banking systems*, introducing revised capital rules.
16 April 2012	The CPSS and IOSCO jointly release Principles for Financial Market Infrastructures, containing new international standards for payment, clearing and settlement systems, including central counterparties.
1 January 2013	The BCBS releases *Guidance for national authorities operating the countercyclical capital buffer* as part of the Basel III framework.
1 March 2013	The BIS International Data Hub (IDH) is created to facilitate the exchange and secure storage of confidential bank data among supervisory agencies and central banks in participating jurisdictions.

(continued)

(continued)

1 September 2014	The Committee on Payment and Settlement Systems (CPSS), first created in 1990, changes its name to the Committee on Payments and Market Infrastructures (CPMI).
7 December 2017	The Basel Committee's oversight body, the Group of Central Bank Governors and Heads of Supervision (GHOS), endorses the outstanding Basel III post-crisis regulatory reforms.
1 January 2019	Implementation of the new Article 27 of the BIS Statues, broadening the composition of the BIS Board of Directors.
30 June 2019	The BIS announces the creation of the BIS Innovation Hub to foster international cooperation on innovative financial technology within the central-banking community. Innovation Hub centres are subsequently established in collaboration with the HKMA in Hong Kong SAR (18 September 2019), with the SNB in Switzerland (8 October 2019) and with the MAS in Singapore (13 November 2019).
30 June 2019	The BIS announces plans to establish in 2020 a dealing room in the BIS Representative Office for the Americas to allow the Bank to comprehensively serve client central banks across all time zones.
May–July 2020	The BIS celebrates its ninetieth anniversary.

BIS-Based Committees – Membership, Chairs and Secretaries, 1962–2020

1 Gold and Foreign Exchange Committee (1962–2002)/Markets Committee, MC (since 2002)

At the end of 1961, seven European central banks (those of Belgium, France, Italy, Germany, the Netherlands, Switzerland and the United Kingdom), all members of the BIS, and the US Federal Reserve System, decided to pool some of their gold reserves for the purpose of selling (and buying) gold on the free gold market in London in order to keep the gold price on the market in line with the official price of gold (at that time fixed at \$35 per ounce of fine gold). Gold and foreign exchange experts from the participating central banks started meeting regularly at the BIS in 1962 to discuss the operations of the so-called Gold Pool and the prospects for the gold market generally. In 1964, gold and foreign exchange experts from the central banks of Canada, Japan and Sweden joined their Gold Pool colleagues for regular meetings at the BIS to discuss the situation on the international gold and foreign exchange markets. This was the origin of the BIS Gold and Foreign Exchange Committee as a G10 Committee. These meetings have continued to take place at the BIS ever since (whereas the operations of the Gold Pool were discontinued in 1968).

In 2002, the Gold and Foreign Exchange Committee was renamed the Markets Committee (MC). Its current remit is 'discussing financial market developments beyond gold and foreign exchange, and cooperating closely in assessing current events as well as longer-term structural trends that may have implications for financial market functioning and central bank operations'. See: www.bis.org > Committees & associations > Markets Committee.

Membership

From 1964	National Bank of Belgium, Bank of Canada, Bank of France, Deutsche Bundesbank, Bank of Italy, Bank of Japan, Netherlands Bank, Sveriges Riksbank, Swiss National Bank, Bank of England, Board of Governors of the Federal Reserve System, Federal Reserve Bank of New York. Occasionally, other advanced and emerging-market economy central-bank representatives attended meetings as invited participants.
From 1997	All of the above plus the following invited participants attending regular 'enlarged' Gold and Foreign Exchange Committee/ MC meetings: Reserve Bank of Australia, Central Bank of Brazil, People's Bank of China, European Central Bank (1998), Hong Kong Monetary Authority, Reserve Bank of India, Bank of Korea, Bank of Mexico, Monetary Authority of Singapore, Bank of Spain. Occasionally, other advanced and emerging-market economy central-bank representatives attended meetings as invited participants.
From 2006	Formalisation of the membership of all invited participants attending the regular 'enlarged' meetings as listed above. Occasionally, other advanced and emerging-market economy central-bank representatives attended meetings as invited participants.
From 2020	Formalisation of the membership of Bank Indonesia, Central Bank of Malaysia, Central Bank of the Russian Federation, South African Reserve Bank and Central Bank of the Republic of Turkey, taking the number of central bank members to 27.

Chairs and Secretaries

Chair	Tenure	Head of Secretariat (BIS)	Tenure
JHO Graaf van den Bosch (Netherlands Bank)	1962–1966		
Johannes Tüngeler (Deutsche Bundesbank)	March 1966		
Charles A Coombs (Federal Reserve)	May 1966		
MP André (National Bank of Belgium)	September 1966		
MM Théron (Bank of France)	November 1966		
Hans Mandel (BIS)	1967–1972		
Donald H MacDonald (BIS)	1972–1973	Richard T P Hall	1973–1992
Johannes Tüngeler (Deutsche Bundesbank)	1974–1976		
Pieter Timmerman (Netherlands Bank)	1976–1981		
J L Sangster (Bank of England)	1981–1982		
K Rodebäck (Sveriges Riksbank)	1982–1985	Marten de Boer	1992–1995
Shijuro Ogata (Bank of Japan)	1985–1986	Svein Andresen	1995–1998
J A Sillem (Netherlands Bank)	1986–1990	Claudio Borio	1998–2000
Fabrizio Saccomanni (Bank of Italy)	1990–1991	Gabriel Sensenbrenner	2000–2001
Thomas Franzén (Sveriges Riksbank)	1991–1995	Ingo Fender	2001–2004
Ian Plenderleith (Bank of England)	1995–2001	Chris Aylmer	2004–2005
Bruno Gehrig (Swiss National Bank)	2001–2003	Bruno Tissot	2006
Sheryl Kennedy (Bank of Canada)	2003–2006	François-Louis Michaud	2006–2009
Hiroshi Nakaso (Bank of Japan)	2006–2013	Corrinne Ho	2009–2013
Guy Debelle (Reserve Bank of Australia)	2013–2017	Morten Bech	2013–2016
Jacqueline Loh (Monetary Authority of Singapore)	2017–present	Andreas Schrimpf	2016–present

2 Euro-currency Standing Committee, ECSC (1971–1999)/ Committee on the Global Financial System, CGFS (since 1999)

From the early 1960s, central banks meeting at the BIS started to monitor the rapid growth of the so-called eurocurrency market, that is, the market for short-term deposits and credits denominated in a currency different from that of the country in which the deposit-taking and credit-giving bank was located (at that time usually banks located in Europe conducting such operations in US dollars). Annual meetings of central bank experts on the eurocurrency market took place at the BIS from the mid-1960s onwards. In 1971, the G10 central-bank Governors, concerned about the rapid growth of the international eurocurrency markets, created the G10 Euro-currency Standing Committee (ECSC). Its remit was 'to consider policy problems arising out of the existence and operations of the Euro-currency market'.

In 1999, the ECSC was renamed the Committee on the Global Financial System (CGFS) and adopted the following mandate: 'The CGFS is a central bank forum for the monitoring and examination of broad issues relating to financial markets and systems with a view to elaborating appropriate policy recommendations to support the central banks in the fulfilment of their responsibilities for monetary and financial stability. In carrying out this task, the Committee will place particular emphasis on assisting the Governors in recognising, analysing and responding to threats to the stability of financial markets and the global financial system.' See: www.bis.org > Committees & associations > Committee on the Global Financial System.

Membership

From 1971	National Bank of Belgium, Bank of Canada, Bank of France, Deutsche Bundesbank, Bank of Italy, Bank of Japan, Netherlands Bank, Sveriges Riksbank, Swiss National Bank, Bank of England, Board of Governors of the Federal Reserve System, Federal Reserve Bank of New York. Occasionally, other advanced and emerging-market economy central banks attended meetings as invited participants.
From 1982	All of the above plus Commissaire au Contrôle des Banques/Institut Monétaire Luxembourgeois.

(continued)

(continued)

From 1997	All of the above plus Central Bank of Luxembourg (1998) and European Central Bank (1998), as well as the following invited participants attending regular 'enlarged' ECSC/CGFS meetings: Reserve Bank of Australia, Central Bank of Brazil, European Central Bank (1998), Hong Kong Monetary Authority, Bank of Korea, Bank of Mexico, Monetary Authority of Singapore, Bank of Spain.
From 2005	All of the above plus People's Bank of China, Reserve Bank of India, with all invited participants attending all regular CGFS meetings.
From 2009	Formalisation of the membership of all regular meeting attendees = all of the central banks listed above.
From 2020	Formalisation of the membership of the Central Bank of Argentina, Central Bank of the Russian Federation, Saudi Arabian Monetary Authority, South African Reserve Bank and Bank of Thailand, taking the number of central bank members to 28.

Chairs and Secretaries

Chair	Tenure	Head of Secretariat (BIS)	Tenure
René Larre (BIS)	1971–1979	Michael Dealtry	1971–1990
Alexandre Lamfalussy (BIS)	1980–1993	Helmut Mayer	1990–1992
Andrew Crockett (BIS)	1994–1996	Svein Andresen	1992–1998
Toshihiko Fukui (Bank of Japan)	1997–1998	Claudio Borio	1998–2000
Yutaka Yamaguchi (Bank of Japan)	1998–2002	Allen Frankel	2000–2005
Roger W Ferguson (Fed Reserve Board)	2003–2006	Stefan Gerlach	2005–2007
Donald L Kohn (Fed Reserve Board)	2006–2010	Dietrich Domanski	2007–2010
Marc Carney (Bank of Canada)	2010–2011	Ingo Fender	2011–2015
William C Dudley (Fed Res Bank New York)	2012–2018	Kostas Tsatsaronis	2015–present
Philip Lowe (Res Bank Australia)	2018–present		

3 Committee on Banking Regulations and Supervisory Practices (1974–1990)/Basel Committee on Banking Supervision, BCBS (since 1990)

The rise of financial stability risks after the end of the Bretton Woods system of fixed exchange rates in 1971–1973 – and more particularly the high-profile failures of Bankhaus Herstatt and Franklin National Bank in 1974 – prompted the G10 Governors gathered in Basel in December 1974 to create a Standing Committee on Banking Regulations and Supervisory Practices. The Committee's first discussions concerned the sharing of supervisory responsibility for banks' foreign activities between host- and home-country authorities, and led to the 1975 Basel Concordat. The Committee then focused its attention on bank capital standards, elaborating the 1988 Basel Capital Accord (Basel I), which introduced a credit risk measurement framework for internationally active banks that became a globally accepted standard.

Renamed Basel Committee on Banking Supervision (BCBS) in 1990, the committee subsequently issued the Core Principles for Effective Banking Supervision (1997). The Basel Capital Accord was overhauled twice, leading to the adoption of the Basel II (2004) and, in response to the 2007–2009 financial crisis, Basel III (2011–2017) frameworks. To this day, the BCBS is the primary global standard setter for the prudential regulation of banks and provides a forum for cooperation on banking supervisory matters. Its mandate is to strengthen the regulation, supervision and practices of banks worldwide with the purpose of enhancing financial stability. Its membership comprises representatives from central banks and supervisory authorities. See: www.bis.org > Committees & associations > Basel Committee on Banking Supervision.

Membership

From 1974	Belgium, Canada, France, Germany, Italy, Japan, Luxembourg, Netherlands, Sweden, Switzerland, United Kingdom, United States.
From 1995	All of the above plus European Commission as observer.
From 1998	All of the above plus European Central Bank.
From 2001	All of the above plus Spain.
From 2006	All of the above plus Committee of European Banking Supervisors (later European Banking Authority) as observer.

(continued)

(continued)

From 2009	All of the above plus Argentina, Australia, Brazil, China, Hong Kong SAR, India, Indonesia, South Korea, Mexico, Russia, Saudi Arabia, Singapore, South Africa, Turkey; plus International Monetary Fund as observer.
From 2012	All of the above plus Basel Consultative Group as observer.
From 2014	All of the above plus Chile, Malaysia, United Arab Emirates as observers.

Chairs and Secretaries

Chair	Tenure	Head of Secretariat	Tenure
George Blunden (Bank of England)	1974–1977	Michael Dealtry	1974–1984
Peter Cooke (Bank of England)	1977–1988	Chris Thompson	1984–1988
Huib Muller (Netherlands Bank)	1988–1991	Peter Hayward	1988–1992
E Gerald Corrigan (Fed Res Bank New York)	1991–1993	Erik Musch	1992–1998
Tommaso Padoa-Schioppa (Bank of Italy)	1993–1997	Danièle Nouy	1998–2003
Tom de Swaan (Netherlands Bank)	1997–1998	Ryozo Himino	2003–2006
William J McDonough (Fed Res Bank New York)	1998–2003	Stefan Walter	2006–2011
Jaime Caruana (Bank of Spain)	2003–2006	Wayne Byres	2012–2014
Nout Wellink (Netherlands Bank)	2006–2011	William Coen	2014–2019
Stefan Ingves (Sveriges Riksbank)	2011–2019	Carolyn Rogers	2019–present
Pablo Hernández de Cos (Bank of Spain)	2019–present		

4 Group of Experts on Payment Systems (1980–90)/Committee on Payment and Settlement Systems, CPSS (1990–2014)/Committee on Payments and Market Infrastructures, CPMI (since 2014)

As from 1969, a group of central-bank computer experts began to meet regularly at the BIS. Their discussions on payment system issues prompted the G10 Governors to set up a separate Group of Experts on Payment Systems in 1980. In 1989, an ad hoc Committee on Interbank Netting Schemes was created, chaired by BIS General Manager Alexandre Lamfalussy, to study the policy issues related to cross-border and multicurrency interbank netting schemes. As a follow-up to the work of this committee, in 1990 the G10

Governors decided to turn the existing Group of Experts on Payment Systems into a full-fledged G10 Committee on Payment and Settlement Systems (CPSS), reporting directly to them. In its early years, the CPSS focused on the reduction of foreign exchange settlement risk ('Herstatt risk') and on the global move towards real-time gross settlement systems (RTGS).

In 2014, in the light of the committee's enhanced standard-setting activities, its mandate was reviewed and the CPSS was renamed the Committee on Payments and Market Infrastructures (CPMI). The CPMI's mandate is to promote the safety and efficiency of payment, clearing, settlement and related arrangements, thereby supporting financial stability and the wider economy. To this end, the CPMI monitors and analyses developments in these arrangements, both within and across jurisdictions. It also serves as a forum for central-bank cooperation in related oversight, policy and operational matters, including the provision of central-bank services. The CPMI is also a global standard setter in this area. It aims to strengthen regulation, policy and practices regarding such arrangements worldwide. The CPMI Charter, describing its mandate, membership, governance and organisation, was published in September 2014. See: www.bis.org > Committees & associations > Committee on Payments and Market Infrastructures.

Membership

From 1990	National Bank of Belgium, Bank of Canada, Bank of France, Deutsche Bundesbank, Bank of Italy, Bank of Japan, Netherlands Bank, Sveriges Riksbank, Swiss National Bank, Bank of England, Board of Governors of the Federal Reserve System, Federal Reserve Bank of New York.
From 1997	All of the above plus Hong Kong Monetary Authority, Monetary Authority of Singapore.
From 1998	All of the above plus European Central Bank.
From 2009	All of the above plus Reserve Bank of Australia, Central Bank of Brazil, People's Bank of China, Reserve Bank of India, Bank of Korea, Bank of Mexico, Central Bank of the Russian Federation, Saudi Arabian Monetary Authority, South African Reserve Bank, Central Bank of the Republic of Turkey.
From 2018	All of the above plus Central Bank of Argentina, Bank Indonesia, Bank of Spain.

Chairs and Secretaries

Chair	Tenure	Head of Secretariat (BIS)	Tenure
George Blunden (Bank of England)	1980–1982		
Hans Meyer (Swiss NB)	1983–1988		
Wayne Angell (Fed Reserve Board)	1988–1994	Paul Van den Bergh	1989–1998
William McDonough (Fed Res Bank New York)	1994–1998		
Wendelin Hartmann (Deutsche Bundesbank)	1998–2000	Gregor Heinrich	1998–2002
Tommaso Padoa-Schioppa (ECB)	2000–2005	Marc Hollanders	2002–2007
Timothy Geithner (Fed Res Bank New York)	2005–2009	Denis Beau	2007–2008
William C Dudley (Fed Res Bank New York)	2009–2012	Daniel Heller	2009–2012
Paul Tucker (Bank of England)	2012–2013	Klaus Löber	2012–2016
Benoît Cœuré (ECB)	2013–2019	Morten Bech	2016–2020
Jon Cunliffe (Bank of England)	2020–present		

Annex 3

BIS Balance Sheet, 1980–2019

The BIS was created in 1930 as a company limited by shares. As on 31 March 2019, the Bank's issued capital amounted to SDR 698.9 million, consisting of 559,125 shares (with each share having a par value of SDR 5,000 but only being paid up to 25 per cent). The total authorised capital of the Bank amounts to 600,000 shares, equivalent to a total of SDR 3 billion (if fully paid up). The 559,125 shares issued as on 31 March 2019 were held by the BIS member central banks, with 1,000 shares being held in treasury by the BIS itself.

The BIS was set up as a bank in order to allow it to fulfil its original objective of receiving, administering and distributing the annuities payable by Germany under the so-called Young Plan (plan for the definitive settlement of the First World War reparation payments due by Germany, as adopted at the Hague Conference in January 1930). As these annuities were paid to the BIS by the German Reichsbank on behalf of Germany, and distributed by the BIS to the central banks of the allied nations, all central banks concerned opened accounts with the BIS and vice versa. The Bank's Statutes also assigned to the BIS the objective of 'providing additional facilities for international financial operations'. The type of banking operations the BIS is allowed to carry out on its own behalf or on behalf of its customers – central banks and international organisations – is specified in articles 20 to 25 of the current Statutes. On this basis, the BIS offers a wide range of financial services specifically designed to assist central banks and other official monetary institutions in the management of their foreign exchange reserves. These services include money market instruments, BIS tradable instruments, foreign exchange and gold services, and asset management services, as well as trustee or agency functions in connection with international financial arrangements. The BIS's banking business is managed with particular regard to maintaining liquidity and therefore retains assets appropriate to the maturity and character of its liabilities. The Bank's Statutes do not allow the BIS to open current accounts in the name of, or make advances to, governments. The Bank's customers are exclusively central banks and other public sector entities.

The BIS balance sheet closed on 31 March 2019 (end of financial year 2018–19) with total assets of SDR 291.1 billion.

From 1930 until 2003, the Bank's accounts were expressed in gold francs, which was in fact the Swiss gold franc as it existed before its devaluation on 26 September 1936 (i.e. one Swiss gold franc being equivalent to 0.29032258 grams of fine gold). As from 1934, the value of the gold franc was calculated on the basis of the official US Treasury selling price for gold of $35 per ounce of fine gold. In December 1971, as a result of the monetary realignment agreed at the Smithsonian summit, the new gold parity of $38 per ounce was adopted for converting US dollars into gold francs. In February 1973, the dollar was devalued again to $42.22 per ounce. This reference basis was used until mid-1979. As a result, the official gold price used by the Bank for converting its accounts in gold francs became increasingly removed from the market price. In June 1979, the BIS decided to update the price to $208 per ounce of fine gold to reflect the change in the market price. This resulted in a fixed rate of 1 gold franc = $1.94149, which remained in place until March 2003. Since April 2003 (start of the financial year 2003–04), the Bank's accounts have been expressed in the SDR or Special Drawing Right, a basket of the main currencies used in international trade and finance, as defined by the International Monetary Fund. During the first nine months of 2019, the value of 1 SDR averaged $1.388.

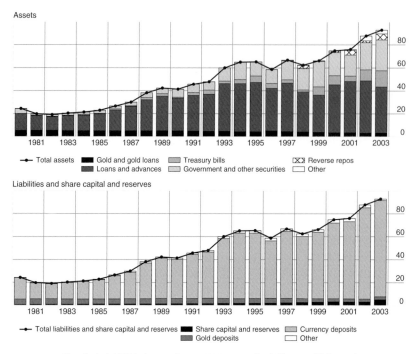

Graph A.1 BIS balance sheet, 1980–2003 (in billion gold francs)

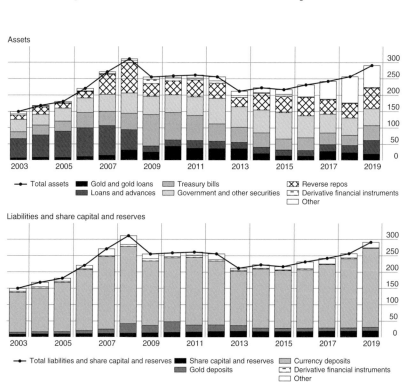

Graph A.2 BIS balance sheet, 2003–2019 (in billion SDR)

Notes:

As mentioned above, until the financial year ending on 31 March 1979 the BIS converted the gold franc, used in its accounts, on the basis of the official US dollar gold price of $42.22 per ounce determined in February 1973. For that reason, the Bank's balance sheet from 1973 to 1979 is not comparable one-for-one with the balance sheet for the period 1980 to 2003, when the BIS applied a gold-dollar conversion rate of $208 per ounce of fine gold.

For ease of comparison, Graph A.1 only provides the balance sheet figures for the period 1980–2003. For the BIS balance sheet totals for the period 1930–1979, the reader is referred to Toniolo 2005: 647–60.

The relatively strong growth in share capital and reserves in 2003 (Graph A.1) reflects a change in accounting practices, under which what had previously been hidden reserves were made transparent and included in the total reserves position.

Annex 4

Current and Former Functionaries of the BIS Board
of Directors and BIS Management, 1973–2020

Chair of the BIS Board of Directors

Jens Weidmann	Nov 2015–present
Christian Noyer	Mar 2010–Oct 2015
Guillermo Ortiz	Mar 2009–Dec 2009
Jean-Pierre Roth	Mar 2006–Feb 2009
Arnout H. E. M. Wellink	Mar 2002–Feb 2006
Urban Bäckström	Mar 1999–Feb 2002
Alfons Verplaetse	Jul 1997–Feb 1999
Willem F. Duisenberg	Jan 1994–Jun 1997
Bengt Dennis	Jan 1991–Dec 1993
Willem F. Duisenberg	Jan 1998–Dec 1990
Jean Godeaux	Jan 1985–Dec 1987
Fritz Leutwiler	Jan 1982–Dec 1984
Jelle Zijlstra	Jul 1967–Dec 1981

Vice-Chair of the BIS Board of Directors

Raghuram G. Rajan	Nov 2015–Sep 2016
Masaaki Shirakawa	Jan 2011–Mar 2013
Hans Tietmeyer	Jun 2003–Dec 2010
Robin Leigh-Pemberton	Jun 1996–Jun 2003
Carlo A. Ciampi	Jul 1994–May 1996
Lamberto Dini	Sep 1993–May 1994
Gordon Richardson	Nov 1991–Jun 1993
Bernard Clappier	Aug 1989–Nov 1991
Paolo Baffi	Nov 1988–Aug 1989
Gordon Richardson	Nov 1985–Nov 1988
Bernard Clappier	Jul 1983–Nov 1985
Leslie K. O'Brien	Mar 1979–Jun 1983
Henri Deroy	Nov 1970–Jan 1979

Current and former senior members of BIS Management
General Manager

Agustín Carstens	Dec 2017–present
Jaime Caruana	Apr 2009–Nov 2017
Hervé Hannoun (*Acting General Manager*)	Oct 2008–Mar 2009
Malcolm D. Knight	Apr 2003–Sep 2008
Andrew Crockett	Jan 1994–Mar 2003
Alexandre Lamfalussy	May 1985–Dec 1993
Günther Schleiminger	Mar 1981–Apr 1985
René Larre	May 1971–Feb 1981

Assistant General Manager/Deputy General Manager (since 2000)

Luiz Awazu Pereira da Silva	Oct 2015–present
Hervé Hannoun	Jan 2006–Sep 2015
André Icard	Jan 1996–Dec 2005
Remi Gros	Feb 1992–Dec 1995
Richard Hall	May 1985–Jan 1992
Alexandre Lamfalussy	Mar 1981–Apr 1985
Günther Schleiminger	Jan 1978–Feb 1981
Antonio d'Aroma	Jan 1975–Dec 1977

Secretary General

Monica Ellis	Jan 2017–present
Peter Dittus	Jan 2005–Dec 2016
Gunter D. Baer	Sep 1994–Dec 2004
Giampietro Morelli	Jun 1978–Aug 1994
Günther Schleiminger	Jan 1975–May 1978
Antonio d'Aroma	Jan 1962–Dec 1974

Head of Banking Department

Peter Zöllner	May 2013–present
Günter Pleines	Apr 2005–Apr 2013
Robert D. Sleeper	Feb 1999–Mar 2005
George Malcolm Gill	Apr 1995–Jan 1999
Remi Gros	May 1985–Mar 1995
Richard Hall	Jan 1974–Apr 1985
Donald Macdonald	Oct 1972–Dec 1973

Economic Adviser/Head of Monetary and Economic Department (MED)

Hyun Song Shin (Economic Adviser and Head of Research)	May 2014–present
Claudio Borio (Head of MED)	Dec 2013–present
Stephen G. Cecchetti	Jul 2008–Nov 2013
William R. White	May 1995–Jun 2008
Horst F. W. Bockelmann	May 1985–Apr 1995
Alexandre Lamfalussy	Jan 1976–Apr 1985
Milton Gilbert	Nov 1960–Dec 1975

Legal Adviser/General Counsel (since 1997)

Diego Devos	Oct 2009–present
Daniel Lefort	Jan 2006–Sep 2009
Mario Giovanoli	Mar 1989–Dec 2005
Frédéric-Edouard Klein	Oct 1974–Dec 1986
Henri Guisan	Apr 1955–Sep 1974

Annex 5

Shareholding Members of the BIS as on 1 July 2020

Year	BIS member central bank	Country
1930	Board of Governors of the Federal Reserve System[1]	USA
	National Bank of Belgium	Belgium
	Bank of England	UK
	Bank of France	France
	Deutsche Bundesbank	Germany
	Bank of Italy	Italy
	Netherlands Bank	Netherlands
	Sveriges Riksbank	Sweden
	Swiss National Bank	Switzerland
	Central Bank of the Republic of Austria	Austria
	Bulgarian National Bank	Bulgaria
	Danmarks Nationalbank	Denmark
	Bank of Finland	Finland
	Bank of Greece	Greece
	Magyar Nemzeti Bank	Hungary
	Narodowy Bank Polski	Poland
	National Bank of Romania	Romania
	Bank of Estonia	Estonia
	Bank of Latvia	Latvia
1931	Bank of Lithuania	Lithuania
	Central Bank of Norway	Norway
1950	Central Bank of Iceland	Iceland
	Central Bank of Ireland	Republic of Ireland
1951	Bank of Portugal	Portugal
	Central Bank of the Republic of Turkey	Turkey
1960	Bank of Spain	Spain
1970	Bank of Canada	Canada
	The Bank of Japan[2]	Japan
	Reserve Bank of Australia	Australia
1971	South African Reserve Bank	South Africa
1993	Czech National Bank[3]	Czech Republic
	National Bank of Slovakia[3]	Slovakia
1996	The People's Bank of China	China
	Hong Kong Monetary Authority	Hong Kong SAR
	Reserve Bank of India	India
	Bank of Mexico	Mexico

(continued)

(continued)

Year	BIS member central bank	Country
	Central Bank of the Russian Federation	Russia
	Saudi Arabian Monetary Agency	Saudi Arabia
	Monetary Authority of Singapore	Singapore
1997	Bank of Korea	Republic of Korea
	Central Bank of Brazil	Brazil
	Croatian National Bank[4]	Croatia
	National Bank of the Republic of Macedonia[4]	Macedonia
	Bank of Slovenia[4]	Slovenia
	Central Bank of Bosnia and Herzegovina[4]	Bosnia and Herzegovina
1999	Central Bank of Malaysia	Malaysia
	European Central Bank	Euro area
2000	Central Bank of Argentina	Argentina
	Bank of Thailand	Thailand
2003	Bank of Algeria	Algeria
	Reserve Bank of New Zealand	New Zealand
	Bangko Sentral ng Pilipinas	Philippines
	Central Bank of Chile	Chile
	Bank Indonesia	Indonesia
	Bank of Israel	Israel
2009	National Bank of Serbia[4]	Serbia
2011	Central Bank of Colombia	Colombia
	Central Bank of Luxembourg	Luxembourg
	Central Reserve Bank of Peru	Peru
	Central Bank of the United Arab Emirates	United Arab Emirates
2020	Central Bank of Kuwait	Kuwait
	Bank of Morocco	Morocco
	State Bank of Vietnam	Vietnam

[1] The US Federal Reserve System was one of the founding central banks of the BIS. However, the BIS shares issued in its name were not subscribed by the Federal Reserve but rather offered for public subscription via a consortium of US private banks. These privately held shares were withdrawn in 2001, without affecting the rights of representation and voting rights of the Federal Reserve System.

[2] The Bank of Japan had been a BIS member central bank since 1930. However, the shares issued in its name had been subscribed by a consortium of Japanese private banks. In 1952 the Bank of Japan relinquished its BIS membership as a result of the San Francisco Peace Treaty of 1951. The Bank of Japan again became a shareholding member of the BIS in 1970.

[3] The Czechoslovak National Bank was a BIS member central bank from 1930. In 1993, it was legally succeeded as BIS member central bank by both the Czech National Bank and the National Bank of Slovakia.

[4] The National Bank of Yugoslavia joined as a BIS member central bank in 1931. Its membership was in abeyance from 1991 to 1992 as a result of the civil war and dissolution of the Yugoslav Republic. The legal succession of the National Bank of Yugoslavia as BIS member central bank was resolved in 1997–2009, with the central banks of Croatia, Macedonia, Slovenia, Bosnia-Herzegovina and Serbia all becoming BIS member central banks.

COMMENTS

The Bank of Danzig was a BIS member from 1930. The Free City of Danzig ceased to exist in 1939, and the Bank of Danzig was liquidated thereafter. The BIS shares issued in the name of the Bank of Danzig were cancelled by decision of the Extraordinary General Meeting of 11 June 1979.

The National Bank of Albania was a BIS member from 1931 until it withdrew its membership in 1977.

Note on Sources

The contributions in this book are based on original research undertaken by the authors on the basis of the BIS's own publications, academic literature and primary source material.

The vast majority of the BIS's own publications are available at www.bis.org.

With regard to its archives, the BIS applies a thirty-year access restriction for external researchers (see: www.bis.org > About BIS > History > Archive collections). In addition, for the purpose of this volume, the authors were given access to more recent material – in some cases up to 2019 – on the condition that they respected certain confidentiality limitations that still apply to such materials.

The exact references to these archival sources can be found in the endnotes at the end of each chapter, where 'BISA' stands for 'Bank for International Settlements Archive'. The majority of archival materials up to 2010 are preserved in hardcopy (paper-based) format and can be consulted only on the premises of the BIS in Basel. For any enquiries, please contact archive@bis.org.

In addition to privileged access to the Bank's archives, the authors benefited from discussions with and input from BIS staff, past and present, who were closely involved with the events and developments described in this volume.

Bibliography

Any references to Bank for International Settlements publications can be located at www.bis.org.

Abbott, K. W. and S. Duncan (2000). Hard and Soft Law in International Governance. *International Organization*, 54(3), 421–56.

Abdelal, R. (2006). The IMF and the Capital Account. In E. M. Truman, ed., *Reforming the IMF for the 21st Century*. Washington, DC: Institute of International Economics, 185–97.

Abreu, D. and M. K. Brunnermeier (2003). Bubbles and Crashes. *Econometrica*, 71(1), 173–204.

Adrian, T. and M. K. Brunnermeier (2010). Co VaR: A Systemic Risk Contribution Measure. Technical Report, Princeton University and Federal Reserve Bank of New York, Staff Reports, No. 348.

Adrian, T. and H. S. Shin (2010). Liquidity and Leverage. *Journal of Financial Intermediation*, 19(3), 418–37.

Alexander, K., R. Dhumale and J. Eatwell (2006). *Global Governance of Financial Systems: The International Regulation of Systemic Risk*. Oxford: Oxford University Press.

Allen, F., C. Bean and J. De Gregorio (2016). *Independent Review of BIS Research: Final Report*. Basel: Bank for International Settlements, 23 December.

Arner, D. W. and M. W. Taylor (2009). The Global Financial Crisis and the Financial Stability Board: Hardening the Soft Law of International Financial Regulation? Asian Institute of International Financial Law, *Working Paper*, No. 6. See www.law.hku.hk/aiifl/research/documents/AIIFLWorkingPaper6June2009.pdf.

Baer, G. D. (1994). The Committee of Governors as a Forum for European Central Bank Cooperation. In A. F. Bakker, H. Boot, O. Sleijpen and W. Vanthoor, eds., *Monetary Stability through International Cooperation: Essays in Honour of André Szász*. Amsterdam: De Nederlandsche Bank, 147–57.

Baker, A. (2013). The New Political Economy of the Macroprudential Ideational Shift. *New Political Economy*, 18(1), 112–39.

Baker, A. (2014). The G20 and Monetary Policy Stasis. *International Organizations Research Journal*, 9(4), 19–31. See http://iorj.hse.ru/data/2014/12/28/1103785194/3.pdf.

Baker, A. (2015). Varieties of Economic Crisis, Varieties of Ideational Change: How and Why Financial Regulation and Macroeconomic Policy Differ. *New Political Economy*, 20(3), 342–66.

Baker, A. (2017). Esteem as Professional Currency and Consolidation: The Rise of the Macroprudential Cognoscenti. In L. Seabrooke and L. Henriksen, eds., *Professionals and Organizations in Transnational Governance*. Cambridge: Cambridge University Press, 149–64.

Baker, A. (2018). Macroprudential Regimes and the Politics of Social Purpose. *Review of International Political Economy*, 25(3), 293–316.

Bank for International Settlements (BIS AR) (1973–2019). *BIS Annual (Economic) Reports*, from 1973 until 2019.

Bank for International Settlements (BIS) (1983). The International Interbank Market: A Descriptive Study. *BIS Economic Papers*, No. 8, July.

Bank for International Settlements (BIS) (2009). Addressing Financial System Procyclicality: A Possible Framework. Note for the FSF group on Market and Institutional Resilience. See www.fsb.org/wp-content/uploads/r_0904e.pdf.

Bank for International Settlements (BIS) (1930–2016), Statutes of the Bank for International Settlements. See www.bis.org/about/statutes-en.pdf.

Barr, M. S. and G. P. Miller (2006). Global Administrative Law: The View from Basel. *European Journal of International Law*, 17(1), 15–46.

Basel Committee on Banking Supervision (1997). *Core Principles for Effective Banking Supervision*. Basel: Bank for International Settlements, September.

Basel Committee on Banking Supervision (2011a). *Global Systemically Important Banks: Assessment Methodology and the Additional Loss Absorbency Requirement*. Basel: Bank for International Settlements. See www.bis.org/publ/bcbs207.pdf.

Basel Committee on Banking Supervision (2011b). *Basel III: A Global Regulatory Framework for More Resilient Banks and Banking Systems*. Basel: Bank for International Settlements, June. See www.bis.org/publ/bcbs189.pdf.

Bayoumi, T. (2017). *Unfinished Business: The Unexplored Causes of the Financial Crisis and the Lessons Yet to Be Learned*. New Haven: Yale University Press.

Bayoumi, T. and B. Eichengreen (1993). Shocking Aspects of European Monetary Unification. In F. Torres and F. Giavazzi, eds., *Adjustment and Growth in the European Monetary Union*. Cambridge: Cambridge University Press.

Bederman, D. (1988). The Bank for International Settlements and the Debt Crisis: A New Role for the Central Bankers' Bank. *Berkeley Journal of International Law*, 6(1), 92–121.

Bernholz, P. (2009). Are International Organizations Like the Bank for International Settlements Unable to Die? *Review of International Organisations*, 4(4), 361–81.

Bhattacharya, S., C. Goodhart, D. Tsomocos and A. P. Vardoulakis (2015). A Reconsideration of Minsky's Financial Instability Hypothesis. *Journal of Money, Credit and Banking*, 47(5), 931–73.

Bird, G. (1998). The Political Economy of the SDR: The Rise and Fall of an International Reserve Asset. *Global Governance*, 4(3), 355–79.

Blyth, M. (2002). *Great Transformations: Economic Ideas and Institutional Change in the Twenty First Century*. Cambridge: Cambridge University Press.

Bordo, M. D. and H. James (2017). Partial Fiscalization: Some Historical Lessons on Europe's Unfinished Business. In L. Odor, ed., *Rethinking Fiscal Policy after the Crisis*. Cambridge: Cambridge University Press, 232–57.

Bordo, M. D. and L. Jonung (2003). The Future of EMU: What Does the History of Monetary Unions Tell Us? In F. H. Capie and G. E. Wood, eds., *Monetary Unions: Theory, History, Public Choice*. London, New York: Routledge, 42–69.

Borio, C. (2003). Towards a Macroprudential Framework for Financial Supervision and Regulation? *CESifo Economic Studies*, 49(2), 181–215.

Borio, C. (2006). Monetary and Prudential Policies at a Crossroads? New Challenges in the New Century. *BIS Working Papers*, No. 216.

Borio, C. (2008). The Financial Turmoil of 2007–?: A Preliminary Assessment and Some Policy Considerations. *BIS Working Papers*, No. 251.

Borio, C. (2011a). Rediscovering the Macroeconomic Roots of Financial Stability: Journey, Challenges and a Way Forward. *BIS Working Papers*, No. 354.

Borio, C. (2011b). Implementing a Macroprudential Framework: Blending Boldness and Realism. *Capitalism and Society*, 6(1), 1–23.

Borio, C. (2014). The International Monetary and Financial System: Its Achilles Heel and What to Do About It. *BIS Working Papers*, No. 456, August.

Borio, C. (2018). Macroprudential Frameworks: Experience, Prospects and a Way Forward. Speech at the BIS Annual General Meeting, 24 June. See www.bis.org/speeches/sp180624a.pdf.

Borio, C. and P. Disyatat (2011). Global Imbalances and the Financial Crisis: Link or No Link? *BIS Working Papers*, No. 346, May.

Borio, C. and M. Drehmann (2009). Towards an Operational Framework for Financial Stability: 'Fuzzy' Measurement and Its Consequences. *BIS Working Papers*, No. 284.

Borio, C., C. Furfine and P. Lowe (2001). Procyclicality of the Financial System and Financial Stability Issues and Policy Options. *BIS Papers*, No. 1, 1–57.

Borio, C. and P. Lowe (2002). Asset Prices, Financial and Monetary Stability: Exploring the Nexus. *BIS Working Papers*, No. 114.

Borio, C. and I. Shim (2007). What Can (macro-)Prudential Policy Do to Support Monetary Policy? *BIS Working Papers*, No. 242.

Borio, C. and G. Toniolo (2006). One Hundred and Thirty Years of Central Bank Cooperation: A BIS Perspective. *BIS Working Papers*, No. 197.

Borio, C. and G. Toniolo (2008). One Hundred and Thirty Years of Central Bank Cooperation: A BIS Perspective. In C. Borio, G. Toniolo and P. Clement, eds., *The Past and Future of Central Bank Cooperation, Studies in Macroeconomic History Series*. Cambridge: Cambridge University Press, 16–75.

Borio, C. and W. R. White (2004). Whither Monetary and Financial Stability? The Implications of Evolving Policy Regimes. *BIS Working Papers*, No. 147.

Borio, C., G. Toniolo and P. Clement, eds. (2008). *Past and Future of Central Bank Cooperation*. Cambridge: Cambridge University Press.

Bossone, B. (2008). *IMF Surveillance: A Case Study on IMF Governance*. BP/08/10. Washington, DC: International Monetary Fund, Independent Evaluation Office (IEO).

Bozo, F. (2009). *Mitterrand, the End of the Cold War, and German Unification*. New York: Berghahn Books.

Brummer, C. (2014a). *Minilateralism: How Trade Alliances, Soft Law and Financial Engineering Are Redefining Economic Statecraft.* Cambridge: Cambridge University Press.

Brummer, C. (2014b). *Soft Law and the Global Financial System.* Cambridge: Cambridge University Press.

Brunnermeier, M. K., A. Crockett, C. Goodhart, A. D. Persaud and H. S. Shin (2009). The Fundamental Principles of Financial Regulation. Geneva Report on the World Economy. Geneva: International Centre for Monetary and Banking Studies, London: Centre for Economic Policy Research.

Brunnermeier, M., H. James and J.-P. Landau (2016). *The Euro and the Battle of Ideas.* Princeton: Princeton University Press.

Brunnermeier, M. K. and M. Oehmke (2012). Bubbles, Financial Crises, and Systemic Risk. *NBER Working Papers*, No. 18398.

Buiter, W., G. Corsetti and P. Pesenti (1998). Interpreting the ERM Crisis: Country-Specific and Systemic Issues. *Princeton Studies in International Finance*, No. 84, March. International Finance Section, Department of Economics, Princeton University.

Caballero, R. J. and A. Simsek (2017). A Risk-centric Model of Demand Recessions and Macroprudential Policy. *NBER Working Papers*, No. 23614. See https://economics .mit.edu/files/13059.

Carstens, A. (2019a). *The New Role of Central Banks.* Speech at the Financial Stability Institute's 20th Anniversary Conference, Basel, 12 March.

Carstens, A. (2019b). The Future of Money and Payments. Speech at the 2019 Whitaker Lecture, Central Bank of Ireland, Dublin, 22 March.

Caruana, J. (2004). Basel II – A New Approach to Banking Supervision. *BIS Review*, 33, 1–9.

Caruana, J. (2012). *Policy Making in an Interconnected World.* Luncheon Speech to the Annual Economic Policy Symposium of the Federal Reserve Bank of Kansas City, Jackson Hole, Wyoming, 31 August.

Caskey, J. (1989). The IMF and Concerted Lending in Latin American Debt Restructurings: A Formal Analysis. *Journal of International Money and Finance*, 8 (1), 105–20.

Cecchetti, S. G., I. Fender and P. McGuire (2010). Toward a Global Risk Map. *BIS Working Papers*, No. 309.

Cecchetti, S. G., M. S. Mohanty and F. Zampolli (2011). The Real Effects of Debt. *BIS Working Papers*, No. 352.

Claessens, S. (2019). *Moving Forward with Macroprudential Frameworks.* Presentation at the SUERF/Narodowy Bank Polski Conference on Challenges of Interactions between Macroprudential and Other Policies, Warsaw, 15 February.

Clement, P. (2008). Introduction: Past and Future of Central Bank Cooperation. In C. Borio, G. Toniolo and P. Clement, eds., *Past and Future of Central Bank Cooperation.* Cambridge: Cambridge University Press, 1–15.

Clement, P. (2010). The Term 'Macroprudential': Origins and Evolution. *BIS Quarterly Review*, March, 59–67.

Clement, P. and I. Maes (2013). The BIS and the Latin American Debt Crisis of the 1980s. *National Bank of Belgium Working Papers*, No. 247, December.

Clement, P. and I. Maes (2016). The BIS and the Latin American Debt Crisis of the 1980s. In M. Garcia-Molina and H.-M. Trautwein, eds., *Peripheral Visions of*

Economic Development: New Frontiers in Development Economics and the History of Economic Thought. New York: Routledge, 203–28.

Cline, W. (1982–1983). Mexico's Crisis, the World's Peril. *Foreign Policy*, 49, 107–18.

Committee on the Global Financial System (1986). *Recent Innovations in International Banking*. Basel: Bank for International Settlements, 1 April.

Cooke, W. P. (1982). *The Role of the Banking Supervisor*. Bank of England Quarterly Bulletin, December, 547–52.

Crockett, A. (2000a). *In Search of Anchors for Financial and Monetary Stability*. Speech at the SUERF Colloquium, Vienna, 27–29 April. See www.bis.org/speeches/sp000427.htm.

Crockett, A. (2000b). *Marrying the Micro- and Macro-prudential Dimensions of Financial Stability*. Remarks at the 11th International Conference of Banking Supervisors, Basel, 20–21 September. See www.bis.org/speeches/sp000921.htm.

Crockett, A. (2002). *Towards Global Financial Reporting Standards: A Critical Pillar in the International Financial Architecture*. Lecture at the US-Europe Symposium Rüschlikon, 27 February.

Danielsson, J., P. Embrechts, C. Goodhart, C. Keating, F. Muennich, O. Renault and H. S. Shin (2001). *An Academic Response to Basel II*. Special Paper-LSE Financial Markets Group.

Danielsson, J., H. S. Shin and J.-P. Zigrand (2004). The Impact of Risk Regulation on Price Dynamics. *Journal of Banking and Finance*, 28(5), 1069–87.

De Grauwe, P. (2010). The Scientific Foundation of Dynamic Stochastic General Equilibrium (DSGE) Models. *Public Choice*, 144(3–4), 413–43.

De Grauwe, P. (2012). *The Eurozone's Design Failures: Can They Be Corrected?* Lecture at the London School of Economics and Political Science. See www.lse.ac.uk/lse-player?id=1675

De Lis, F. S., J. Martinez Pagés and J. Saurina (2001). Credit Growth, Problem Loans and Credit Risk Provisioning in Spain. *BIS Papers*, No. 1, 331–53.

Devenow, A. and I. Welch (1996). Rational Herding in Financial Economics. *European Economic Review*, 40(3–5), 603–15.

Dornbusch, R. (1976). Expectations and Exchange Rate Dynamics. *Journal of Political Economy*, 84(6), 1161–76.

Dornbusch, R. and A. Werner (1994). Stabilization, Reform, and No Growth. *Brookings Papers on Economic Activity*, 25(1), 253–297.

Draghi, M. (2012). *Competitiveness – The Key to Balanced Growth in Monetary Union*. Remarks at Treasury Talks 'A European Strategy for Growth and Integration with Solidarity', a Conference Organised by the Directorate General of the Treasury, Ministry of Economy and Finance – Ministry for Foreign Trade, Paris, 30 November.

Drehmann, M. et al. (2016). Recent Enhancements to the BIS Statistics. *BIS Quarterly Review*, September, 35–44

Drehmann, M. and M. Juselius (2014). Evaluating Early Warning Indicators of Banking Crises: Satisfying Policy Requirements. *International Journal of Forecasting*, 30(3), 759–80.

Drehmann, M. and K. Tsatsaronis (2014). The Credit-to-GDP Gap and Countercyclical Capital Buffers: Questions and Answers. *BIS Quarterly Review*, March, 55–73.

Drehmann, M., C. Borio, L. Gambacorta, G. Jimenez and C. Trucharte (2010). Countercyclical Capital Buffers: Exploring Options. *BIS Working Papers*, No. 317.

Eatwell, J. (2009). Practical Proposals for Regulatory Reform. In P. Subacchi and A. Monsarrat, eds., *New Ideas for the London Summit: Recommendations to the G20 Leaders*. Chatham House and Atlantic Council Report, 11–15.

Eichengreen, B. (1998). *Globalizing Capital: A History of the International Monetary System*. Princeton: Princeton University Press.

Eichengreen, B. (2000). The EMS Crisis in Retrospect. *NBER Working Papers*, No. 8035.

Eichengreen, B. (2008). *Globalizing Capital: A History of the International Monetary System*, 2nd edn. Princeton: Princeton University Press.

Eichengreen, B. (2011). *Exorbitant Privilege: The Rise and Fall of the Dollar and the Future of the International Monetary System*. Oxford: Oxford University Press.

Eichengreen, B. and P. Gupta (2018). Managing Sudden Stops. In E. Mendoza, E. Pastén and D. Saravia, eds., *Monetary Policy and Global Spillovers: Mechanisms, Effects and Policy Measures*, 1st edn., Vol. 25. Santiago: Central Bank of Chile, 9–47.

Eichengreen, B. and M. Uzan (1992). The 1933 World Economic Conference as an Instance of Failed International Cooperation. In P. Evans, H. Jacobson and R. Putnam, eds., *Double-Edged Diplomacy: International Bargaining and Domestic Politics*. Berkeley: University of California Press, 71–106.

Embrechts, P., F. Lindskog and A. McNeil (2001). Modelling Dependence with Copulas and Applications to Risk Management. *Rapport technique, Département de mathématiques, Institut Fédéral de Technologie de Zurich, Zurich*.

European Economic Community (1962). *Action Programme for the Second Phase of EEC*, 24 October.

Fama, E. F. (1991). Efficient Capital Markets: II. *The Journal of Finance*, 46(5), 1575–617.

Federal Reserve Bank of Kansas City (2003). *Whither Financial and Monetary Stability? The Implications of Evolving Policy Regimes*. General Discussion: Chair Guillermo Ortiz. Annual Economic Policy Symposium of the Federal Reserve Bank of Kansas City, Jackson Hole, Wyoming. See www.kansascityfed.org/publicat/sympos/2003/pdf/GD32003.pdf.

Feldstein, M. (2012). The Failure of the Euro: The Little Currency That Couldn't. *Foreign Affairs*, January/February.

Felix, D. (1990). Latin America's Debt Crisis. *World Policy Journal*, 7(4),733–71.

Financial Services Authority (2009). *The Turner Review: A Regulatory Response to the Global Banking Crisis*. London: FSA.

Financial Stability Board (2013a). *Policy Framework for Strengthening Oversight and Regulation of Shadow Banking Entities*, August. See www.fsb.org/2013/08/r_130829 c.

Financial Stability Board (2013b). *Policy Framework for Addressing Shadow Banking Risks in Securities Lending and Repos*, August. See www.fsb.org/2013/08/r_130829b.

Financial Stability Board (2015). *Transforming Shadow Banking into Resilient Market-Based Finance: An Overview of Progress*, November. See www.fsb.org/2015/11/transforming-shadow-banking-into-resilient-market-based-finance-an-overview-of-progress.

Financial Stability Forum (2008). *Report of the Financial Stability Forum on Enhancing Market and Institutional Resilience*, April. See www.fsb.org/publications/r_0804.pdf.

Financial Stability Forum (2009). *Report on Addressing Procyclicality in the Financial System*, April. See www.fsb.org/publications/r_0904a.pdf.

Fischer, S. (1997). *Capital Account Liberalization and the Role of the IMF*. Speech at the IMF Seminar on 'Asia and the IMF', 19 September. See www.imf.org/en/News/Articles/2015/09/28/04/53/sp091997.

Fischer, S. (1998). Capital-Account Liberalization and the Role of the IMF. In S. Fischer, R. N. Cooper, R. Dornbusch, P. M. Garber, C. Massad, J. J. Polak, D. Rodrik and S. S. Tarapore, eds., *Should the IMF Pursue Capital-Account Convertibility?* Essays in International Finance, No. 207, 1–10 May. International Finance Section, Department of Economics, Princeton University.

Frankel, J. (2015). *The Plaza Accord, Thirty Years Later*. Unpublished manuscript. Harvard University, December.

Fraser, B. (1995). *Central Bank Cooperation in the Asian Region*. Talk to the 24th Conference of Economists in Adelaide, 25 September, Reserve Bank of Australia. See www.rba.gov.au/speeches/1995/sp-gov-250995.html.

Frenkel, J. and M. Goldstein (1986). A Guide to Exchange Rate Target Zones. *NBER Working Papers*, No. 2113.

Funabashi, Y. (1988). *Managing the Dollar: From the Plaza to the Louvre*. Washington: Institute for International Economics.

Gelpern, A. and M. Gulati (2010). Foreword: Of Lawyers, Leaders, and Returning Riddles in Sovereign Debt. *Law and Contemporary Problems*, 73(4), autumn, i–xii.

Gilbert, M. (1968). The Gold-Dollar System: Conditions of Equilibrium and the Price of Gold. *Essays in International Finance*, No. 70, October. International Finance Section, Department of Economics, Princeton University.

Goodhart, C. (2011). *The Basel Committee on Banking Supervision: A History of the Early Years, 1974–1997*. Cambridge: Cambridge University Press.

Goodhart, C. and J. Danielsson (2001). *The Inter-Temporal Nature of Risk*. 23rd SUERF Colloquium on Technology and Finance: Challenges for Financial Markets, Business Strategies and Policy Makers, Brussels, October.

Gore, C. (2000). The Rise and Fall of the Washington Consensus as a Paradigm for Developing Countries, *World Development*, 28(5), 789–804.

Gros, D. and N. Thygesen (1998). *European Monetary Integration: From the European System to Economic and Monetary Union*, 2nd edn. Upper Saddle River: Prentice-Hall.

Group of Twenty (2009). *G20 Working Group on Enhancing Sound Regulation and Strengthening Transparency: Final Report*, February.

Guzman, A. (2008). *How International Law Works: A Rational Choice Theory*. Oxford: Oxford University Press.

Haas, P. (1992). Introduction: Epistemic Communities and International Policy Coordination. *International Organization*, 46(1), 1–35.

Hall, P. A. (1993). Policy Paradigms, Social Learning, and the State: The Case of Economic Policymaking in Britain. *Comparative Politics*, 25(3), 275–96.

Hall, P. A. (2013). Brother, Can You Paradigm? *Governance*, 26(2), 189–92.

Hanke, T. (1998). Dolchstoß. *Die Zeit*, 20, 7 May.

Healey, D. (1989). *The Time of My Life*. London: Michael Joseph.

Holtrop, M. W. (1957). Is a Common Central Bank Policy Necessary within a United Europe? *De Economist*, 105, 642–61.

Honohan, P. (2012). *A View from Ireland – the Crisis and the Euro*. Address to the David Hume Institute and the Scottish Institute for Research in Economics, Edinburgh, 13 November.

Ingves, S. (2014). *Basel III Implementation: Progress, Pitfalls and Prospects.* Speech at the BCBS-FSI High-Level Meeting for the Americas, Lima, 5 November.

Ingves, S. (2018). *Basel III: Are We Done Now?* Basel Committee on Banking Supervision Keynote Speech at the Institute for Law and Finance Conference, Goethe University, Frankfurt am Main, 29 January. See www.bis.org/speeches/sp180129.pdf.

International Monetary Fund (1978). *The Second Amendment to the Fund's Articles of Agreement.* IMF Pamphlet Series, 25 January.

Issing, O. (2012). Großer Beifall von allen Seiten. *Frankfurter Allgemeine Zeitung,* 3 September.

James, H. (1996). *International Monetary Cooperation since Bretton Woods.* Oxford: Oxford University Press.

James, H. (2012). *Making the European Monetary Union.* Cambridge, MA: Belknap Press of Harvard University Press.

Jeanne, O. (2000). Currency Crises: A Perspective on Recent Theoretical Developments. *Special Papers in International Economics,* No. 20, March. International Finance Section, Department of Economics, Princeton University.

Jordan, C. (2014). *International Capital Markets: Law and Institutions.* Oxford: Oxford University Press.

Kane, E. J. (1994). Incentive Conflict in the International Regulatory Agreement on Risk Based Capital. In C. A. Stone and A. Zissu, eds., *Global Risk Based Capital Regulations,* Book 1 on Capital Adequacy. New York: Irvin Professional Publishers, 98–120.

Kantor, R. M. (2011). How Great Companies Think Differently. *Harvard Business Review,* 89, November, 66–78.

Kenen, P. B. (1969). The Theory of Optimum Currency Areas: An Eclectic View. In R. A. Mundell and A. K. Swoboda, eds., *Monetary Problems of the International Economy.* Chicago: University of Chicago Press, 41–60.

Kenen, P. B. (1995). *Economic and Monetary Union in Europe: Moving beyond Maastricht.* Cambridge: Cambridge University Press.

Kindleberger, C. (1978). *Manias, Panics, and Crashes: A History of Financial Crises.* New York: Basic Books.

Knight, M. (2007). *Now You See It, Now You Don't: Risk in the Small and in the Large.* Speech Delivered at the Eighth Annual Risk Management Convention of the Global Association of Risk Professionals, 27–28 February.

Krugman, P. (1979). A Model of Balance of Payments Crises. *Journal of Money, Credit and Banking,* 11(3), 311–25.

Krugman, P. (1998). It's Baaack: Japan's Slump and the Return of the Liquidity Trap. *Brookings Papers on Economic Activity,* 29(2), 137–87.

Lall, R. (2012). From Failure to Failure: The Politics of International Banking Regulation. *Review of International Political Economy,* 19(4), 609–38.

Lamfalussy, A. (1989a). The Danger: A Protectionist Backlash. *Euromoney,* June, 97–102.

Lamfalussy, A. (1989b). *Macro-Coordination of Fiscal Policies in an Economic and Monetary Union in Europe.* Collection of Papers. Committee for the Study of Economic and Monetary Union, Luxembourg, January, 91–126.

Lebor, A. (2013). *Tower of Basel: The Shadowy History of the Secret Bank That Runs the World*. New York: Public Affairs.

Lipson, C. (1991). Why Are Some International Agreements Informal? *International Organization*, 45(4), 495–538.

Lombardi, D. (2011). *The Governance of the Financial Stability Board*. Washington DC: Brookings Institution, September. See www.brookings.edu/wp-content/uploads/2016/06/FSB_Issues_Paper_Lombardi.pdf.

Lombardi, D. and M. Moschella (2017). The Symbolic Politics of Delegation: Macroprudential Policy and Independent Regulatory Authorities. *New Political Economy*, 22(1), 92–108.

Long Island Business News (2003). *1974: Franklin National Bank Goes Under*. See https://libn.com/2003/04/11/1974-franklin-national-bank-goes-under.

Lowenfeld, A. F. (2010). The International Monetary System: A Look Back Over Seven Decades. *Journal of International Economic Law*, 13(3), 575–95.

Ludlow, P. (1982). *The Making of the European Monetary System*. London: Butterworths European Studies.

Maes, I. (2011a). Alexandre Lamfalussy and the Origins of the BIS Macro-Prudential Approach to Financial Stability. *PSL Quarterly Review*, 63(254), 263–90, 19 April. See https://papers.ssrn.com/sol3/papers.cfm?abstract_id=1815135.

Maes, I. (2011b). The Evolution of Alexandre Lamfalussy's Thought on European Monetary Integration 1961–1993. Paper Prepared for the 31st Aphes Conference, Coimbra, 18–19 November. *Œconomia*, 1–4, 489–523.

Maes, I. and P. Clement (2012). *The Latin American Debt Crisis: At the Origins of the BIS Macro-Prudential Approach to Financial Stability*. Unpublished manuscript. National Bank of Belgium and Bank for International Settlements, September.

Maes, I. and G. Szapàry (2017). *Alexandre Lamfalussy. Selected Essays*. Budapest: Magyar Nemzeti Bank and National Bank of Belgium.

Mayer, H. (1982). The Theory and Practice of Floating Exchange Rates and the Role of Official Exchange-Market Intervention. *BIS Economic Papers*, No. 5, February.

Mayer, H. and H. Taguchi (1983). Official Intervention in the Exchange Markets: Stabilising or Destabilising? *BIS Economic Papers*, No. 6, March.

McCauley, R. N. (1997). The Euro and the Dollar. Unpublished manuscript. Bank for International Settlements, November.

McCauley, R. N. and C. R. Schenk (2014). Reforming the International Monetary System in the 1970s and 2000s: Would an SDR Substitution Account Have Worked? *BIS Working Papers*, No. 444, March.

McCauley, R. N. and C. R. Schenk (2020). Central Bank Swaps Then and Now: Swaps and Dollar Liquidity in the 1960s, *BIS Working Paper* (forthcoming).

McCauley, R. N. and J.-F. Rigaudy (2011). Managing Foreign Exchange Reserves in the Crisis and After. *BIS Papers*, No. 58, October, 19–47.

McKinnon, R. I. (1963). Optimum Currency Areas. *American Economic Review*, 53(4), 717–25.

Minsky, H. P. (1995). Financial Factors in the Economics of Capitalism. *Journal of Financial Services Research*, 9, 197–208.

Mody, A. (2018). *EuroTragedy: A Drama in Nine Acts*. Oxford: Oxford University Press.

Monetary and Economic Department, Bank for International Settlements (1983). The International Interbank Market: A Descriptive Study. *BIS Economic Papers*, No. 8, December.

Morris, S. and H. S. Shin (1999). Risk Management with Interdependent Choice. *Oxford Review of Economic Policy*, 15(3), 52–62.

Morris, S., I. Shim and H. S. Shin (2017). Redemption Risk and Cash Hoarding by Asset Managers. *Journal of Monetary Economics*, 89, 71–87. See www.bis.org/publ/work608.pdf.

Mourlon-Druol, E. (2012). *A Europe Made of Money: The Emergence of the European Monetary System*. Ithaca: Cornell University Press.

Mourlon-Druol, E. (2015). 'Trust Is Good, Control Is Better': The 1974 Herstatt Bank Crisis and Its Implications for International Regulatory Reform. *Business History*, 57 (2), 311–34.

Mundell, R. A. (1961). A Theory of Optimum Currency Areas. *American Economic Review*, 51(4), 657–65.

Nofsinger, J. R. and R. W. Sias (1999). Herding and Feedback Trading by Institutional and Individual Investors. *The Journal of Finance*, 54(6), 2263–95.

O'Neill, J. (2001). Building Better Global Economic BRICs. Goldman Sachs Global Economics Paper, 66, November.

Obstfeld, M. (1994). The Logic of Currency Crises. *Banque de France Cahiers Economiques et Monétaires*, 43, 189–213.

Obstfeld, M. (1996). Models of Currency Crises with Self-Fulfilling Features. *European Economic Review*, 40(3–5), 1037–47.

Ocampo, J. A. (2017). *Resetting the International Monetary (Non) System*. Oxford: Oxford University Press.

Ostry, J. D., A. Ghosh, M. Chamon and M. Qureshi (2012). Tools for Managing Financial-Stability Risks from Capital Inflows. *Journal of International Economics*, 88(2), 407–21.

Persaud, A. (2000). Sending the Herd off the Cliff Edge: The Disturbing Interaction between Herding and Market-Sensitive Risk Management Practices. *The Journal of Risk Finance*, 2(1), 59–65.

Pihlman, J. and H. Van der Hoorn (2010). Procyclicality in Central Bank Reserve Management: Evidence from the Crisis. *IMF Working Paper*, 10/150.

Prati, A. and G. J. Schinasi (1997). European Monetary Union and International Capital Markets: Structural Implications and Risks. *IMF Working Papers*, No. 97/62, May.

Rogoff, K. (1985). Can International Monetary Cooperation Be Counterproductive? *Journal of International Economics*, 18(3–4), 199–217.

Roosa, R. (1983). How to Create Exchange Rate Target Zones. *Journal of Commerce*, 3 June.

Rueff, J. (1978). L'Europe se fera par la monnaie ou ne se fera pas. *Commentaire*, 3, 386–88.

Ruggie, J. (1982). International Regimes, Transactions, and Change: Embedded Liberalism in the Postwar Economic Order. *International Organization*, 36(2), 379–415.

Sarotte, M. E. (2011). *1989: The Struggle to Create Post-Cold War Europe*. Princeton: Princeton University Press.

Schenk, C. R. (2010). *The Decline of Sterling: Managing the Retreat of an International Currency, 1945–1992*. Cambridge: Cambridge University Press.

Schenk, C. R. (2014). Summer in the City: Banking Failures of 1974 and the Development of International Banking Supervision. *The English Historical Review*, 129(540), October: Oxford University Press, 1129–56.

Schwarz, H.-P. (2012). *Helmut Kohl: Eine politische Biographie*. München: Deutsche Verlags-Anstalt.

Seabrooke, L. and L. F. Henriksen, eds. (2017). *Professional Networks in Transnational Governance*. Cambridge: Cambridge University Press.

Segoviano, M. A. and C. Goodhart (2009). Banking Stability Measures. *IMF Discussion Paper Series*, No. 627.

Shaffer, G. C. and M. A. Pollack (2010). Hard Law vs. Soft Law: Alternatives, Complements and Antagonists in International Governance. *Minnesota Law Review*, 94(3), 706–799.

Shin, H. S. (2010). *Risk and Liquidity*. Oxford: Oxford University Press.

Singer, D. A. (2007). *Regulating Capital: Setting Standards for the International Financial System*. Ithaca: Cornell University Press.

Skidelsky, R. (2001). *John Maynard Keynes: Fighting for Freedom 1937–1946*. Vol. 3. New York: Viking.

Slaughter, A.-M. (2004). *A New World Order*. Princeton: Princeton University Press.

Slaughter, A.-M. and D. T. Zaring (2006). Networking Goes International: An Update. *Annual Review of Law and Social Science*, 2, 211–29.

Smets, F. and R. Wouters (2007). Shocks and Frictions in US Business Cycles: A Bayesian DSGE Approach. *American Economic Review*, 97(3), 586–606.

Steil, B. (2013). *The Battle of Bretton Woods: John Maynard Keynes, Harry Dexter White, and the Making of a New World Order*. Princeton: Princeton University Press.

Stoker, G. (1998). Governance as Theory: Five Propositions. *International Social Science Journal*, 50(155), 17–28.

Thiemann, M., M. Aldegwy and E. Ibrocevic (2017). Understanding the Shift from Micro- to Macro-Prudential Thinking: A Discursive Network Analysis. *Cambridge Journal of Economics*, 42(4), 935–62.

Tietmeyer, H. (1996). *Währungsstabilität für Europa*. Baden-Baden: Nomos Verlagsgesellschaft.

Tietmeyer, H. (1999). *International Cooperation and Coordination in the Area of Financial Market Supervision and Surveillance*. Report to the Finance Ministers and Central Bank Governors of the G7 Nations, Deutsche Bundesbank, 11 February. See www.fsb.org/wp-content/uploads/r_9902.pdf.

Toniolo, G. (with P. Clement) (2005). *Central Bank Cooperation at the Bank for International Settlements, 1930–1973*. Cambridge: Cambridge University Press.

Trichet, J.-C. (2011). *Building Europe, Building Institutions*. Speech on Receiving the Karlspreis 2011 in Aachen, 2 June.

Triffin, R. (1957). *Europe and the Money Muddle: From Bilateralism to Near-Convertibility, 1947–1956*. Vol. 7. New Haven: Yale University Press.

Ungerer, H. (1997). *A Concise History of European Monetary Integration: From EPU to EMU*. Westport, Connecticut: Quorum.

Vähämaa, M. (2013). Groups as Epistemic Communities: Social Forces and Affect as Antecedents to Knowledge. *Social Epistemology*, 27(1), January, 3–20.

Vanthoor, W. F. V. (1991). *Een oog op Holtrop: Grondlegger van de Nederlandse monetaire analyse*. Amsterdam: NIBE.

Verdun, A. (2001). The Political Economy of the Werner and Delors Reports: Continuity amidst Change or Change amidst Continuity. In L. Magnusson and B. Stråth, eds., *From the Werner Plan to the EMU: In Search of a Political Economy for Europe.* Brussels: Peter Lang, 73–96.

Welch, I. (2000). Herding among Security Analysts. *Journal of Financial Economics,* 58 (3), 369–96.

Wessel, D. (2009). *In Fed We Trust: Ben Bernanke's War on the Great Panic.* New York: Crown Business.

White House Office of the Press Secretary (2009). Press Release, *Fact Sheet: Creating a 21st Century International Economic Architecture.* Washington, DC, 24 September.

White, W. R. (2002). *Changing Views on How Best to Conduct Monetary Policy.* Speech at the Central Bank Governors' Club Meeting Held in Nafplio, Greece, 18 October.

White, W. R. (2006). Procyclicality in the Financial System: Do We Need a New Macrofinancial Stabilisation Framework? *BIS Working Papers,* No. 193.

Widmaier, W. W. (2016). *Economic Ideas in Political Time: The Rise and Fall of Economic Orders from the Progressive Era to the Global Financial Crisis.* Cambridge: Cambridge University Press.

Wilkens, A. (1999). *Interessen verbinden: Jean Monnet und die europäische Integration der Bundesrepublik Deutschland.* Bonn: Bouvier.

Wilkens, A. (2005). Der Werner-Plan: Währung, Politik und Europa 1968–1971. In F. Knipping and M. Schönwald, eds., *Aufbruch zum Europa der zweiten Generation: Die europäische Einigung 1969–1974.* Trier: Wissenschaftlicher Verlag Trier, 221–22.

Williamson, J. (1977). *The Failure of World Monetary Reform, 1971–74.* London: Thomas Nelson & Sons, Ltd.

Williamson, O. E. (1996). *The Mechanisms of Governance.* Oxford: Oxford University Press.

Woods, N. (2000). The Challenge of Good Governance for the IMF and the World Bank Themselves. *World Development,* 28(5), 823–41.

World Bank Group (2018). *Poverty and Shared Prosperity 2018. Piecing Together the Poverty Puzzle.* Washington, DC: International Bank for Reconstruction and Development.

Zimmermann, H. (2001). The Fall of Bretton Woods and the Emergence of the Werner Plan. In L. Magnusson and B. Stråth, eds., *From the Werner Plan to the EMU: In Search of a Political Economy for Europe.* Brussels: Peter Lang, 49–72.

Index

Other Books in the Series (*Continued from p. ii*)

Peter L. Rousseau and Paul Wachtel, Editors, *Financial Systems and Economic Growth: Credit, Crises, and the Regulation from the 19th Century to the Present* (2017)

Ernst Baltensperger and Peter Kugler, *Swiss Monetary History since the Early 19th Century* (2017)

Øyvind Eitrheim, Jan Tore Klovland, and Lars Fredrik Øksendal, *A Monetary History of Norway, 1816–2016* (2016)

Jan Fredrik Qvigstad, *On Central Banking* (2016)

Michael D. Bordo, Øyvind Eitrheim, Marc Flandreau, and Jan F. Qvigstad, Editors, *Central Banks at a Crossroads: What Can We Learn from History?* (2016)

Michael D. Bordo and Mark A. Wynne, Editors, *The Federal Reserve's Role in the Global Economy: A Historical Perspective* (2016)

Owen F. Humpage, Editor, *Current Federal Reserve Policy Under the Lens of Economic History: Essays to Commemorate the Federal Reserve System's Centennial* (2015)

Michael D. Bordo and William Roberds, Editors, *The Origins, History, and Future of the Federal Reserve: A Return to Jekyll Island* (2013)

Michael D. Bordo and Ronald MacDonald, Editors, *Credibility and the International Monetary Regime: A Historical Perspective* (2012)

Robert L. Hetzel, *The Great Recession: Market Failure or Policy Failure?* (2012)

Tobias Straumann, *Fixed Ideas of Money: Small States and Exchange Rate Regimes in Twentieth-Century Europe* (2010)

Forrest Capie, *The Bank of England: 1950s to 1979* (2010)

Aldo Musacchio, *Experiments in Financial Democracy: Corporate Governance and Financial Development in Brazil, 1882–1950* (2009)

Claudio Borio, Gianni Toniolo, and Piet Clement, Editors, *The Past and Future of Central Bank Cooperation* (2008)

Robert L. Hetzel, *The Monetary Policy of the Federal Reserve: A History* (2008)

Caroline Fohlin, *Finance Capitalism and Germany's Rise to Industrial Power* (2007)

John H. Wood, *A History of Central Banking in Great Britain and the United States* (2005)

Gianni Toniolo (with the assistance of Piet Clement), *Central Bank Cooperation at the Bank for International Settlements, 1930–1973* (2005)

Richard Burdekin and Pierre Siklos, Editors, *Deflation: Current and Historical Perspectives* (2004)